INTERCOMMUNAL WARFARE
AND ETHNIC PEACEMAKING

MCGILL-QUEEN'S STUDIES IN PROTEST, POWER, AND RESISTANCE

Series editor: Sarah Marsden

Protest, civil resistance, and political violence have rarely been more visible. Nor have they ever involved such a complex web of identities, geographies, and ideologies. This series expands the theoretical and empirical boundaries of research on political conflict to examine the origins, cultures, and practices of resistance. From grassroots activists and those engaged in everyday forms of resistance to social movements to violent militant networks, it considers the full range of actors and the strategies they use to provoke change. The series provides a forum for interdisciplinary work that engages with politics, sociology, anthropology, history, psychology, religious studies, and philosophy. Its ambition is to deepen understanding of the systems of power people encounter and the creative, violent, peaceful, extraordinary, and everyday ways they try to resist, subvert, and overthrow them.

1 New Media and Revolution
Resistance and Dissent in Pre-uprising Syria
Billie Jeanne Brownlee

2 Games of Discontent
Protests, Boycotts, and Politics at the 1968 Mexico Olympics
Harry Blutstein

3 Organizing Equality
Dispatches from a Global Struggle
Edited by Alison Hearn, James Compton, Nick Dyer-Witheford, and Amanda F. Grzyb

4 The Failure of Remain
Anti-Brexit Activism in the United Kingdom
Adam Fagan and Stijn van Kessel

5 The Participation Paradox
Between Bottom-Up and Top-Down Development in South Africa
Luke Sinwell

6 Citizens, Civil Society, and Activism under the EPRDF Regime in Ethiopia
An Analysis from Below
Edited by Camille Pellerin and Logan Cochrane

7 Intercommunal Warfare and Ethnic Peacemaking
The Dynamics of Urban Violence in Central Asia
Joldon Kutmanaliev

Intercommunal Warfare and Ethnic Peacemaking

The Dynamics of Urban Violence in Central Asia

JOLDON KUTMANALIEV

McGill-Queen's University Press
Montreal & Kingston · London · Chicago

© McGill-Queen's University Press 2023

ISBN 978-0-2280-1683-0 (cloth)
ISBN 978-0-2280-1805-6 (ePDF)
ISBN 978-0-2280-1806-3 (ePUB)

Legal deposit second quarter 2023
Bibliothèque nationale du Québec

Printed in Canada on acid-free paper that is 100% ancient forest free (100% post-consumer recycled), processed chlorine free

We acknowledge the support of the Canada Council for the Arts.

Nous remercions le Conseil des arts du Canada de son soutien.

Library and Archives Canada Cataloguing in Publication

Title: Intercommunal warfare and ethnic peacemaking : the dynamics of urban violence in Central Asia / Joldon Kutmanaliev.
Names: Kutmanaliev, Joldon, author.
Series: McGill-Queen's studies in protest, power, and resistance ; 7.
Description: Series statement: McGill-Queen's studies in protest, power, and resistance ; 7 | Includes bibliographical references and index.
Identifiers: Canadiana (print) 20220475121 | Canadiana (ebook) 20220475342 | ISBN 9780228016830 (cloth) | ISBN 9780228018056 (ePDF) | ISBN 9780228018063 (ePUB)
Subjects: LCSH: Urban violence—Kyrgyzstan—Osh. | LCSH: Ethnic conflict—Kyrgyzstan—Osh. | LCSH: Uzbeks—Kyrgyzstan—Osh. | LCSH: Kyrgyz—Kyrgyzstan—Osh. | LCSH: Osh (Kyrgyzstan)—Ethnic relations.
Classification: LCC HN670.24.O84 K88 2023 | DDC 363.32095843—dc23

This book was typeset by True to Type in 11.5/13 Arno Pro

Contents

Figures and Tables vii
Preface and Acknowledgments ix

PART ONE: INTRODUCTION AND THEORY

1 The Puzzle and the Argument 3
2 Explaining Communal Violence at the Micro-Spatial Level: Intragroup Policing, Intergroup Nonaggression Pacts, and the Neighbourhood Security Dilemma 29

PART TWO: HISTORICAL CONTEXT AND THE DYNAMICS OF VIOLENCE IN OSH

3 Structural-Historical Context and the Onset of Violence: Conflict Background 59
4 Microdynamics and Patterns of Violence: Conflict Data and Flashpoints of Violence in Osh 87

PART THREE: NEIGHBOURHOOD-LEVEL COMPARISONS

5 Spatial Security during Communal Violence in Osh: How Spatial Factors and the Built Environment Affect the Local Dynamics of Violence and Neighbourhood Security 125
6 Intragroup Balance of Power and Self-Policing in Osh Neighbourhoods 150

7 Security Dilemma and the Variation in Neighbourhood Responses to Uncertainty in Jalalabat   189
8 Conclusions   219

   Notes   231
   References   237
   Index   251

Figures and Tables

FIGURES

1.1 Neighbourhood response strategies to uncertainty under the "emerging anarchy" 8
2.1 Observed paths of pact-making 35
3.1 Map of Kyrgyzstan 61
4.1 Osh city and its neighbourhoods 94
4.2 Property damage clusters in Cheremushki and Kyzyl-Kyshtak. *Source*: Map adapted from UNITAR/UNOSAT data. 99
4.3 Three property damage clusters in the eastern entrance to Osh city: Provinical Hospital, Shark, and Furkat. *Source*: Map adapted from UNITAR/UNOSAT data. 105
4.4 The distribution of the damage clusters in Osh city. *Source*: Map adapted from UNITAR/UNOSAT data. 107
5.1 Central square and a damage cluster in Oshskii Raion. *Source*: Map adapted from UNITAR/UNOSAT data. 133
5.2 Cheremushki and Kalinin neighbourhoods. *Source*: Map adapted from UNITAR/UNOSAT data. 140
5.3 Patterns of property damage in Oshskii raion and Cheremushki. *Source*: Map adapted from UNITAR/UNOSAT data. 142
6.1 Roadblocks in Turan. *Source*: Map adapted from UNITAR/UNOSAT data. 155
6.2 Location of Turan, Uchar, and Toloikon 157
6.3 Nariman and Nurdar 179
7.1 Overview of property damage in Jalalabat. *Source*: Map adapted from UNITAR/UNOSAT data. 194

7.2   The largest cluster of property damage in Jalalabat. *Source*: Map adapted from UNITAR/UNOSAT data.   199

TABLES

1.1   Conceptual operationalization of the June 2010 ethnic violence   25
2.1   Type of response to uncertainty   33
4.1   Ethnic distribution in urban and rural areas in southern regions of Kyrgyzstan (by Kyrgyz and Uzbek populations)   108
4.2   Number of deaths by dates and nationality   109
4.3   Number of deaths by gender   109
4.4   Number of deaths by age   110
4.5   Number of deaths by nationality and type of mortal wound   111
4.6   Violent and non-violent towns in 1990 and 2010   113
6.1   Variation in structural, spatial, and contingent factors and their impact on peaceful/violent trajectories in Toloikon and Uchar   177
6.2   Variation in structural, spatial, and contingent factors and their impact on peaceful/violent trajectories in Turan and Nariman   178
7.1   Divergent defense strategies and responses to emerging anarchy   215

Preface and Acknowledgments

This book is the result of a research program that ended due to tragic events, before it even got started, but which led to something new and unexpected. The focus of the research remained in Kyrgyzstan and with Uzbek and Kyrgyz ethnic communities. As a local scholar from Bishkek, I had always been distinctly interested in Kyrgyzstani, Central Asian, and post-Soviet politics and society. However, this book studies a global phenomenon through a local story.

In 2010, I got a research grant from the Central Asian Research and Training Initiative (CARTI) program, funded by the Open Society Institute, Budapest, to study political linguistics in southern Kyrgyzstan. The research hypothesis I had at the time derived from conversations with ordinary people from the south. According to their accounts, a growing number of Uzbeks – the largest ethnic minority based in southern Kyrgyzstan – were becoming fluent in the Kyrgyz language. For me, it was a sign of increasing political integration of Uzbeks and their rational decision to play a more active role in Kyrgyzstan's social life. I spent the 2010 spring semester at the Davis Center for Russian and Eurasian Studies at Harvard University, studying theoretical foundations of ethnic politics and preparing myself for the ethnographic fieldwork in Osh. Upon return to Kyrgyzstan, in June, I was determined immediately to go to Osh. But then my brother unexpectedly arranged his wedding for 12 June, so I had to postpone my fieldwork. When I woke up in the morning of 11 June, just one day before my brother's wedding, Kyrgyzstan's state TV reported ongoing clashes between Uzbeks and Kyrgyz in Osh. This was the onset of the horrible violence that completely refuted my integration hypothesis. After the active phase of the conflict was over, in a Skype conversation with my then academic mentor, Laura Adams, I decided to go to Osh anyway, this time to find out the situation on the ground.

I arrived in Osh in a shared taxi in a hot summer day in July 2010. The city struck me by a gloomy picture. The taxi drove us along a long row of completely burnt houses in Furkat and Shark – the eastern neighbourhoods in Osh – to the central bazaar, an economic heart of the city, that had also been completely destroyed by communal violence. Although the active violence subsided, the situation was still very tense. There were still random killings and kidnappings that kept local residents in fear, forcing them to rush to their homes as soon as they were done with their business routines in the city center. Walking through the city's deserted streets, I could see multiple traces of recent armed combats, but I also observed neighbourhoods that remained completely untouched by violence. This was a puzzling contrast, considering that violence and intense full-scale armed combats embraced the whole city. Already then, I started talking to people in Osh and even conducted my first three exploratory interviews, gaining invaluable insights into the conflict, including my first interview with Rahman (not his real name), a local Uzbek human rights activist and community leader who actively participated in peace negotiations and pacted agreements on the local level. My first observations of post-conflict Osh led me to the main idea of this study and to the doctoral program at the European University Institute in Florence, Italy, where I conducted the main research for this book.

Many experts were quick to advance the relative deprivation and grievance-based explanations for why the conflict happened. But their accounts did not explain the contrasting picture of the post-conflict Osh that I observed. Two similar and adjacent neighbourhoods located in the same area, Cheremushki and Kalinin, exhibited two strikingly different pictures. Although both neighbourhoods comprised residentially segregated Uzbek and Kyrgyz ethnic communities, Cheremushki was in ruins, completely burned and destroyed, while Kalinin did not show any visible signs of recent firearm combats and property destruction. Despite ethnodemographic and residential similarities and spatial proximity of the two neighbourhoods, these two contrasting images derived from actions, reactions, and interactions of local communities as well as spatial and locational characteristics. In Cheremushki, local Uzbek and Kyrgyz communities became suspicious of each other erecting barricades that would divide them along ethnic lines, descending into an early spiral of intercommunal brawls and preventive skirmishes. Their leaders failed to negotiate non-aggression agreements and reestablish intercommunal trust. Spatially, Cheremushki was also unfortunate to be located between the city center and Zapadnyi, a western neighbourhood that became one of hotbeds for ethnic mobilization for groups from rural and mountainous areas. Residents of Cheremushki blocked the only available strategic streets that connected

Zapadnyi and the city center and preventively confronted outsider groups that attempted to get through those roadblocks to the city center. This preemptive and confrontational strategy became a counterproductive mistake: instead of protecting, it drew destructive attacks on their neighbourhood that eventually resulted in a horrible pogrom. Contrastingly, in neighbouring Kalinin, local communal leaders and residents from both communities agreed to cooperate to counter threat from external groups. They completely closed off the neighbourhood by blocking all entrance streets to the quarters but leaving open those few principal city-level streets. Community leaders established strong control over local residents restraining them from opportunistic behaviour and denying entrance to any outsider groups. By physically isolating the neighbourhood and establishing strong rules for intercommunal nonaggression and cooperation, Kalinin managed to preserve internal peace and avoid attacks from outsiders.

These two examples demonstrate that different reactions by local communities to uncertainty dilemmas and diverse spatial-geographical contexts produce contrasting outcomes in urban neighbourhoods. While the underlying conditions, security environments, and external threats might be the same for local communities, their responses to the outbreak of violence are not. Local neighbourhood communities react in different ways to the emerging threat. Furthermore, variations in violence exist even within towns. My initial plan was to study variations between violent and nonviolent towns and villages. As I did more research, I realized that variations existed even across neighbourhoods and quarters and that there was not as much existing research that would explain armed conflicts in urban areas, especially at the neighbourhood level. So, I wanted to figure out why, in a highly segregated city, ethnic neighbourhood communities chose or were forced to adopt different strategies to deal with the existential threat.

I spent most of the overall ten-month fieldwork time extended across several years (2010–14) in Osh, the largest city in southern Kyrgyzstan and most violent during the conflict, with some time spent in Jalalabat and Uzgen. I became aware that most peaceful neighbourhoods relied on nonaggression pacts with their out-group neighbours. The scale of destruction and killings also suggested that this conflict was not just conventional violent riots but a communal warfare that had full capacity of turning into a civil war. Accordingly, I wanted to determine how the behaviour of local groups and neighbourhood affected the escalation of violence. Consequently, I visited almost all neighbourhoods, documenting the differences in their spatial and built environments and talking to local residents. These visual inspections of urban neighbourhoods helped me to build the overall picture and recognize differences in spatial patterns and environmental conditions. After that, I selected case studies that were representative of other similar neighbourhoods for a more-focused research.

What happened in Osh is not unique to Kyrgyzstan and is a general pattern in multiple communal conflicts across the globe. Reading through numerous of accounts of communal conflicts in sub-Saharan Africa, the Middle East, south and south-east Asia, one can recognize not only common patterns and dynamics of violence but also observe that communal violence is often spatially selective.

One such example is the communal violence between various Muslim and Christian ethno-communal groups in Plateau, Benue, Kaduna and other states of the Middle Belt in central Nigeria. These conflicts share many similar patterns and structural characteristics with the one in Osh, Kyrgyzstan. They are recent, non-internationalized, and high death toll conflicts. Intense armed fighting between communal groups take place mainly in segregated urban environments, such as the heavily concentrated in provincial capital cities of Jos, Kaduna, and other towns.

In contrast to the short-term conflict in Osh, communal violence in Jos (Plateau) and other neighbouring cities has been recurrent, producing horrible and high-causality outbreaks of violence. Several conflicts occurred between 2001 and 2018, each time bringing this region to the brink of a regional civil war between local communal groups. The escalation has already shifted this conflict to the regional scale diffusing the violence to other Middle Belt states. In the first quarter of 2018 alone, 1,078 people died in armed communal clashes (HRW 2018). In terms of intensity, the conflict in Plateau, Kaduna, and other Middle Belt states has significantly outpaced the death toll of the civil war with Boko Haram in northeastern Nigeria. The conflict is increasingly framed in religious-communal terms, risking to trigger a large-scale civil war and potentially to merge with the Boko Haram insurgency. Communal conflicts similar to ones that took place in Osh and in the Middle Belt Nigerian cities have highly devastating potential to spark bigger armed conflicts at the national and even regional levels.

The communal wars in Nigeria with around 20,000 battle-related deaths and continuous violence leans toward the civil war trajectory. This underlines the tendency of increasing security threat coming from ethnically divided cities. And yet, despite their high intensity and war-like nature of these armed conflicts, violence distributes itself unevenly, even across urban neighbourhoods in such violence-prone cities and towns in conflict-prone regions and countries around the world as Osh, Jos, Kaduna, Kinshasa, Mogadishu, Aligarh, and Ahmedabad.

Therefore, this volume's focus on urban neighbourhoods in southern Kyrgyzstan can be justified by three reasons.[1] First of all, the chessboard-like urban segregation patterns of southern Kyrgyzstan are also common to a number of conflict-ridden towns in Nigeria, Indonesia, Liberia, Kenya, India, Uganda and many other countries. Consequently, a better understanding of conflict dynamics in southern Kyrgyzstan might help us to develop a model that fits with neighbourhood dynamics of urban violence and warfare. Second, such a context-specific study should provide us with a good starting point for a general model of neighbourhood conflicts which can help us to better understand the mechanisms of spatial diffusion of urban communal violence.

Third, the conflict outcomes in southern Kyrgyzstan in 2010 show that communal groups have agency. They can and do react differently to the deterioration of urban security environments. Therefore, a better understanding of local conflict management and the effects of neighbourhood relations, including embedded social institutions and practices, might help us to develop local peace strategies with cumulative effects at the urban, regional, and potentially even national level. Therefore, it is important to understand why urban communities respond differently to ethnic fears and uncertainty. Urban neighbourhoods in southern Kyrgyzstan provide us with an important starting point for this type of research.

A final caveat is that this book does not aim to identify the general causes of this conflict, nor does it imply to identify who is responsible for this bloodshed or to blame one of the parties. The goal of this book is different – it aims to identify and explain mechanisms of the escalation and spread of violence across neighbourhoods to elucidate the variance in the reactions of the local-level urban ethnic communities to intercommunal warfare. Explaining these mechanisms can help us to understand many other intercommunal conflicts that take place in urban settings and prevent, or at least to mitigate their consequences.

*　*　*

My acknowledgements go to people who supported me and shared with me good moments as well as stress throughout the process of writing this book. I am sure that I forgot to name some, especially those with whom I have not recently been in contact. For this, I would like to apologize in advance.

First of all, I feel grateful to my respondents in Osh, Jalalabat, Uzgen, and other towns and villages of Kyrgyzstan for their willingness to share their thoughts with me. Without their honest responses, I would never reach this point of writing this book.

This book journey started with my dissertation research the European University Institute's (EUI) doctoral program in Florence. Therefore, the role of my doctoral supervisor, Donatella della Porta, was critical for this book. I would like to thank Donatella for leading me through six years of my doctoral study. Not only did she provide me with excellent academic supervision, but she also morally supported and encouraged me when I was frustrated and unconfident with my research. She gave me unlimited freedom to explore potential routes of my research and periodically deviate from my planned direction. I am grateful to Donatella for her trust and support.

I would like to thank the members of jury panel – professors David Waddington, Mark Beissinger, and Olivier Roy – for spending their invaluable time to read and critically comment on my work. Their critical and at the same time, friendly comments helped me to improve the quality of my doctoral dissertation that became a basis for this book. Mark Beissinger has long stayed in touch even after my thesis defence to provide me with professional advice and academic support.

A research grant provided by the CARTI and people associated with this program: Sasha Shtokvych, John Schoeberlein, and Laura Adams, allowed me to start my preliminary research in southern Kyrgyzstan. Sasha was very flexible and supportive to arrange my fellowship even after I changed my research project. John encouraged me to focus my research project on ethnic politics in southern Kyrgyzstan. Laura was my academic mentor during my research fellowship at Harvard University. When ethnic violence broke out in southern Kyrgyzstan in June 2010 and it became clear that I could not continue my research project on political linguistics in Osh, she was first to suggest me to look at and explain cases with peaceful outcomes.

My stay at the EUI and in Florence was one of the best periods in my life. This is mostly because I found there many great people. Particularly, I would like to highlight friends and voluntary "babysitters" of my children: Vera, Antonio, Leonidas, Chiara, Frank, Pancho, Bogi, Nick, Maskeiko (Francis), Pietro, Alberto Caselli, and many others. I met these great people at the EUI in a capacity of my classmates, teammates, drink mates, and so on. I hope my children never forget them.

My football team Cinghiali (Cinghialisti) and a legendary group of Collettivo Prezzemolo at the EUI were instrumental in helping me meet my friends Leonidas, Pancho, Pietro, Frank O'Connor, Frank McNamara, Vincent, Afroditi, Alberto, Semih, Dani, Lorenzo, Eliska, Hugo, Johanne, Trajche, Cat, Joseph, Kivanc, Daniela, Helge, Bogdan, Ksenia, Markos, Myrssini, and others.

My fieldwork in Osh was very much facilitated by the logistical support of my uncle – Azamat Kutmanaliev, who at that time worked in Osh. He also introduced me Mukhtar Irisov, Zamir Aldashev, and Graziella Pavone who became my good friends. Conversations with them and my other friends Sanjar Tajimatov, Rasul Avazbek uulu, and Sardor Makhmudov helped me enjoy my time in Osh and better understand local context. Sanjar hosted me in his house in July 2010 when other housing options were not available. I would also like to thank Alisher Khamidov for giving me invaluable advice on ethnographic fieldwork in the context of Osh.

Several organizations facilitated my fieldwork in the Osh city. The regional Office of Organization for Security and Co-operation in Europe (OSCE) in Osh and the Iret NGO permitted me to observe trainings of local mediators from the "Yntymak Jarchylary" (Heralds of Peace) NGO's peacebuilding network established by the OSCE. Aziza Abdrasulova, a head of Kylym Shamy human rights organization, shared with me her materials and data. Janyl Jusupjan from Radio Azattyk provided me with first interview contacts in Osh. My friends in Bishkek cheered me every time I arrived from Italy. I wish my best friend Jyrgal could celebrate the publication of this book with me.

Several scholars, Nick Megoran, Andreas Hasenclever, Matteo Fumagalli, and John Heathershaw, were particularly important to help me refine my theoretical arguments by giving constructive feedbacks. Furthermore, Nick and John invited me to participate in an organized workshop and a conference panel related to the problem of peacekeeping in the Central Asian context and to contribute to their edited volume on conflict prevention. These were good opportunities to share and test the findings of my research. During my study at the EUI, Stefan Malthaner, Lorenzo Bosi, Xabier Itcaina, Leonidas Oikonomakis, and Frank O'Connor read and commented on parts of my thesis. Before my first fieldwork trip to Kyrgyzstan, Stefan provided me with many invaluable tips about how to conduct ethnographic research and interviews in post-conflict settings. Lorenzo and Frank also helped me to improve the content of my book proposal, years later after I finished my study program.

This book benefited a lot from valuable comments from members of the doctoral international relations colloquium at the Institute of Political Science at the University of Tubingen in Germany, among them: Natalie Pawlowski, Maike Messerschmidt, and especially Christine Andra who provided me with several excellent written feedbacks on the content of this book and on the book proposal.

I would particularly like to thank Andreas Hasenclever, a true mentor, for his moral, academic and institutional support throughout the book-writing journey. His excellent comments helped me immensely to improve the content of the book. He and Jeanne Feaux de la Croix supported me in getting a postdoctoral fellowship in the final year of my doctoral study. Furthermore,

Andreas hosted me at the Institute of Political Science, providing me with all necessary resources. This was crucial since this position gave me an opportunity not to worry about finances and to finish this book. I am grateful to Andreas and will never forget his support in difficult times of my life.

Positive and helpful feedback given to me by three anonymous reviewers improved the content of this book. My editor Richard Baggaley was flexible and supportive by generously providing me with additional time to write this book and useful tips and advice. Simon Watmough made language corrections of my dissertation that became a basis for this subsequent book and Nicki Owtram linguistically proofed my article that became a basis for chapter 5 in this book. Abha Agarwal provided editorial support for this book.

In Kyrgyzstan, people are happily embedded in dense networks of extended families. My case is not an exception because I also enjoyed unconditional support of my family that particularly includes my brothers Tilek (Tika) and Ajike (Ajimurat) and their families. My mother- and father-in-law, Sabira Chargynova and Usupjan Baialiev, took care of my children in Kyrgyzstan during my fieldwork trips and when they visited us in Florence and Tubingen. It is through their stories I got interested in local-level ethnic politics in southern Kyrgyzstan.

My deepest gratitude goes to my family: my mother Roza, my wife Gulzat, and my children Aybike, Aykut, and Ayluna. They tolerated, and were patient to, my long absences from the family life when I was busy with my research. My mother Roza devoted three years of her life to help my family in everyday routine issues in Florence, especially when Gulzat had to leave Florence to study a one-year master's program in political science at the Central European University in Budapest, Hungary. Gulzat, besides taking the main burden in family duties and being busy with her own professional and research activities, helped me with my research tasks from transcribing my interviews, to formatting the final version of my dissertation, to creating a digital version of maps used in this book. Her assistance and support have been immense. I could not have a better friend and companion in life. Without her support and encouragement, this book would have never been written. My late father, Bolot Kutmanaliev, would have been happy to see this book.

This book is dedicated to my family: my mother Roza Mukasheva, my wife Gulzat (Buru), my children Aybike, Aykut, and Ayluna, and to the memory of my father Bolot Kutmanaliev.

PART ONE

Introduction and Theory

1

The Puzzle and the Argument

URBAN COMMUNAL WAR IN SOUTHERN KYRGYZSTAN, JUNE 2010

On 10 June 2010, hundreds of Uzbeks gathered in the central streets in Osh – the largest city in southern Kyrgyzstan – following a brawl between few Uzbek and Kyrgyz youths in a local casino. The crowd, mostly Uzbeks, grew increasingly hostile. Some in the crowd started beating Kyrgyz passersby and throwing stones at the police that arrived at the location and at a nearby university dormitory that was mostly inhabited by Kyrgyz female students. This stone attack against the female dormitory produced powerful rumours about an alleged mass rape of Kyrgyz female students by the Uzbeks. As the situation on the scene grew tense, the police dominated by Kyrgyz officers opened fire against the Uzbek crowd. This was the beginning of the violent conflict that turned into urban intercommunal war between the Kyrgyz and the Uzbeks.

The conflict raged in the city for several days and then spread to several neighbouring towns and villages with mixed Kyrgyz and Uzbek populations. However, the distribution and intensity of violence across space were uneven. Not all ethnically mixed and segregated settlements experienced violence. Some towns suffered property damage but no deaths; some towns remained peaceful. Even in Osh – the epicenter of the conflict – some districts saw bloodshed and suffered from property damage, while other districts remained free of violence.

The most active phase of the 2010 mass violence continued for four days, from 11 to 15 June. Sporadic violence in the form of kidnapping, hostage-taking, and random killing continued for several more weeks. This conflict was characterized by an extremely high intensity of violence with around 500 people killed and several thousand wounded, large-scale destruction of more than 2,000 buildings and houses, and more than 400,000 refugees and internally displaced individuals (KIC 2011, ii).

The conflict was mostly limited to urban areas and affected cities with Uzbek and Kyrgyz populations. The housing policy and practices of town administrations conducted since the 1960s transformed many towns of southern Kyrgyzstan into a chessboard-like, highly ethnically segregated urban areas. The boundaries of ethnic neighbourhoods became too well-distinguishable and were easily recognized by local residents and even by outsiders. This created a unique situation – once violence broke out and fear induced by uncertainty divided the people across ethnic lines, the segregated neighbourhoods transformed into ethnic strongholds and enclaves with divergent violent dynamics.

As violence escalated, armed clashes looked increasingly as full-scale military combats with intensive use of firearms. However, the first massive wave of strong ethnic mobilization of Kyrgyz people from rural mountainous areas was triggered by a rumour about alleged mass rape of Kyrgyz female students. The Kyrgyz mobilization from rural areas was also strongly driven by retaliatory emotions based on attacks against Kyrgyz residents by Uzbek militants or false rumours. Uzbek groups initially dominated urban streets in Osh in big crowds, engaging in violence against Kyrgyz including killing some of them. Many rural Kyrgyz, who came to Osh to evacuate their children and relatives, were unable to enter the city because of gunfire from Uzbek roadblocks on city entrances. Being insufficiently armed, the antagonized Kyrgyz groups stormed several military depots in various locations across the southern region. After they got weapons, including two or three APCs (armoured personnel carriers), the dynamics of violence changed. The balance of power shifted toward the rural Kyrgyz, now armed sufficiently to fight with Uzbek groups, some of them, also armed with firearms.

On 12 June, violence escalated to its peak, spreading across several neighbourhoods. Kyrgyz rural militants started massive attacks on Uzbek *mahalla*s (communities). Their attacks were now more organized, "and demonstrated some planning, unlike the previous day, when the attackers were driven by strong emotions ... The character of Uzbek defences also changed, becoming more conscious. The Uzbeks did not try to move around the city, but concentrated on defence of their mahallas and mounted a few successful counterattacks" (Matveeva, Savin, and Faizullaev 2012, 24).

Residents in some neighbourhoods cooperated among themselves to prevent violence and aggression from outside groups. Virtually all communities and neighbourhoods constructed barricades where it was possible to do so. Consequently, many neighbourhoods turned into isolated ethnic enclaves.

The Kyrgyz attacks on the Uzbek mahallas were characterized by intensive gunfire, killings, and mass arson. In a number of cases, opportunistic behaviour included atrocities such as gang rapes and tortures. Uzbek groups retaliated against Kyrgyz residents living in Uzbek-dominated neighbourhoods which also involved gang rapes and torture. The real extent of sexual violence is difficult to establish.

The attacks on mahallas were facilitated by two APCs, which the Kyrgyz participants seized from the military. The APCs demolished barricades and opened way for militants to get deeper inside the mahallas. At the same time, the military's some attempts to restore order turned to be counterproductive. In several cases reported by the Human Rights Watch (HRW), the Kyrgyzstan Inquiry Commission (KIC), and Memorial Human Rights Center (hereafter Memorial), the military demolished some barricades without protecting residents inside mahallas. On the other hand, Uzbek groups used armoured trucks to counterattack the armed Kyrgyz groups. In general, the role of the police and military during this conflict was ambiguous and mostly inefficient. These institutions failed to curb violence in initial stages of the conflict. At the number of hotspots, their actions contributed to the violence rather than preventing it. They were especially ineffective in very tense situations but more effective in clashes in which participants were weakly armed and/or were in small numbers. Communal violence and sporadic killings continued in the Osh city on 13 and 14 June. Violence diffused to Jalalabat – the second largest city in southern Kyrgyzstan. Although the scale of violence was less intense, Jalalabat still significantly suffered from armed interethnic clashes and property destruction.[1]

THE PUZZLE(S)

The central puzzle that guides this research is why did ethnic violence affect or break out in some urban neighbourhoods but not in many others? Why did neighbourhoods with similar ethnic composition and social and economic contexts exhibit a variation in, and different levels of, ethnic violence?

In this book, I address this puzzle by studying this case of communal warfare in southern Kyrgyzstan. The main aim is to explain the dynamics of communal warfare and ethnic peacemaking in highly segregated towns and why urban communal groups and neighbourhoods respond to uncertainty in different ways. This study suggests that two main mechanisms – intracommunal policing and intergroup nonaggression pacts – were key to bolstering local-level peace and helped local leaders and mediators to prevent violence.

However, if in-group policing and intergroup pacts are key to local-level peace, then the question remains: why do all neighbourhood-level groups not utilize these mechanisms to prevent violence? To explain this puzzle, this study seeks to answer the following questions. What conditions and mechanisms can explain why only some local communities manage to conduct robust in-group policing and nonaggression pacts? What explains divergent responses of the urban neighbourhoods to emerging violence? What factors/mechanisms account for efficient in-group policing and is it in fact conducted efficiently? Why do peaceful negotiations and nonaggression pacts take place only in some instances? In addition, this book seeks to assess the impact of spatial and micro-strategic factors by answering the following questions: How does urban spatial differentiation or the security dilemma account for the spread and dynamics of violence? How was violence prevented in peaceful towns and in certain neighbourhoods within the violent towns? These questions suggest the importance of analyzing micro-scale spatial variations in violence.

By micro-variations here, I imply the variance in the intensity of violence, or in the occurrence or non-occurrence of violence across spaces and locations such as urban district neighbourhoods, and even quarters. Various neighbourhoods were exposed to different degrees and forms of violence or displayed divergent trajectories. Some neighbourhoods and quarters in Osh and Jalalabat experienced practically no violence or only minor violent incidents while other neighbourhoods in the same city or even in the same urban district suffered from varying levels of communal violence and full-scale armed fighting. While violence broke out in some neighbourhoods as a result of spiralling interactions between local communal groups, other neighbourhoods were attacked by outsiders, yet some other neighbourhoods were affected by spillover effects from neighbouring quarters or by the complex combination of all above factors.

This study provides analytical accounts for the spatial variation in violence and explains the causes of violence and peace across urban neighbourhoods by analyzing micro-scale factors and conditions that produced divergent security dynamics in each location. The importance of such analysis is emphasized by its contributions to the studies of microdynamics of violence, urban conflicts, peace studies – especially to its urban-geographical dimension and spatial, known as a "spatial turn" – and, last but not the least, to the Central Asian studies, where the book contributes to the regional literature on pacts and informal institutionalism (Collins 2006; Jones Luong 2002); communal mobilization and norms (Radnitz 2012); civil war and armed conflict (Driscoll 2015; Epkenhans 2018; Kılavuz 2009); ethnic politics and nationalism (Lewis and Sagnayeva 2020; Megoran 2017; Reeves 2014); peace and security (Heathershaw 2009; Owen et al. 2018), Osh and urban development (Fumagalli 2007; Liu 2012; Megoran 2013); and evidently on communal violence in 2010, which, so far, has not received much attention (Khamidov, Megoran, and Heathershaw 2017). This study is the first book that systematically analyzes this armed conflict.

Furthermore, the analysis of the communal violence in southern Kyrgyzstan identifies several gaps in the literature on microdynamics of violence, peace studies, and urban warfare. First, the analysis of the conflict should focus not only on the town-level but also on the neighbourhood-level (or a neighbourhood community) since variations in violence exist even across neighbourhoods within one town. Second, the variation in community responses to violence is greater than just the binary categories of "violent" and "nonviolent" reactions. As this book shows, there are at least three major types of responses to violence by local communities (see figure 1.1). The analysis should reflect on this complexity. Third, there is not always just one fixed outcome across various neighbourhoods along the violent or nonviolent categories. Local communities experience different dynamics and trajectories of violence in the course of a conflict. Some neighbourhoods manage to restore order after initially being exposed to violent outbreaks and later curbing violence and thus turning into nonviolent locations. Others descended into violence at the later stages after initially not experiencing breakouts of violence. So, the same neighbourhood can transition from one outcome category to another. Four, the conflict in Kyrgyzstan shows that ethnic groups are not monolithic. We need to disaggregate ethnic groups into smaller units – communal subgroups – to understand the complexity of interactions. Ethnic groups can fractionalize, and various (fractionalized) subgroups may have divergent preferences and interests depending on the community-based contexts and security dynamics in the locations of their residence. Thus, there is the variation in local contexts and groups' behaviour and responses to a crisis. This, too, should be taken into account.

To reflect on these important points, this book identifies local conditions and processes that explain these divergent outcomes, dynamics, and trajectories by conducting a comparative analysis of across neighbourhoods and, thus, presenting the analysis across chapters.

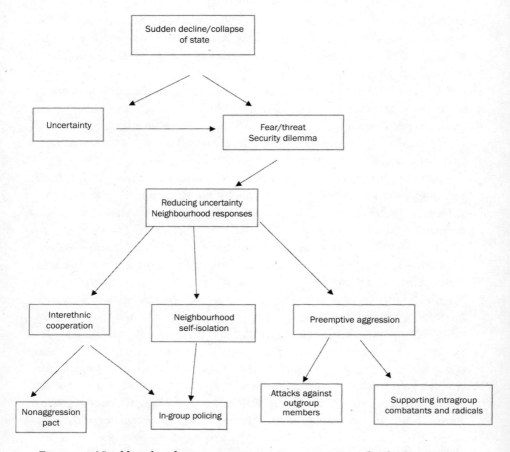

Figure 1.1 Neighbourhood response strategies to uncertainty under the "emerging anarchy"

NEIGHBOURHOOD RESPONSES TO EMERGING VIOLENCE: DIVERGENT MICRO-SCALE OUTCOMES UNDER SIMILAR ENVIRONMENTAL CHANGES

The dependent variable that this book aims to explain is neighbourhoods' divergent responses to emerging violence and uncertainty. These communal responses often determine local-level outcomes in the respective neighbourhoods. The variation in neighbourhood responses to exogenous shocks can generally be juxtaposed to neorealist studies that deal with the security dilemma at the higher scales of aggregation.

The literature on the security dilemma and civil wars argues that the "decision to fight, to negotiate, or to remain at peace" is contingent on the strategic environment (Walter 1999, 2). Accordingly, the change(s) in environmental conditions can induce actors and groups to start a war or to negotiate a peaceful agreement to reduce uncertainty and fears caused by sudden collapse of the state or an exogenous shock. These are meso-level responses to the changing macro-level environmental conditions and external threat. However, in this book, I maintain that despite the similar environmental changes, responses to these changes can be different across various local-level (sub)groups. I show how the temporal breakdown of the central state and the "emerging anarchy" produced divergent outcomes across towns in southern Kyrgyzstan and urban neighbourhoods in the violent cities of Osh and Jalalabat. To understand the divergent responses by various neighbourhoods to the emerging violence, I analyze the urban communal conflict in Kyrgyzstan relying on theoretical assumptions offered by the neorealist scholarship on civil wars and large-scale intrastate conflicts as well as on theoretical insights offered by urban studies.

The absence of the central state, which resulted from disengagement and inability of state to deal with communal violence during the 2010 conflict, produced similar situation of the emerging anarchy – a necessary condition for the security dilemma model. The central state had already been declining in the southern provinces of Kyrgyzstan since the violent regime change on 7 April 2010 that had taken place just two months before the June 2010 conflict. After first ethnic riots broke out in the southern city of Osh on 10 June 2010, state authorities lost control of the situation. The police and military failed to contain the violence and were completely paralyzed. Law enforcement troops were inefficient and often afraid of the raging crowds, and thus failing to actively intervene to prevent communal violence. As the local population realized that the state was not capable (or not willing) to provide protection for the civilian population, neighbourhood-level communities in Osh – and later in Jalalabat and other towns – erected barricades and roadblocks to protect themselves from aggressive mobs and possible attacks from the territory of adjacent neighbourhoods. As a result, entire neighbourhoods in such cities as Osh, Jalalabat and some other smaller towns "had been turned into isolated enclaves, where roads of entry had been closed off" (Memorial 2012, 82).

Neighbourhood Responses

During those days of anarchy, such isolated neighbourhoods acted much like individual units or states do in world politics and pursued the same kinds of strategies. These neighbourhood interactions with out-group members were conditioned and motivated by concerns of physical survival and existential insecurity. Strategic dilemmas and interactions between ethnic neighbourhoods and intragroup dynamics produced different micro-scale outcomes across urban quarters, districts, and even towns and triggered divergent responses from the neighbourhoods. External developments – outside respective neighbourhoods – forced local communities to re-evaluate communal security concerns and responses to the crisis. Rising insecurity concerns triggered either more aggressive responses pushing some groups to expect the worse from their neighbours – sometimes preventively striking against out-group members or induced groups to negotiate with the out-groups. Accordingly, as I discussed above, the survival strategies produced three types of response outcomes, typically discussed in the neorealist literature on large-scale interethnic conflicts: (1) confrontational attitudes and preemptive attacks against adjacent out-group members and communities; (2) interethnic cooperation, mostly in ethnically mixed neighbourhoods, based on neighbourhood solidarity and the formation of interethnic alliances against outsiders and; (3) nonaggression pacts between residentially segregated ethnic neighbourhoods.[2] In many cases, outcomes were determined not only under influence of strategic factors but also, in combination with local-level, spatial, and neighbourhood-specific conditions.

Thus, despite the similar threat, urban neighbourhoods in Osh and other towns chose different responses to uncertainty and strategies to deal with existential insecurity depending on:

(a) opportunities and constraints for negotiating nonaggression pacts in intergroup interactions;
(b) the strength of local self-policing and communal norms and intragroup shifts in balance of power between radicals and moderates; and
(c) neighbourhood-specific characteristics such as the location, the built environment, and social and ethnic composition of the neighbourhoods.

These factors can reveal why towns and neighbourhoods in southern Kyrgyzstan responded to the emerging violence in different ways.

THE ARGUMENT

In this book, I argue that the micro-spatial variation in violent and nonviolent outcomes across urban neighbourhoods, districts, and even quarters within the towns can be explained to the great extent by the presence (or absence) of intragroup policing and nonaggression intergroup pacts among neighbourhood-scale subgroups of both ethnic communities. In-group policing, a theoretical concept advanced by Fearon and Laitin (1996) is a crucial mechanism for understanding ethnic violence and peace in southern Kyrgyzstan. By itself, effective in-group policing – even in the absence of a nonaggression pact with out-group members – increases the likelihood of peaceful outcome or significantly decreases the possibility of intensive violent outbreaks in respective localities. Intracommunal policing is a necessary, but not a sufficient, condition for local-level peace and for negotiating efficient intercommunal pacts as strong in-group policing establishes firm discipline and order within communities and signals to an out-group about commitment to the terms of a pact. On the other hand, pacts reduce uncertainty and lessen fears (McFaul 2002, 217) by re-embedding trust and signalling peaceful intentions among residentially segregated rival communities.

The linkage between in-group policing and out-group nonaggression pacts requires analysis of the dynamics of intragroup and intergroup interactions. This logic of two-level game of interethnic and intraethnic cooperation corresponds to international and domestic arenas in international relations (IR) (see Christia 2012; Evans, Jacobson, and Putnam 1993; Lake and Rothchild 1998; Putnam 1988). However, whether intergroup pacts and in-group policing are successful depends also on several contingent and micro-structural factors and the spatial environment of neighbourhoods that I explain in more detail below and in the theoretical review in chapter 2.

In-group Policing

Successful in-group policing during the violence was complemented with intercommunal nonaggression pacts among the Uzbek and the Kyrgyz neighbourhood leaders and elders between adjacent neighbourhoods and neighbouring villages. Pacts, on the other hand, are meaningless without effective self-policing. Negotiating parties must guarantee nonaggression and punishment of culprits. Pacts complement self-policing and the strength of self-policing indicates commitment and creates trust between communities. The success and failure of in-group policing and intercommunal agreements are often determined in the dynamics of intergroup and within-group strategic interactions and are also contingent on local-level spatial and structural factors.

In-group policing is essential in the absence of interethnic everyday connections and civic links among ethnically segregated neighbourhoods. In many instances, peaceful outcomes can be explained by successful self-policing by traditional community leaders in stable residential neighbourhoods. However, in neighbourhoods with high residential mobility and non-stable migrant population, community policing was either difficult or nearly impossible due to weak social networks and non-compliance with local social norms and non-legitimacy of traditional authority of local leaders. Some of the latter neighbourhoods suffered from violent opportunism during the conflict. Finally, initially successful policing was broken in the neighbourhoods that experienced an influx of outsiders such as militants from outside areas and embittered refugees from distressed zones. Outsiders in local neighbourhood communities thus serve as a crucial factor that affects the efficiency of local in-group policing and they can tip the intragroup balance of power toward radicals.

This book identifies the following conditions that increase chances of successful in-group policing: (1) a majority of neighbourhood residents who share and comply with local communal and social norms; (2) the presence of locally recognized and legitimate community leaders and mediators; (3) social homogeneity of local constituency (such as the absence of outsiders and residential stability) and presence of preferably small and socially homogenous communities; (4) radical outsiders including internal migrants, militants from outside areas, displaced persons, refugees and so on do not infiltrate local communities and thus, do not interfere in activities of local leaders, and; (5) physical self-isolation of the community during conflict that is supplemented by such measures as construction of barricades on non-principal streets, restriction of freedom of movement, avoidance from direct contacts with other groups of different ethnic communities, denying transit, and preventing human flow through the neighbourhood's territory.

In-group policing is a key and necessary condition/element in pact-making. It enforces peaceful pact by mitigating the problem of credible commitment. Effective self-policing, which includes within-group sanctions against violators of pact, is critical for establishing or restoring mutual trust under a condition of intergroup uncertainty. What is important is that in-group sanctions must be visible or perceptible to out-group members (Fearon and

Laitin 1996, 723). By restraining radicals and punishing violators, leaders of one group signal to the other group that they are credibly committed to the conditions and rules of the pact. Although, this model does not explicitly address the question of intergroup nonaggression negotiations, it shows how competing ethnic groups reach an agreement in the form of an informal pact or mutual understanding or "equilibrium," according to Fearon and Laitin (ibid.).

Nonaggression Pacts

Uncertainty between ethnic neighbourhoods can be reduced by intercommunal nonaggression pacts negotiated by ethnic neighbourhood leaders. Pacts formed under broken trust in interethnic relations indicate attempts to recover cooperation. Leaders provide security to their constituencies by negotiating pacts with out-group leaders and reassuring them of peaceful intentions. A pacted agreement helps to prevent intergroup violence by mitigating the security dilemma and reducing the level of mutual distrust and fear. The model formulates its assumptions based on relations between segregated ethnic groups.

The evidence from Kyrgyzstan demonstrates that those ethnic communities that managed to utilize intercommunal nonaggression pacts and efficiently conduct in-group policing substantively increased their chances to keep their neighbourhoods peaceful.

Pacts between ethnic neighbourhoods create a set of rules that reduces uncertainty, fear, and distrust – essential components of security dilemma – in interethnic relations at local community level (micro-scale) that were triggered by communal violence among ethnic communities at national level (macro-scale). According to the evidence drawn from my interviews with local leaders, intercommunal nonaggression pacts that were negotiated between leaders of ethnic neighbourhoods usually included the following terms: abstention from violence and appealing to outsiders (non-alignment), restraining radicals, and implementing in-group sanctions against violators. Essentially, these terms of nonaggression constitute the core components of in-group policing, also highlighted in the literature on policing of mass protests and demonstrations (della Porta, Peterson, and Reiter 2006; della Porta and Reiter 1998; Waddington 1989, 2007) and pacted democratic transitions (O'Donnell 1986; O'Donnell and Schmitter 1986). This demonstrates that the same mechanisms and components of in-group policing operate across different forms of contentious politics (Tilly and Tarrow 2007). Consequently, in this conflict, the main term of the nonaggression pacts brokered by group leaders was the requirement to conduct self-policing as effective in-group control enforces the terms of a pact and signify credible commitment of ethnic leaders to the conditions of a pact.

Informal brokerage by local mediators – usually community leaders – allowed the rebuilding of trust between local ethnic communities under circumstances of growing fear and uncertainty in intercommunal relations. Mediators from both sides negotiated nonaggression pacts in several cases. Coupled with effective self-policing, intercommunal pacts became a successful strategy in peaceful negotiations between the Uzbek ethnic leaders in the town of Uzgen and the Kyrgyz from surrounding villages, as well as between the Uzbek and the Kyrgyz community leaders in some neighbourhoods in Osh and Jalalabat. Many urban neighbourhoods and towns avoided violence to great extent due to strong self-policing conducted within ethnic neighbourhoods and nonaggression pacts negotiated between ethnic community leaders. However, the patterns of the meso-level responses to the macro-level environmental changes were different in various ethnically segregated and mixed neighbourhoods. This highlights the importance of local-level spatial-structural factors. In highly ethnically segregated neighbourhoods and districts, Uzbek and Kyrgyz communities were exposed to fears against each other which, in some instances, erupted into preemptive violence. However, in other instances fears were managed by nonaggression pacts mediated by local leaders.

In few ethnically mixed neighbourhoods, Uzbeks and Kyrgyz cooperated on the grounds of neighbourhood solidarity with or without involvement of traditional ethnic community leaders. They formed interethnic alliances against outsiders (see chapters 5 and 7). Local residents blocked entrances to neighbourhoods by way of improvised barricades and roadblocks. Where local traditional community leaders managed these interethnic alliances, they conducted strong community policing and restrictive measures such as prohibiting local residents from going outside their neighbourhoods, closing access to outsiders, and denying the transit through the territory of the respective neighbourhoods. The different patterns of strategic responses to fears of intercommunal violence in ethnically mixed and segregated neighbourhoods display the importance of intercommunal civic engagement as hypothesized by Varshney (2002) regarding the Hindu-Muslim intercommunal violence in India. Intense intercommunal civic ties increase cooperation and solidarity based on common interests rather than on ethnic affiliation.

This book identifies three conditions that should be present for forming intergroup pacts: (1) a shared perception of threat that induces negotiations; (2) availability of legitimate brokers/mediators and ethnic neighbourhood leaders; and (3) favourable intragroup and intergroup balance of power (Collins 2006).

A threat that arises out of situations of uncertainty and fear can act not only as a trigger for violent conflict but also as a trigger for negotiations. The literature on pacts underlines the importance of (external) threat to the political and economic interests and/or physical safety of elites and ethnic and identity groups as a main trigger and incentive that pushes the political elites and ethnic leaders to negotiate a pact among themselves, often with the involvement of a third-party mediator or broker. Hartzell and Rothchild (1997, 153) refer to the notion of threat and rising costs are as a necessary condition for pact-making.

The second condition highlights the importance of leaders for the production and stability of nonaggression pacts. Why were the intergroup pacts negotiated only at the leaders' level? One of the main reasons was that intercommunal civic ties and contacts between ordinary residents were practically absent in segregated neighbourhoods. The virtual absence of intercommunal quotidian and civic links was well recorded and analyzed in anthropological studies on the relations between the Kyrgyz and the Uzbeks in Osh (Liu 2012; Megoran 2013). The model on interethnic cooperation proposed by Fearon and Laitin (1996) explains the importance of local-level ethnic leaders who in the absence of contacts between segregated ethnic groups represent and police their respective communities in intercommunal relations. In operating at the meso-level, they connect the macro-level divisions with micro-level incentives (Christia 2012, 5). Low intercommunal social capital stemming from residential, economic, and spatial segregation of two ethnic communities increases local elites' intragroup importance and their utility in intergroup relations. Under such circumstances, leaders act as brokers in intercommunal relations. Using their intragroup prominence and status they can mediate intercommunal agreements or on the contrary, abuse their power by subverting intercommunal relations.

The third condition refers to the intragroup and intergroup balance of power. The intragroup balance was critical for the pact occurrence when local allied groups of radicals and moderates emerged in each locality under the emergent violence. If a local leader attempted to negotiate an agreement with the out-group, it was important that they had the support of in-group moderates. Leaders used the moderate constituency to control and police local communities and, if necessary, to counteract challenges from radicals and to enforce sanctions against violators of intercommunal pacts and in-group security measures. The local intergroup balance of power was also important, although to less extent. It induced local actors to negotiate pacts; however, it was less relevant as the dynamics of violence brought about a high volatility of power shifts. The complicating factor was that local balance of power was often conflated by the general (town-level) balance of power. Macro-scale and micro-scale balances of power can be different and nested; the former can affect the latter.[3] So, on the ground, it is difficult to calculate the volatile power distribution, and, therefore, the views on intergroup power shifts were formed more by perceptions affected by rumours and real events.

Whether there was a violent or a nonviolent outcome in such small-scale localities as neighbourhoods and villages was often established as result of local-level intra- and intercommunal interactions. The intragroup balance of power and intergroup brokerage affected the probability of pact occurrence and its effect on a peaceful outcome in the respective locations. Since terms and conditions of a nonaggression pact negotiated between communal leaders should be enforced on the members of the respective communities, the mechanisms of pact enforcement are effective when intragroup balance of power favours moderate leaders inclined to keep peaceful relations with their out-group neighbours. However, this type of interaction and the possibility to negotiate an intercommunal pact and to conduct effective self-policing can be constrained by spatial and structural factors.

Structure, Spatiality, and Agency

This research assesses a highly dynamic episode of violence as opposed to sustained forms of mass violence such as civil wars. Studying such volatile dynamics of events requires us to place more focus on interactional and contingent factors. In other words, the explanatory power of interactional and contingent variables significantly increases in the analysis of short-term and highly dynamic events. However, this does not imply that structural, spatial, and environmental conditions are not important. They played an important role by shaping, constraining, and providing context for the interactions among actors. I move beyond the structure versus agency framework (Jones

Luong 2002) and argue that structural and agency-based factors together explain violent, low-violent, and nonviolent outcomes in neighbourhoods.

The preconditions literature underemphasized collective decisions and strategic interactions but stressing only agency renders too much voluntarism to the nature of human interactions. The choice under uncertainty is always inhibited and conditioned by historical, institutional, structural and spatial constraints (Karl 1990, 6). For example, housing patterns, demography, ethno-social composition, and residential stability in neighbourhoods influence the strength of communal social norms that are key to the level of the efficiency of communal policing and consequently, to the probability of pact occurrence. The level of local civil society, bonding (intragroup) and bridging (intergroup) social capital (Putnam, Leonardi, and Nanetti 1994; Varshney 2002), and the strength of local social norms (Petersen 2001; Radnitz 2012) critically affected the success rate of local leaders in building pacts and exerting social control in local communities. Social structures present constraints and opportunities on contingent choices (Karl 1990, 7). Without focusing on structural explanations, pact-making "would appear to be simply the result of skillful bargaining by astute political leaders" (Karl 1990, 7; see also Jones Luong 2002). Overly structural or contingency-based arguments present too deterministic or too voluntaristic explanations. Choices and options available for leaders are conditioned by institutional, spatial, and structural constraints and opportunities established in the past (Jones Luong 2002).

In this communal conflict, the structural and spatial factors mainly relate, but not only, to neighbourhood characteristics. They include geographical and locational characteristics of the neighbourhoods (such as proximity to the border with Uzbekistan, to highway roads, to main streets, frontier zones), their ethnic composition, housing patterns, and the social homogeneity/integrity of the population that is dependent on the presence/absence of internal migrants, residential mobility rates in the neighbourhood, the extent of development and experience of interethnic ties between local community ethnic leaders, especially with the geographically adjacent neighbourhoods. The latter factors have impact on intra- and intercommunal trust. Other structural and spatial factors include availability of broad communication roads and streets and the presence of commercial objects such as bazaars, cafes, and shops. Wide streets provided space for the movement of combatants, rioters, and the military, and the commercial objects attracted looters. The built environment and landscape of the cities can either facilitate or hinder the spread of violence and provide the context for strategic interactions.

When violence broke out in Osh, the residents built barricades and roadblocks to protect themselves from the aggressive mobs. In Osh, a highly ethnically segregated town, construction of barricades along ethnic spatial lines turned entire neighbourhoods and residential districts into isolated ethnic enclaves (Memorial 2012, 82). Barricades created new temporal physical boundaries in the city, changed the urban landscape and the built environment of the whole neighbourhoods, and constrained human mobility, including the mobility of combatants, militants, residents, refugees, and the police. All this had its impact on the dynamics and spatial variation of violence across neighbourhoods. While in many cases, the placement of barricades and roadblocks saved local communities from the opportunistically behaving violent mobs, in other places, their construction was counterproductive as they triggered attacks by militants. Physical isolation through building makeshift barricades in many neighbourhoods enabled local leaders to impose greater social control and informal power over the territory. Such neighbourhoods were now turned into isolated spaces with their own emergency rules and increased power of local informal leaders. These spatial-structural factors are mainly discussed in chapter 5 and also in chapters 6 and 7.

Consequently, the variation in local outcomes is contingent on the combination and interplay of three main factors: (1) efficient in-group policing, (2) efficient intergroup pacts, and (3) the spatial differentiation and neighbourhood effects in each locality.

Other Factors

Other contingent factors such as rumours, the presence or absence of barricades, the decision by the military to remove some barricades but not the others, and opportunist behaviour of conflict participants significantly affected the dynamics of violence at local level. For example, rumours and news on notorious killings and sexual violence created focal points for ethnic mobilization by emotionally inducing hundreds and thousands of ordinary people to join radicals and militants in revenge against rival groups. They escalated violence in certain neighbourhoods and directed raging mobs at certain places. Rumours – and also news on actual infamous events – triggered mobilization and strong emotions of revenge, outrage, and fury, not only among militants and radicals but also among ordinary residents, who were witnesses to shocking and psychologically traumatic events.

However, it is difficult to measure the impact of such factors. Apparently, rumours are important in explaining dynamics of violence but the challenge here is to find conditions favourable for the spread of rumours and mechanisms that would translate such rumours into violence (Bhavnani, Findley, and Kuklinski 2009; Wilkinson 2009). Studies that draw on diffusion/contagion theories use spatial distance indicators and assume that depending on transportation and organizational links and the degree of media segregation by language, the information about an initial riot can quickly disseminate to respective towns, neighbourhoods, and villages (Wilkinson 2009, 340). However, the 2010 conflict shows that the assumptions of the rumour contagion/diffusion theory work with some reservations. At its simplest, the model cannot explain the micro-spatial variation in violence at locations with similar conditions and spatial distances. Although I do not systematically analyze such contingent factors, I pay considerable attention to them in various chapters.

THE IMPORTANCE OF UNDERSTANDING URBAN WARFARE AND NEIGHBOURHOOD-LEVEL VIOLENCE

Studying violent ethnic conflict in urban areas and at the neighbourhood scale is an important added value that allows us to analyze neighbourhood effects on micro-strategic behaviour and divergent group-level responses to communal violence in cities. This book argues that local communal subgroups can act differently as independent units depending on locally ingrained, neighbourhood-level structural conditions. Consequently, the analysis of their strategic interactions and the neighbourhood's effects, including locally embedded social structures and institutions, can explain the security dynamics in each locality and might aggregate into conflict management strategies on the regional as well as national levels. Since the ethnocommunal violence in June 2010 in Kyrgyzstan exhibits variation in violence even within particular towns, micro-spatial analysis of local-level institutions and strategic interactions at the neighbourhood level is key to understand the causes of violence and its spatial diffusion.

The research observes and explains why neighbourhoods respond differently to emerging violence and what causes or prevents the process of violent escalation in intercommunal urban warfare between micro-level communal groups. Disaggregated analysis is important to understand the actions and reactions of local ethnic communities in response to an outbreak of violence. My key assumption is that their cumulative actions determine the violence dynamics of the conflict and the final aggregated outcome of strategic interactions – violent escalation to large-scale armed conflict or de-escalation of violence. Thus, the main goal of this micro-comparative research is to explain how local communities are able or not able to avoid highly violent escalation of urban communal conflicts.

This book contributes to the analysis of neighbourhood dynamics in communal armed conflicts and to contextualization of these dynamics within the broader field of the microdynamics of conflict research. Until now, however, the focus of most studies has been either on rural and non-urban violence (Kalyvas 2006; Roessler 2016; Straus 2006; Tajima 2014; Wood 2003), including land conflicts (Boone 2014; Klaus and Mitchell 2015) and cross-regional comparisons (Brosché 2022; Elfversson 2019), or on electoral incentives models of violence (Brass 2003; Varshney 2002; Vinson 2017; Wilkinson 2006). The logic of the electoral incentives model emphasizes the causal link between communal violence and democratic elections. Regional politicians instrumentalize intercommunal tensions, polarize groups, and incite violence to win elections by influencing undecided voters (Wilkinson 2006). So far, however, related studies almost exclusively deal with higher scales of aggregation at the provincial, district, and cross-town levels.

Several studies identified community as the key level of analysis in explaining large-scale conflicts (Bunte and Vinson 2016; Petersen 2001; Straus 2006; Tajima 2014; Vinson 2017; Wood 2003). However, very few studies have analyzed communal warfare in urban settings and on the neighbourhood level, and have sought to explain micro-variations of violence within a town's level (Dhattiwala 2016; 2019; Kutmanaliev 2015; 2017; 2018; Krause 2018; Madueke 2019; Madueke and Vermeulen 2018). These studies make an important step forward in the ethnographic and case-specific understanding of urban armed conflict, yet this problem needs more systematic cross-neighbourhood analysis.

Notably, this gap results both from methodological and theoretical shortcomings. Methodologically, the studies lack valid instruments to distinguish group behaviour at the neighbourhood level. Theoretically, they failed to develop heuristic models to systematically investigate neighbourhood dynamics. One reason for this deficit might be their overall top-down perspective and their "statist" bias: many studies focus on the state's response to violence ignoring local-level factors such as community cohesion (Petersen 2001), efficacy and resilience (Kaplan 2017), urban landscape and the built environment (Dhattiwala 2016), or intra- and intercommunal strategic interactions (Christia 2012; Tajima 2014). Consequently, we still have to develop the necessary tools for the analysis of intense urban fighting in places such as Ahmedabad, Beirut, Kampala, Monrovia, Aligarh, Baghdad, Kaduna, Karachi, and more recently Jos, Mosul, Aleppo, Mariupol, and other cities (Brass 2003; Elfversson, Gusic, and Höglund 2019; Kutmanaliev 2020; Madueke and Vermeulen 2018; Vinson 2017; Weidmann and Salehyan 2013).

Another contribution of this study is to explore the multifaceted interactions among urban communal micro-groups and local conditions that determine their self-survival strategies (resilience) in high-risk situations. Existing literature that explores civil wars and communal conflicts in towns generally considers local communal groups as unitary actors, ignoring their multilateral relations and in-group interactions. However, groups previously considered as unitary actors can fractionalize into subgroups and actually engage in multilateral diplomacy creating alliances with other subgroups, not necessarily on the basis of common ethnic identity (Christia 2012; Tajima 2014). This kind of disaggregated analysis of groups has not been replicated at lower scales of analyses and certainly not in urban settings. In an urban environment, even if one city is represented only by two major ethnic groups, there are many communal subgroups based in different and often segregated neighbourhoods that interact with each other. The complexity and density of interactions and the divergent number of local groups makes the analysis complex. These interactions are often multilateral and difficult to trace, making the measurement challenging and problematic. This creates additional difficulties in distinguishing the neighbourhood-level groups. This methodological problem can partly explain why so many micro-comparative studies focus on communal conflicts in rural areas or on larger units but very rarely analyze urban communal groups.

To address these shortcomings, this volume presents one of the first cross-neighbourhood comparative analyses of large-scale violent conflict in urban settings that seeks to bridge the mentioned methodological and theoretical gaps. Moreover, this study is also the first systematic micro-comparative study of the 2010 communal conflict in Kyrgyzstan, which, despite its intensity and theoretical significance, has hitherto remained understudied. The aim is to shed light on the above gaps and contribute to "micro-comparative turn," "spatial turn," and "urban turn" (Elfversson and Höglund 2021; Raleigh 2015) research within peace and conflict studies.

The analysis in this book draws on extensive ethnographic observations and interview data (N=111) – collected during my research fieldwork between 2010 and 2014 – with ethnic community leaders, ethnic mediators, local officials, police officers, and ordinary citizens from both ethnic groups. The fieldwork also included participant and spatial observations in ethnic communities and urban neighbourhoods. The ethnographic observations are supplemented by satellite images of violent destruction. I started my fieldwork in the immediate aftermath of the communal violence, in July 2010. To my best knowledge, no other academic study has investigated this conflict systematically using first-hand insights acquired through intensive ethnographic research. In chapter 4, I provide a detailed section on the research methodology of this study.

I compare various violent and nonviolent neighbourhoods in Osh and Jalalabat.[4] I selected several pairs of Kyrgyz-Uzbek subgroups to observe how strategic interactions produce escalation and de-escalation of violence and local-level outcomes in the neighbourhoods of the most affected cities. The selected pairs represent violent and nonviolent dyads and are compared across different environmental contexts. This allows me to identify causal mechanisms and evaluate the effect of micro-structural conditions on the respective outcomes in violent and nonviolent neighbourhoods.

DEFINITIONS: ETHNIC RIOTS OR CIVIL WAR

For analytical clarity, we need to classify the type and the form of violence that this communal conflict entails. Below, I briefly discuss the definitions of communal riots and civil war and operationalize the form of violence in this conflict according to quantitative indicators proposed by the literature on civil war. Based on these indicators, I define the June 2010 conflict in southern Kyrgyzstan as communal warfare because it combines the attributes of both civil war and communal riots. In fact, the 2010 ethnic violence in Kyrgyzstan had every chance of being transformed into a full-fledged civil war had it not been contained in the short term by the local communities and by the late efforts of the government.

Different forms of violence assume varying degrees of intensity, organization, and state involvement, as well as specific types and the scope of collective action (Beissinger 2002, 305). In fact, the conflict in Kyrgyzstan comprises multiple forms of violence separated from each other by a sequence of events and/or by geographical distance. Violent mobilization during the communal conflict in Osh started in the form of riots, however, it very quickly progressed into a more violent and organized form. In the course of the events, communal violence escalated into an armed conflict. In the locations where the local Uzbek groups got defeated, ethnic violence transformed into ethnic pogroms. The ethnic violence in Kyrgyzstan largely embraces elements of both civil war and ethno-communal riots.

Ethnic riots and communal violence assume mobilization of rioters along ethnic, racial, communal, or religious lines (Brubaker and Laitin 1998; Horowitz 2001; Olzak 1992; Varshney 2002; Wilkinson 2009). Religious, ethnic, and communal affiliations play an important role as the onset of violence tends to reify group differences and group identities. Victims and target groups are carefully chosen based on their group affiliation. However, "[e]thnicity is not the ultimate, irreducible source of violent conflict ... [r]ather, conflicts driven by struggles for power between challengers and incumbents are newly ethnicized, newly framed in ethnic terms" (Brubaker and Laitin 1998, 425). According to Horowitz (2001, 1), a "deadly ethnic riot" is "an intense, sudden, though not necessarily wholly unplanned, lethal attack by civilian members of one ethnic group on civilian members of another ethnic group, the victims chosen because of their group membership."

On the other hand, Gersovitz and Kriger (2013, 160–1) define civil war as "a politically organized, large-scale, sustained, physically violent conflict that occurs within a country principally among large/numerically important groups of its inhabitants or citizens over the monopoly of physical force within the country." The temporal and spatial dimensions contained in this definition reflect main conceptual criteria found in the relevant literature. Studies have been generally focused on two main indicators: (1) a death threshold that distinguishes civil war from other internal conflicts, and (2) the duration of civil war. Although these threshold indicators are arbitrary cut-off points aimed at operationalization and coding for cross-national quantitative analyses of civil war, they help us to structure our conceptual analysis.

According to the first indicator, the June 2010 ethnic violence falls short of being categorized as civil war. While most scholars determine 1,000 deaths as the threshold for counting violent conflict as a civil war (Doyle and Sambanis 2000, 783; Fearon and Laitin 2003, 76; Kirschner 2014, 34; Licklider 1995, 682), this conflict's death toll of nearly 500 reached just in four days of violence. On the other hand, some studies proposed much lower thresholds with range of 500–1,000 deaths, combined with a large-scale destruction (Sambanis 2004, 820). It does not reach the classic cut-off point of 1,000 deaths but it does reach the threshold proposed by Sambanis (2004), Fearon and Laitin (2003), and Gleditsch et al. (2002). This specification brings us to the second indicator – the duration of civil war. To be counted as civil war, violence has to be sustained. If the ethnic violence in southern Kyrgyzstan were sustained, it could be qualified as civil war.

Yet there are other indicators in the literature that can help us distinguish the type of the ethnic conflict in Kyrgyzstan. Important criteria that this conflict meets for qualifying as civil war are "effective resistance" measured by 100 deaths on the side of the stronger party (Fearon and Laitin 2003; Sambanis 2004, 823–5), large-scale destruction (Sambanis 2004, 820), and mass-scale internal and external displacement of civilians and refugees as an additional measure of human cost (Doyle and Sambanis 2000; Sambanis 2004, 823). This conflict estimates for more than 100 deaths registered on the side of the Kyrgyz – the "stronger" side in this conflict, more than 2,000 buildings razed and burnt, and around 400,000 of refugees and internally displaced persons on both sides. These values highlight the high intensity of the conflict in Kyrgyzstan and can be comparable to thresholds applied to civil wars.

Another indicator that makes this ethnic conflict resemble a civil war is the fact that both sides used automatic weapons (Kalashnikovs and rifles) – nearly three-quarters of all deaths resulted from gunshots rather than from stabbing and cerebral injuries common in riot violence (see death toll statistics in chapter 3). Moreover, some heavy weapon such as armoured personnel carriers (APCs, discussed ahead) and armoured lorries were used in these clashes. Mobilized Kyrgyz who came to Osh from various rural areas captured three APCs from military garrisons to attack Uzbek mahallas, while Uzbek self-defence groups used armoured lorries to counteract these attacks. On the other hand, most participants were weakly organized and armed with knives, sticks, axes, and other simple self-invented weaponry, common in riot violence. Other important indicators such as neutrality of state and level of organization of armed groups suggest that the violence in Kyrgyzstan falls short of being labelled as civil war. In civil wars, normally state is actively involved in fighting against rebels and armed groups are relatively well organized.

The ambiguity of this ethnic conflict as a form of violence was also reflected in my conversations with ordinary people. Many referred to the June 2010 violence as a "war" [*sogush*],[5] while other respondents regarded it as a "disorder" [*topolong*]. This underlines the 2010 ethnic violence as a borderline case which

Table 1.1
Conceptual operationalization of the June 2010 ethnic violence

Indicators	Riots	Civil war
Number of deaths		+
Duration of violence	+	
Neutrality of state	+	
Scale of destruction		+
Level of armament	+	+
Effective resistance		+
Level of organization	+	
Refugees		+

Source: Based on the author's own research.

contains patterns of both civil war and ethnic rioting. The intensity of violence during the conflict in southern Kyrgyzstan approximate it to a short but an intensive civil war. As a result, some of theoretical assumptions normally applied to the analysis of civil wars can also be employed in the current study.

Table 1.1 shows that by the intensity of violence, the death toll, and the number of wounded people, refugees, and internally displaced persons this conflict can be qualified as a civil war. However, the characteristics of spontaneous outbreaks of violence, poor organization of the violent mobs, and the duration of the conflict have more in common with rioting. Although this ethnic conflict falls short of definition of civil war, the similarity with both forms of violence makes the analysis of this conflict more complex but equally interesting. This complex association between these two forms of violence in Kyrgyzstan is laconically reflected in Varshney's notes (2007, 279): "Riots or pogroms typically precede civil wars ... but all riots and pogroms do not lead to civil wars." Given this complexity, this book draws theoretical and empirical insights from both fields of study.

Most studies rarely explain instances of prevented civil wars in which high-scale violence was contained – de facto a terminated onset of civil war in positive cases (see Fearon and Laitin (1996) and Varshney (2007, 276) for the same observation regarding ethnic conflicts). As the ethnic violence in Kyrgyzstan fully fulfills criteria for the onset of civil war, we can regard it a prevented case. Assuming the existing selection bias, this study's one possible contribution is to show how local-level mechanisms of mediation and informal institutions help to prevent the escalation of the local armed conflict into a full-scale civil war.

Some scholars of civil war included several studies on the Hindu-Muslim riots in India conducted by Varshney (2002), Wilkinson (2006), and Brass (1997; 2003) in influential theoretical reviews on civil wars contributing to the rise of the research program on microdynamics of violence and microcomparative turn in civil war studies (Kalyvas 2008; Roessler 2016; Tarrow 2007). Several other works on Indonesia, Nigeria, Sudan, Uganda, DR Congo and many other countries can easily be classified and fit the same category (Brosché and Elfversson 2012; Bunte and Vinson 2016; Klinken 2009; Roessler 2016). This has been an important development in the theoretical literature on civil wars as it shows an increasing appreciation of the studies on ethnic riots by scholars of political violence and the exchange of theoretical insights between both fields of studies.

Correspondingly, the factual significance of the communal conflict in southern Kyrgyzstan is highlighted not only by the high levels of property destruction (around 2,000) but also by the high death toll (around 500), number of injured people (several thousand), and hundreds of thousands internally displaced people just in four days of ethnic violence. This is especially evident when compared with some notorious violent riots that took place in other parts of the world. For example, the total death toll for Aligarch, one of the most riot-prone cities in India, was 195.[6] This comprises all victims killed throughout Aligarh's history of Hindu-Muslim violence for the entire period from 1925 to 1995, in more than twenty large-scale riots that broke out in this city (Brass 2003, 63). This is considerably smaller than in Osh which experienced higher mortality rate just in one conflict episode. The same is true for other riot-prone Indian cities. In just two Indian cities – Mumbai (formerly Bombay) and Ahmedabad – the total death toll (1,137 and 1,119 killings respectively; Varshney 2001, 372), in a half-century-long Hindu-Muslim violence (1950–95) exceeded the number of killings in the single episode of ethnic violence in Kyrgyzstan in June 2010. Other examples of intercommunal violence include racial and commodity riots in the United States (US) in the 1960s, resulting in 250 deaths in about 500 riots (Waddington 2007, 61). Fifty-two people were killed in three days during the infamous Los Angeles riots in 1992, the most murderous, racial riots in the history of interracial violence in the US (Waddington 2007, 60). Approximately 1,300 people were killed in all ethnic conflicts in the entire Soviet Union during the breakdown of the multinational empire from January 1988 through May 1991 (Beissinger 2002, 276). This comparison highlights the highly violent nature of communal conflict in Kyrgyzstan. The high death toll was due to the paralysis of the central state and inefficiency of the local police but was also the result of the widespread use of firearms. Around three-quarters of all killings in the June 2010 violence resulted from gunshot wounds (see table 4.5 in chapter 4). That such a high number of killings resulted from gunshots from automatic weapons, guns, and even APCs gives us grounds to qualify this violent episode as a full-scale armed conflict – a communal warfare.

PLAN OF THE BOOK

The following chapters explain the various determinants of spatial variations in ethnic violence. Chapter 2 places this research within the interdisciplinary literature, identifying common theoretical insights and mechanism-based explanations drawn from disciplines and fields such as urban sociology, IR and security studies, democratization and regime transitions, studies on social disorder and policing of mass protests, ethnic politics, and civil wars in relation to intragroup policing and intergroup pacts. Such interdisciplinary insights include, for instance, the concepts of the balance of power and credible commitment drawn from the neorealist literature in IR to enrich the analysis of neighbourhood-level intergroup interactions.

Chapter 3 discusses the structural-historical context of the relations between Kyrgyz and Uzbek communities at the macro level and provides background to the onset of the 2010 violence in southern Kyrgyzstan. This chapter demonstrates that growing tensions between Kyrgyz and Uzbeks produced uncertainty and fear among these two ethnic groups and triggered ethnic mobilization and escalation of tensions at the national level exacerbated by the weakness of the central state, uncertainty, and power vacuum.

Chapter 4 provides a thorough overview of the dynamics of ethnic violence in the city of Osh. The chapter displays how critical events and contingencies produced uneven spatial distribution and different intensity levels and forms of violence across the city's districts and neighbourhoods. Consequently, the variance in forms of violence was determined by local-level dynamics and conditions in each location and neighbourhood. To adopt Jones Luong's (2002) terminology, chapters 3 and 4 provide structural-historical and immediate strategic contexts, respectively, for the dynamics of ethnic violence and actors' strategic interactions. The last part of chapter 4 discusses descriptive conflict statistics and the research methodology employed for this study.

In the next chapters, this book analyzes urban neighbourhoods' responses to the emerging violence in the city of Osh. In chapters 5 and 6, I conduct paired comparisons of typical neighbourhoods in Osh, one violent and the other nonviolent in each pair. The pairs compare neighbourhoods across different dimensions. These paired comparisons demonstrate similar dynamics of violence in many other neighbourhoods.

Chapter 5 starts with theoretical analysis of the impact of space on violent conflict, thus, complementing the theoretical discussion from chapter 2. Then it compares two neighbourhoods in Osh with different spatial structures and built environments. The chapter demonstrates how differences in the built environment, urban landscape, and spatial infrastructure produce divergent long-term social and structural effects and provide local communities and their leaders with uneven favourable and unfavourable conditions to deal with emerging violence in these typical neighbourhoods in Osh. The difference in spatial characteristics and geographical locations within the city makes some neighbourhoods more vulnerable to violence, while enabling other neighbourhoods to build more effective defence against armed groups.

Chapter 6 presents two paired comparisons and examines the effect of contingency and strategic interactions – both within and between groups – on violent dynamics across Osh's neighbourhoods. It analyzes how local communal groups' divergent strategies in dealing with external threats through in-group policing and intercommunal pacts in two similar districts in Osh produced different outcomes. Furthermore, it also analyzes the impact of environmental and spatial factors on the variation in violence.

Chapter 7 analyzes how the security dilemma and ethnic fears affected the dynamics of violence in the city of Jalalabat, an administrative center of the Jalalabat oblast (province). In 2010, it was the second most violent town after Osh. Neighbourhoods in Jalalabat adopted strategies/responses that were of confrontational, cooperative, self-isolationist, and/or neutral character, and the type of response to uncertainty that they chose affected the spatial dynamics of the conflict and the (non)violent outcomes in neighbourhoods. This chapter displays the variation in types of responses to the diffusion of violence across Jalalabat's four neighbourhoods.

Chapter 8 outlines the contributions of this book. The chapter suggests how the research findings of this book can extend the research program on local-level violence and proposes new directions for future research. It considers the implications of the research findings for policymakers and peacebuilding initiatives.

2

Explaining Communal Violence at the Micro-Spatial Level

Intragroup Policing, Intergroup Nonaggression Pacts, and the Neighbourhood Security Dilemma

This chapter examines the linkage between in-group policing and nonaggression pacts and how it affects the probability of violence occurrence or its prevention in conflict-prone locations. It discusses causal mechanisms and conditions that make these factors (in)efficient in hindering local-level communal violence. This two-level approach for analyzing the linkage between intra- and intergroup interactions has been rarely employed in the relevant literature on microdynamics of violence. I argue that neither intragroup nor intergroup factors can explain the variation in outcomes on their own. Some assumptions of this approach – namely, the importance of constellation of in-group forces for external negotiations and the linkage between intragroup and intergroup levels in mediation/negotiation processes – are key to the analysis of violent dynamics in each location.

Among the micro-comparative literature on communal violence produced in recent two decades, an electoral incentives model argument has been especially influential. According to this model, local politicians and ethnic entrepreneurs instigate intercommunal violence by strategically exploiting tensions between local ethnic communities in order to achieve their electoral goals. In contrast to the top-down electoral model, Varshney (2002) and Berenschot (2011, 2020) argue that violence flourishes in communities where local social capital and patronage networks in everyday life are organized around intraethnic leaders, institutions and organizations. Those communities exclusively connected to ethnic organization are more likely to be manipulated by ethnic entrepreneurs and divisive leaders. Lacking intercommunal social bridges with out-group members, ethnically segregated communal groups have few chances to bridge their differences and build cooperative relations in times of acute crisis. This variance in the degree of segregation and the density of intercommunal ties explains why violence erupts with different intensity across various communities. However, this book presents a non-electoral model and displays the missing part in Varshney's and Berenschot's respective arguments by demonstrating that even segregated communal groups have conflict resolving mechanisms such as in-group policing and intercommunal pacts. This book analyzes micro-scale institutional (in-group policing), interactive (pact-making), and spatial factors and how they determine local outcomes, and presents a theoretical discussion of these factors and related set of variables.

As noted in the previous chapter, very few studies analyze communal violence at the neighbourhood level. However, recently several studies engaged in the micro-comparative analysis of communal conflicts at the level of rural communities (Tajima 2014), districts (Bunte and Vinson 2016), and neighbourhoods (Berenschot 2011; Krause 2018). Most studies dealing with micro-spatial variations in violence neglect the spatial factors that could considerably impact the geographical or locational distribution of violence. Few exceptions include studies with detailed analysis of spatial characteristics of cross-neighbourhood variations in violence in the Indian city of Ahmedabad (Dhattiwala 2016) and analysis of various spatial and locational dimensions of communal violence in the Nigerian city of Jos (Madueke 2018, 2019; Madueke and Vermeulen 2018). However, in this chapter I do not discuss the impact of space in connection to violence. I discuss theoretical implications of space in chapter 5, along with relevant comparative analysis of neighbourhoods in Osh.

By combining the analysis of contingent, spatial, and structural factors, this book consolidates various analytical dimensions examined by scholars of communal conflicts but, at the same time, presents an integrated theoretical approach that was largely lacking in the previous studies. The following sections present theoretical propositions of this study.

INTERGROUP PACTS

Pacts can prevent intrastate violence and resolve conflicts. Pact is usually an elitist and exclusivist and usually short-term agreement among a select set of actors (O'Donnell and Schmitter 1986, 37) intended to prevent or resolve costly violent conflict between competing forces.

In ethnic politics, pacted democracy is a form of mutual security agreements among ethnic elites and pacts are fragile and temporary coalitions with minimal security reassurances to ethnic minorities (Rothchild and Lake 1998, 207–8). Scholars of ethnic conflict and civil war place great emphasis on pacts' mutual guarantees of physical security and political and economic interests of elites or identity groups. As Lake and Rothchild (1998, 13) put it: "Stable ethnic relations can be understood as based upon a 'contract' between groups. Ethnic contracts specify, among other things, the rights and responsibilities, political privileges, and access to resources of each group. These contracts may be formal constitutional agreements or simply informal understandings between elites. Whatever their form [be], ethnic contracts specify the relationship between the groups and normally channel politics in peaceful directions."

Sometimes, once a pact is negotiated between narrow circle of leaders, it then should be endorsed by a wider public or elites' ethnic constituencies (O'Donnell 1986, 12). In general, a pact is a fragile temporary coalition which can breakdown if conditions and factors that led to a negotiated settlement change or if one of the parties does not credibly commit to the conditions of the negotiation (Fearon 1998; Hartzell and Rothchild 1997; Lake and Rothchild 1998).

Each pact incorporates some necessary elements. According to O'Donnell and Schmitter (1986, 38), "At the core of a pact lies a negotiated compromise under which actors agree to forgo or underutilize their capacity to harm each other by extending guarantees not to threaten each other's corporate autonomies or vital interests. This typically involves clauses stipulating abstention from violence, a prohibition on appeals to outsiders (the military or the masses), and often a commitment to use pact-making again as the means for resolving future disputes."

However, as per Rothchild and Lake (1998, 208) "[i]f poorly negotiated and implemented, the incomplete ethnic contracts may be rejected eventually by the groups they are designed to protect." In general, a pact is not a remedy to intergroup conflicts but only a temporary solution which allows actors to build upon more robust and longer-term solutions to ethnic conflicts.

In ethnic politics, pacts are not full-fledged ethnic cooperation. They do not signify robust interethnic civic engagement (see Varshney 2002). In the context of ethnic violence in Kyrgyzstan, a pact is the result of negotiations between small number of communal leaders. The main goal of these negotiations was to guarantee ethno-communal security. They signalled commitment by ethnic leaders to nonaggression and ethnic peace. By committing to peace through pacts, communal leaders sought to increase trust between local ethnic communities and reduce uncertainty.

Importance, Effects, and Outcomes of Pacts

Political pact plays an important role in conflict resolution. Around one-fourth of civil wars that took place since the Second World War ended with negotiated settlements (Licklider 1995, 684). One of the most important aims of a pact is to reduce uncertainty of elites or an identity group toward their physical survival and political-economic security.

The literature in general considers pacts between national-level or ethnic-group-level elites. In this, the present study is different by analyzing small-scale ethnic community leaders. It does not consider the issue of long-term stability of pacts. It only concerns very short-term security pacts.

According to the democratic transitions literature, pacts play an important role as they keep outsiders away, marginalize radicals from decision-making, "limit the role of radicals and the masses in the negotiation process" (McFaul 2002, 218), "reduce uncertainty about actors' ultimate intentions," and "lessens the fears" (ibid., 217).

In ethnic politics pacts do not substitute full-fledged ethnic cooperation. This reflects peaceful outcomes observed in the mixed and segregated neighbourhoods in Osh and Jalalabat, where residents in ethnically mixed neighbourhoods cooperated based on neighbourhood solidarity. Pacts emerged where grassroots cooperation was absent (i.e., in areas of segregated neighbourhoods without mass-level interethnic interactions), while in ethnically mixed neighbourhoods, people cooperated without negotiating pacts at the interleader level.

One important element/aim of a pact is restriction on participation of outsiders in decision-making. A pact at all levels involves "a commitment for some period to resolve conflicts arising from the operation of the pact by renegotiating its terms, not by resorting to the mobilization of outsiders or the elimination of insiders" (O'Donnell and Schmitter 1986, 41; see also McFaul 2002, 217). As evidence shows, when negotiating intercommunal pacts in Osh and other towns, community leaders demanded that the other side does not involve strangers and outsiders in local issues. According to conditions of nonaggression pacts, neighbouring communities negotiated to protect each other from aggressive groups coming from outside areas.

Table 2.1
Type of response to uncertainty

	Peaceful	*Violent*
Leader-level	Pact and ingroup policing	Instigation
Mass-level	Ethnic cooperation/neutrality	Violent confrontation

Source: Based on the author's own research.

Pacts are not causal determinants of peace and can lead to divergent outcomes. However, they play important role in reducing uncertainty and tensions. Although pacts do not guarantee peace, they increase the likelihood of peaceful outcome if the actors involved in these pact negotiations are in a position to control and police their respective groups. A scholar of democratization argued that "[t]hough a pact is not a necessary condition for a successful democratic transition, it enhances the probability of success ... A democratic outcome is most likely when soft-liners and moderates enter into pacts that navigate transition from dictatorship to democracy ... If transition is not pacted, it is likely to fail" (McFaul 2002, 216). Equivalently, pact in ethnic politics is not a necessary condition for peace but greatly enhances the probability for peaceful outcome – particularly, if negotiated between moderate leaders and communal activists from both sides.

As table 2.1 illustrates, intergroup arrangements keep outsiders away and marginalize radicals from decision-making by limiting "the role of radicals and the masses in the negotiation process" (ibid., 218). However, when masses play a primary role, this can result either in mass violence or grassroots-level ethnic cooperation. The latter is a more robust condition for peace than a pact negotiated between elites.

Requisite Conditions for Pact-Making (Production of Pacts)

In order to analyze the efficiency of pacts in containing, preventing, and resolving intrastate violent conflicts, we need to distinguish two different phases in pact-making process. One concerns the process of the production of pacts (pact-making) and the other deals with the problem of pact efficiency. To analyze these phases, I distinguish the following related questions: Under what conditions are pacts likely to be negotiated? What accounts for the efficiency and stability of these pacts? In this section, I discuss various conditions that lead to the emergence and durability of pacts. I then analyze their theoretical implications for the nonaggression pacts conducted by ethnic-neighbourhood-community leaders in southern Kyrgyzstan.

The theoretical literature identifies three main conditions required for the production of political pacts: (1) existence of external threat for elites and their constituencies; (2) availability of legitimate brokers or third-party intermediaries who have connections to the contending parties; and (3) the balance of power between contending groups. Threat acts as a trigger condition for initiating pacts, legitimate leaders and brokers negotiate pacts, and equal balance of power provides favourable condition for negotiation and durability of the pact.

Pacts in clan-based societies emerge in response to instability which usually comes with an exogenous shock such as sudden decline of the central. If exogenous shock or violence occurs, pacts maintain durable and peaceful but not necessarily friendly relations between groups. Collins (2006, 50) argues that clan elites are likely to negotiate pacts when the following three conditions are met: "(1) a shared external threat induces cooperation among clans who otherwise would have insular interests; (2) a balance of power exists among the major clan factions, such that none can dominate; (3) a legitimate broker, a leader trusted by all factions, assumes the role of maintaining the pact and the distribution of resources that it sets in place."

The second stage of pact politics concerns the problem of stability and durability of agreements. Stability of pacts depends on two main factors: (1) shifts in the balance of power between competing forces, and (2) compliance with the conditions of pact. In the first scenario, shifts in the distribution of power produce incentives for the side that increasing its power to renegotiate the pact or to stop complying with its conditions. This brings us to the second scenario. When one side stops to enforce the pact conditions, the other side in the pact does not see the reason to continue with the agreement. As a result, the pact breaks down. To make a pact durable, both sides must show credible commitment to the rules established by mutual agreement. Figure 2.1 outlines the paths of pact-making as observed during the 2010 communal conflict in Kyrgyzstan. It demonstrates the various paths that lead to different outcomes in terms of pact-making.

Pacts occur between leaders in situations where there are weak or absent interethnic civic ties between two local communities. The leaders make a pact to prevent violent conflict and to marginalize radicals from the power and the process of decision-making. In the following section, I examine the conditions that explain both pact-making and durability of pacts in detail and

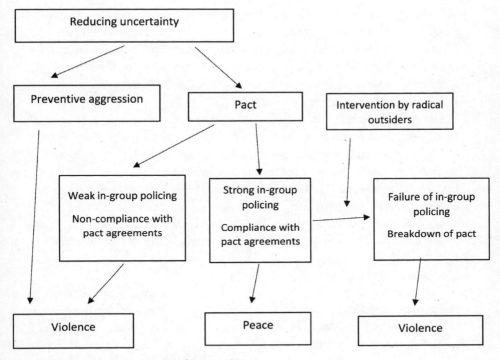

Figure 2.1 Observed paths of pact-making

then discuss their theoretical implications for the intercommunal pacts conducted by ethnic community leaders in southern Kyrgyzstan.

Uncertainty and Fear

Pact-making has strong relation to the notions of uncertainty and fear. The communal conflict in southern Kyrgyzstan broke out in the context of the breakdown of the central state that occurred after a popular uprising against President Kurmanbek Bakiev's corrupt regime in capital city of Bishkek. The regime change shook Bakiev's extensive patronage networks, particularly strongly embedded in the southern regions. The power vacuum produced acute political uncertainty and caused power struggles that involved Kyrgyz and Uzbek political and business elites eventually leading to intercommunal tensions and fears.

Uncertainty and fear are inherent mechanisms explaining security dilemma model. Booth and Wheeler (2008) distinguish between these terms defining uncertainty as an existential human condition and fear as a primordial emotion. These conditions trigger (i.e., produce incentives for) leaders and groups to reduce vulnerability by either conducting preventive attacks against their adversaries and repressions against the opposition or by negotiating pacted agreements and settlements. Both options allow reductions in uncertainty and lessen fear.

Uncertainty includes analysis of the crisis and responses to them. It "concerns the beliefs of decision makers, and ... arises when decision makers are not fully informed about parameters of the game and when information is asymmetrically distributed. Traditionally, game theory assumes that all players are fully informed about relevant parameters, including the strategies available to an opponent and the opponent's preferences – or at least that they all share the same 'imperfect' view" (Niou, Ordeshook, and Rose 1989, 58). Fear is a primordial emotion and is often based on past interactions (Booth and Wheeler 2008). Past interactions may mitigate intergroup engagement or exacerbate past hostilities.

The relationship between fear and uncertainty is complex but both often result from "emerging anarchy" (Posen 1993) produced by exogenous shocks – contingent and unexpected events such as natural disasters, death of nationwide leaders, or sudden decline of the central state (Collins 2006; McAdam, Tarrow, and Tilly 2001). Exogenous shocks produce "sudden and unpredictable decisions, high level of uncertainty, and new combinations of threat and opportunity" (McAdam, Tarrow, and Tilly 2001, 223). These contingent events trigger environmental changes and create conditions that can be perceived by actors both as threat or opportunity.

The collapse of the central state produces emerging anarchy and the relevant effects and conditions. According to Lake and Rothchild (1998, 8), "When central authority declines, groups become fearful for their survival. They invest in and prepare for violence, and thereby make actual violence possible ... state weakness is a necessary precondition for violent ethnic conflict to erupt." One consequence of the state collapse is that many ethnic groups and communities become geographically isolated and feel vulnerable surrounded by the territories of a rival group.

Another consequence of state decline is an exogenous shock that often changes the balance of power and creates an external threat to the interests of identity groups and elites. The presence or absence of the central state is an important condition for understanding the role of fear and uncertainty in intergroup relations. As Walter (1999, 5) states, "Groups have little to fear from each other when the central government can effectively enforce rules and arbitrate disputes." External threat becomes a trigger that pushes elites to negotiate pacts or to make preemptive attacks against rival forces.

Anarchy is "the absence of political authority in international politics above that of the sovereign state" (Booth and Wheeler 2008, 2) and a key condition of security dilemma. In domestic politics, anarchy would mean absence of the central state. It is "a world of uncertainty, weapons, and fear" (ibid., 2). The importance of anarchy as a key condition in IR and ethnic politics makes application of IR approaches useful in the analysis of ethnic conflict. Survival is the main motivation here: "an anarchic system – a system in which no organization or constraints on action are imposed exogenously" (Niou, Ordeshook, and Rose 1989, 62).

Double Effect of Uncertainty

Uncertainty (and fear) can either produce negotiated settlement or trigger violent conflict and preemptive aggression. According to McFaul (2002, 224), "uncertainty generated by relatively balanced forces facilitated the emergence of democratic institutions [in southern Europe] … [but] this same uncertainty produced the opposite effect – conflict [in eastern Europe]." When distribution of power is unequal there is a more certain pathway or what McFaul calls a "non-cooperative strategic situation." This is important observation that shows how uncertainty produces different outcomes. The twofold effect of uncertainty can lead to pacts or to confrontation. Uncertainty "provides opportunities for claim making but also threatens established groups, leading to competition among claimants for political space" (McAdam, Tarrow, and Tilly 2001, 66), and "the heightened sense of threat or opportunity associated with uncertainty prompt[s] all established parties to the conflict to monitor one another's actions closely and engage in reactive mobilization on an escalating basis" (ibid., 97). The key question is "how different settings on the ground might affect groups' decision to fight, to negotiate, or to remain at peace" (Walter 1999, 2).

The fear-producing environments activate security dilemma between ethnic groups and consequently, "the decision to go to war is based on a group's assessment of how malicious or benign a potential rival might be" (Walter 1999, 9). As de Figueiredo and Weingast (1999, 263) observe, fear is a driving mechanism that forces people to forgo the benefits of social cooperation and economic interests when they feel external threat to their lives and families.

Normally ordinary people's support for aggressive leaders will increase as perception of insecurity increases. However, this study shows how responses to uncertainty from local communities can be different despite similar environmental changes.

Uncertainty introduces unpredictability. The absence of predictable rules of the game makes strategic calculation difficult and increases the importance of contingent choice. "During regime transitions, all political calculations and interactions are highly uncertain. Actors find it difficult to know what their interests are, who their supporters will be, and which groups will be their allies or opponents" (Karl 1990, 6). Therefore, uncertainty can trigger different responses. Local communities in southern Kyrgyzstan responded in divergent ways to uncertainty. One way to reduce uncertainty was to strike against the out-group members with preemptive attacks and another strategy was to transcend uncertainty by rebuilding trust and establishing cooperative relations. Yet, other communities kept neutrality by completely self-isolating their neighbourhoods. Radicals' strategy to reduce uncertainty is to preemptively attack their rivals, while moderates' strategy is to de-escalate tensions by reassuring the other side of their peaceful intentions and to rebuild trust. In this context, the value of strategic interactions and negotiations between competing forces becomes highly significant for the final outcome.

The Role of Brokers in Production of Pacts

The availability of legitimate leaders[1] is another important factor in successful pact-making. Scholars emphasize the importance of leaders in negotiating and producing pacts in order to prevent violent conflicts (Hartzell and Rothchild 1997, 147). Leaders have direct influence on decisions to respond to uncertainty. The decision and response strategy to reduce uncertainty and conditions for such response vary from cooperation and pacted agreement to violent confrontation. The decisions made by leaders at key moments of uncertainty highly influence the outcomes of contingent events.

Influential individuals and leaders can act as brokers and mediators to produce pacts between competing political forces and ethnic communities, provided that they have in-group legitimacy and recognition by an out-group. Legitimate leaders broker pacts between competing forces. Brokerage is one of key mechanisms that links "two or more previously unconnected social sites by a unit that mediates their relations with one another and/or with yet other sites" (McAdam, Tarrow, and Tilly 2001, 26).

Who are brokers and mediators and who have legitimacy to negotiate pacts? As Hartzell and Rothchild (1997, 149) argue, "Elites negotiating a pacted arrangement are normally those who possess enough power to do harm to each other's vital interests. This does not mean, however, that pacts are totally inclusive settlements. Those leaders whom dominant elites judge to lack significant bargaining power may be excluded from both the pact-making process and the institutions of governance." Therefore, pacts are negotiated if leaders participating in negotiation have significant bargaining power with sufficient level of authority and influence within their local ethnic community and ability to police their constituencies. Negotiating with leaders who lack these features is less efficient for the prospects of peace. Weak leaders without in-group legitimacy and external recognition by the out-group will engender a problem of credible commitment. The other side will simply not believe in the ability of such leaders to implement conditions of pact and importantly, to police their constituency and to restrain it from aggression. For this reason, O'Donnell and Schmitter (1986, 40) emphasize the importance of well-recognized leaders in mediation of pacts. As per them, legitimate leaders are "respected, prominent individuals who are seen as representative of propertied classes, elite institutions, and/or territorial constituencies and, hence, capable of influencing their subsequent collective behaviour – seem to offer the best available interlocutors with whom to negotiate mutual guarantees."

In countries where formal institutions are weak, it is the leaders and elites who possess a great deal of informal power who determine and structure local politics. They act as legitimate political brokers between competing clans and factions to manage a stable pact (Collins 2006, 171).

The level of political and social authority of group leaders has important implications for the in-group balance of power and self-policing as a pact is only viable if leaders manage their constituencies. Such legitimate neighbourhood-level communal leaders became critical actors in the situation of deep uncertainty when communal warfare raged in urban settings between local communities in southern Kyrgyzstan.

In many cases, a neutral broker is necessary to mediate and maintain a pact. External brokers are especially efficient under conditions of uncertainty and information failures (Lake and Rothchild 1996). Third-party mediators "can present a solution which is agreeable to both sides but which the disputants may be unwilling to propose for fear of appearing 'weak.'" (Fearon and Laitin 1996, 730). Some examples include during transitional uncertainty in Central

Asian countries in the 1990s – "a pact incorporating powerful clan factions was key to maintaining regime durability in the absence of consolidated regime institutions [and] a neutral broker who balanced power and resources was key to maintaining that pact, and that a shared external threat made it more likely that clan elites would support the pact and the regime" (Collins 2002, 269). Another example comes from medieval Genoa, where competing clans under threat of mutual elimination agreed to invite each year a neutral broker – the podesta – who would govern the city and manage internal conflicts and maintain a peaceful pact (Greif 1998).

Strategic dilemmas can be mitigated and solved through mediation by neutral brokers. Information failure is a strategic dilemma which arises when individuals or groups try to misrepresent their real preferences in order to prevent violence but competing interests can trigger suspicions and violent conflict (Lake and Rothchild 1998, 11; see also Kuran 1998). The dilemma of information failure hinders negotiations between rival groups as private information and group preferences are usually known within group but unknown to the outsider group. When the state weakens, the problem of information failure becomes acute; intergroup suspicions arise about intentions of others. This dilemma can be transcended and solved through third-party brokerage. Neutral mediators reveal groups' real preferences and inform them to other parties, thus achieving a favourable ground for interethnic cooperation (Lake and Rothchild 1998, 13). Pacts as a solution to the information problem "may be accomplished in many instances through professional mediators who know one or both groups well and who specialize in extracting precise information from disputing parties to design finely calibrated compensation packages that prevent spiraling violence" (Fearon and Laitin 1996, 729).

Two-Level Negotiation Game

Neutral mediators are, however, not always available, especially during sudden outbreaks of violence. Nonetheless, intergroup cooperation can be sustained through in-group mediators. In this case, each group's mediator coordinates interactions at two levels: intra- and intergroup communications. Mediators negotiate intergroup pacts and manage intragroup interactions directly with their immediate constituencies. The history of past interactions and trust between leaders/mediators are important. If communication between leaders is not well organized, they have difficulties in reaching pacted agreement as information problems follow from a lack of efficient communication between elites. Rare and sporadic interactions among leaders that are characterized by deep insecurity and suspicions result in the inability to negotiate peaceful pacts and the taking of extreme and destructive measures against rivals, including killings and instigation of violence in order to protect themselves (Higley and Burton 1989, 19). This argument can be extended to the interactions between deeply segregated ethnic groups which are alienated from each other by the absence of regular intergroup communication.

Although the literature on pacts has paid sufficient attention to the problem of interelite interactions and intergroup balance of power, it has insufficiently studied the problem of two-level interactions. In a two-level negotiation game, the role of leaders is twofold. On the one hand, they must deal with leaders of other groups in intergroup relations. On the other hand, they should reflect on the situation in domestic politics and control local constituencies and value their interests and preferences. Both intra- and intergroup interactions can pose challenges for negotiating agreement. Situations of emerging anarchy and violence arise out of the strategic interactions between and within groups.

According to Lake and Rothchild (1998, 8), three different strategic dilemmas can cause violence to erupt between groups: information failures, problems of credible commitment, and incentives to use force preemptively, also known as the security dilemma. These dilemmas are fundamental causes of ethnic conflict. Within-group strategic interactions include political and ethnic entrepreneurs' attempts to outbid moderate politicians, "thereby mobilizing members, polarizing society, and magnifying the intergroup dilemmas. 'Nonrational' factors such as emotions, historical memories, and myths can exacerbate the violent implications of these in-group interactions" (ibid., 8).

The logic of two-level games provides many parallels with IR. One is the critical role of state leaders in connecting interstate and domestic policy preferences. Constraints on presidents from shifting domestic forces changes leaders' behaviour during negotiations (Kaplan 1998, 252). Moravcsik (1993, 24) asks the following questions, related to double-edged diplomacy, slightly paraphrased here: Under what conditions can leaders act independently of constituent pressures? How can leaders employ issue linkage and side-payments to alter domestic constraints? How do interest group configurations, representative institutions, and levels of uncertainty affect the strategies of leaders?

These questions lead the discussion toward the issues of intra- and intergroup balance of power, which I discuss next.

Balance of Power in Communal Conflict

The distribution of power between competing forces directly affects the probability of pact occurrence and durability of pact. Studies on political settlements in democratic transitions emphasize one particular condition that is conducive for pact-making – an equal balance of power between competing groups. The cause of pacts is uncertainty produced by the equal distribution of power between the regime and opposition (O'Donnell and Schmitter 1986). Distribution of power should be equal and uncertain: "Uncertainty enhances the probability of compromise, and relatively equal distributions of power create uncertainty" (McFaul 2002, 219). Stalemated pacts serve as causal force for driving democracy. As McFaul (ibid., 220) argues, new institutions emerge because of bargaining which can be considered as positive-sum game, where all sides benefit.

However, there are also other factors that should be considered. First, while the literature on ethnic pacts pays much attention to the intergroup balance of power, it insufficiently discusses the intragroup distribution of power and the dynamics of intragroup discussions and struggles between moderates and radicals. Second, while scholars analyze distributions of power between ethnic groups at national level, they tend to neglect power balances at local levels. The balances of power can vary at different levels and locations, and they can interplay across levels and spaces. Third, power shifts occur both between and within groups. Scholars of ethnic conflicts tend to focus on intergroup power shifts but not on intragroup power dynamics. Dynamics of power shifts and the linkage between intra- and intergroup distribution of power make it difficult for involved actors to calculate distribution of power in a situation of uncertainty, especially during dynamic situations.

Identified by McAdam et al. (2001) as a "radical flank effect," this mechanism marginalizes radicals and conservatives from intergroup negotiating process and allows moderates from both sides to negotiate a peaceful pact. Because neither side has capacity to impose its first-choice preferences, strategic interactions between competing forces become a causal variable for producing pacts (McFaul 2002, 219).

Another factor not sufficiently discussed in the literature on democratic and transitional pacts is the distribution of power between radicals and moderates within one group, as this has an important role in explaining the success and failure of intercommunal pacts. There is linkage between intra- and intergroup strategic interactions and balances of power in ethnic politics which corresponds to international and domestic arenas in two-level game models (see Evans, Jacobson, and Putnam 1993; Putnam 1988). McFaul (2002, 222) argues that successful peaceful transitions depend not only on the balance of power two groups but also on the distribution of power within each group. If there are no moderates in either side, then pacts do not work. Similarly, if radicals dominate one of the sides, then pacts are practically impossible to negotiate. In-group mobilization and cooperation in society play more important role than interelite negotiations (ibid.). Furthermore, the outcome of pacted transition is determined in the three sets of strategic interactions: (1) between the government and opposition (intergroup); (2) between reformers and conservatives (softliners and hardliners) in the government, and; (3) between moderates and radicals in the opposition (Huntington 1993, 123-4). These interactions are important for determining the overall outcome – contingent on the combination of distributions of power in each set of interactions. The outcome is successful only if moderates are stronger within each group (ibid., 124).

So, why is in-group balance of power important? There is one fundamental difference in the way radicals and moderates deal with uncertainty. Radicals want to reduce uncertainty by preemptive attacks and repressions while moderates do it by reassuring the other side in peaceful intentions and rebuilding trust. What accounts for the breakdown of pacts and self-policing when these have been already negotiated between contending forces? Or what factors can explain the instances when some successful pacts occur after initial outbreaks of violence? The micro-scale evidence from Osh suggests that shifts in power between moderate and radical factions within local ethnic communities can explain sudden breakdown of self-policing and intercommunal pacts.

Power Asymmetry

In general, scholars agree that equal distribution of power is conducive for pact-making. When the intergroup balance of power is asymmetrical, then pact-making is more difficult but still possible. However, asymmetry in power may change conditions for pact-making. There are different views on how asymmetrical distribution of power affect the probability of pact occurrence, its stability, and under what conditions sides agree to enter a pact. The main dilemma is the problem of credible commitment that inhibits pacts (Fearon 1998; Hartzell and Rothchild 1997). In asymmetrical relations, larger and more powerful groups have more capacity to impose the terms of contract.

What, then, induces weak parties to enter into a pact? One factor is rising costs of the conflict. A weaker group is reluctant to negotiate a pact because it expects the stronger group's defection from the pact. Nevertheless, according to one hypothesis, it enters pact because "[f]or those cases of prolonged intrastate conflict that have not produced a military victor, elites are most likely to negotiate pacts when the balance of bargaining power is asymmetrical" (Hartzell and Rothchild 1997, 153). Fearon and Laitin (1996, 726) instead claim that the weaker side is more interested in negotiating a pact. Larger groups may coax cooperation from small groups through the threat of spiral punishment. Since the cost of conflict is higher for a smaller group, the latter "will be more likely to evolve in-group policing strategies to try to avoid the costs of group punishment, while the threat of indiscriminate punishments will be more typical of how large groups give members of small groups an incentive to cooperate" (ibid.). So, for Fearon and Laitin, minorities have less power to determine conditions of the pact and must be more careful in self-policing. However, most accounts, including that of Fearon and Laitin, agree on the point that asymmetry in power makes pacts less stable because of the stronger side's incentives to defect.

Intragroup Power Balance

The communal conflict in southern Kyrgyzstan shows that outcomes in violence are often contingent on the distribution of power between radicals and moderates within local-level communal groups. In his micro-comparative study of the Rwandan genocide, Straus (2006) explains the district-level variation in violence by specific configurations of power in each district. The balance of power between moderates and radicals and power shifts determined violent outcomes and timing of mass ethnic violence across Rwandan districts and "the violence spread as a cascade of tipping points, and each tipping point was the outcome of local, intraethnic contests for dominance" (ibid., 92–3). Hutu hardliners took power both at national and local levels making violence easily spread across space, however, in those districts where moderates resisted longer the onset of genocidal violence was delayed until the moment when moderates were physically eliminated or forcibly coopted by radicals coming from outside. As Straus (2008, 317) puts it, "intra-Hutu struggles for power were a central dynamic as a precursor to the violence against Tutsis."

Shifts in Power

The dynamics of power shifts matter for explaining violence – rapid shifts during ongoing violence increase the sense of uncertainty and confusion and make it difficult for competing sides to do well-calibrated calculations about their responses to the crisis. Under such conditions, parties are willing to secure short-term security pacts due to perceptions of rising costs of conflict or to strike first, if they perceive that a preventive attack would make them less vulnerable. Moreover, the interplay between general and local-level distribution of power is important. Particularly, dynamics of violence at the macro-scale may affect the power dynamics in various locations. At times, many local Kyrgyz and Uzbek groups had difficulties in evaluating intergroup balances. Power shifts under uncertainty trigger a threat for ethnic groups exactly because of the problems of evaluation of relative strength, the degree of vulnerability and prediction of direction of power shifts.

However, as this book shows, intracommunal balance and power shifts are equally important for the type of response to uncertainty that groups choose. Focusing analysis only on either intergroup or in-group dynamics cannot explain the response strategy of the groups. Both intergroup and in-group interactions and power shifts affect the groups' type of responses to uncertainty. The two are interconnected. If intragroup struggle between moderates and radicals determines the willingness of the group to negotiate, intergroup shifts trigger the problem of credible commitment.

Particularly, local-level intragroup power shifts can occur as a result of intergroup dynamics of violence. One scenario is when intergroup power shifts at the macro level may produce similar shifts within ethnic communities in localities. Another scenario is when spillover effects and diffusion of intercommunal violence in particular locations change the balance of power in the neighbouring areas. Examples of in-group power shifts in particular locations produced by both scenarios can be found in few works on ethnic conflicts (Christia 2012; Straus 2006, 2008) and are discussed in the next chapters based on the evidence from the communal warfare in southern Kyrgyzstan. One example comes from the analysis of the Rwandan genocide. Straus (2006, 2008) shows that the dynamics of civil war between Hutus and

Tutsis at national and transborder scales produced power shifts between radicals and moderates within Hutu communities in the districts and communes at local level. In the second scenario, the balance of power changes because of local dynamics of violence. Spillover effects and diffusion of intercommunal violence come from the neighbouring areas in the form of thugs, aggressive crowds, armed groups, and vengeful refugees (Lake and Rothchild 1996). As these groups are outsiders to the local population, their arrival induces both intergroup and in-group power shifts.

Outsiders as an External Factor

One of the key findings of this book is that radical outsiders significantly influence power shifts in neighbourhood-based communities and cause failure of in-group policing, making violent outcome more likely. Radical outsiders are an important external factor that can change both local intergroup and intragroup balances of power. In Rwanda, as an example, the balance of power in many districts tipped toward radicals after the latter were aided by militant hardliners and soldiers coming from outside districts. In some localities with an initial anti-violence stance, the balance shifted toward pro-violent dynamics due to intervention of outside forces. At the national-level, a prime minister and other top hardliners encouraged attacks against Tutsis and thus helped to shift power to radicals at the local-level, in neutral and violence-resistant districts. These power shifts often occurred due to involvement of outsiders such as "a military or militia incursion, an invasion from a neighbouring commune, or direct pressure from prefectural or national authorities" (Straus 2008, 319). Thus, the factor of external forces is important for both intergroup and in-group power shifts.

Balance of Power at Macro- and Micro-Scales

Another complicating factor for assessing balance of power is its geographical dimension. Scholars of IR distinguish between the local and the general balance of power when it comes to the geographical distribution of power. Power is not evenly scattered across space and a general balance of power should be differentiated from local balances of power that emerge in particular locations (Little 2007, 137). At the local level, balance of power can vary across different locations and communities depending on local contexts. What counts is not only general distribution of power between groups but also local-context distributions. The question is how the dynamics of violence at general and local scales affect and change the balance of power and create incentives for some leaders to produce pacts. Therefore, micro-scale analysis brings new factors and variables into consideration.

In divided societies, the distribution of power between two identity groups can be different at the national level and in particular locations. Wilkinson (2006), for example, discusses the problem of town-level balance of power between ethnic groups based on examination of some earlier works, and his own studies on ethnic riots. His observation of several studies on the Hindu-Muslim conflict in India suggests that ethnic violence is likely to break out in towns where there is approximately an equal size of ethnic groups. This argument is based on the demographic balance-security dilemma hypothesis that takes into account the relative size of local groups (Wilkinson 2006, 32–3). However, in general, it is difficult to calculate intergroup balance of power at a disaggregated level. One reason is that there are difficulties in defining and measuring what exact categories should be included in the calculation of balance. Scholars indicate the size of population, territory, available resources, and structures/institutions of ethnic mobilization as indicators of strength (Fearon and Laitin 2003; Hardin 1997; Toft 2002, 2006; Walter 1999). However, because urban neighbourhoods are not nation states or well-defined political entities or groups, it is not clear how we should measure the boundaries of the ethnic neighbourhoods and clusters.

One large ethnic cluster can contain several neighbourhoods with decentralized and dispersed decision-making centers that can have shared networks with one shared key interest – common security. Yet, this does not necessarily imply that the various neighbourhood communities in such ethnic cluster would respond to external threat in a highly coordinated fashion, having divergent preferences and interests. Here the spatial factor is important. Ethnic enclaves and the territories located closer to the frontline or violent zone would be more concerned with their security than communities located in ethnic strongholds or hinterland zones. Varying degrees of uncertainty, vulnerability and perceptions of threat as well as potential costs in case of preventive or retaliatory attacks from rival groups make the security assessments and response strategies of the various neighbourhoods accordingly divergent. Distinct security assessments of threat between residents living in the frontline and in the hinterland areas of an ethnic cluster lead to divergent response strategies deriving from diverse and sometimes contrasting motivating concerns and related costs of/for prospective actions. Depending on the situation and the degree of severity and nature of the threat, the residents of the frontier areas will either invest more in building cooperative relations with the out-groups on the other side of the border or conversely, will be more willing to make preemptive attacks against their neighbours in order to reduce uncertainty.

Correspondingly, residents living in the hinterland areas will have less interest in negotiations with the borderline population of the out-group if the risk of them being involved in war or retaliation attacks is small. With small chances of being reached by retaliation attacks, the center fraction can actually even promote preemptive attacks in the border areas. Same logic applies to some diaspora groups who tend to radically support guerilla war in their home country against competing identity group. For example, the Kurdish activists in Europe and western Turkey tend to support more radical actors in promoting armed struggle against Turkish authorities (O'Connor 2015, 2021). Kalyvas' (2006) model of territorial control applies the same logic in explaining varying intensity of violence used by combatants against civilians in the frontier and hinterland zones.

One major obstacle with operationalization of local balances of power is measurement problems. Unlike situations of regime transitions, traditional interstate wars, and macro-scale ethnic conflicts, it is difficult to calculate local balances of power between neighbourhoods because the relations between two neighbourhoods cannot be isolated from exogenous factors – namely, the violent dynamics unfolding in the scale of the whole city. The developments in other parts of the city influence perceptions of power distribution in localities. Rumours, sporadic police interventions, refugee flows, and the attacks of combatants coming from outside of the city alter the balance of power between ethnic neighbourhoods. This corresponds to multiparty civil wars, such as in Syria and Libya with heavy involvement of external actors, when the domestic distribution of power depends on exogenous factors such as the international and regional contexts and the position of the external powers and actions of transnational armed groups. Equivalently, the local balance of power between two ethnic neighbourhoods should take into account the developments and contextual factors on the town, regional, and national levels. Local balance of power depends on developments at the national and town levels and in neighbouring communities.

The character of violence in southern Kyrgyzstan suggests that factors affecting the micro-scale balance of power are complex and include both structural and contingent dimensions: such as the size of local neighbourhoods and their ethnodemographic composition; the built environment and urban spatial infrastructure; the location of a neighbourhood; and external factors including rumours, intervention by outsiders, and high-publicity events. Case studies given later in this book show how these factors alter the intergroup balance of power.

IMPLEMENTATION OF PACTS:
THE LINKAGE BETWEEN A NONAGGRESSION PACT
AND SELF-POLICING

In-group Policing and Nonaggression Pacts

In this section, I argue that in-group policing – Fearon and Laitin's (1996) theoretical concept of interethnic cooperation – explains why some towns and urban neighbourhoods in southern Kyrgyzstan remained peaceful during the ethnic violence in June 2010 while others suffered horrible violence. One of the central puzzles addressed by Fearon and Laitin (1996, 730) in their model on interethnic cooperation is the following: "Why in some cases do interethnic relations often remain cooperative for a long time yet periodically break down in the form of spiraling violence, while in other cases peace is quickly restored after violence breaks out?" In accord with Fearon and Laitin, I argue that utility of communal policing norms in some neighbourhoods helped local leaders and mediators to prevent violence at the local level.

In-group policing is a necessary but not a sufficient condition for the success of an intergroup agreement and political or social control of the constituency is key to the implementation of in-group policing. In the context of high communal segregation, a basic precondition is the presence of strong leaders and legitimate brokers able to control the constituency and the absence of outsiders who can challenge moderate leaders. An alternative to that implies that there should be strong and organized activists and socially active local population with strong interethnic civic engagement that make grassroots-based interethnic cooperation possible with or without involvement of local leaders. This situation distinguishes few non-segregated neighbourhoods in Osh and Jalalabat where local residents directly cooperated to prevent violence. In areas with weak social control, with uncontrolled groups and weak leaders, pacts are difficult to negotiate and implement and therefore they are often doomed to failure.

Fearon and Laitin elaborated a theoretical model of ethnic violence and peace based on social norms of interethnic cooperation at the local level.

According to this model, in ethnically polarized societies, tense and hostile relations between ethnic communities are mitigated by in-group social control and social norms which help to contain intergroup violence. A weak state provides space for local and informal institutional mechanisms such as social norms for resolving problems of opportunism among individuals from polar ethnic communities.

An intergroup nonaggression pact is at the core of the intragroup policing cooperation model: "Under the in-group policing regime, the two groups in effect make a deal that benefits both sides. By adopting a policy of 'you identify and punish your miscreants and we will do the same,' they take advantage of the fact that each group has better information about the behaviour of its own members than about the other group and so can target individuals rather than whole groups" (Fearon and Laitin 1996, 722).

This book's findings show that community outsiders can undermine intracommunal policing. They are tempted to behave opportunistically as they have a small chance to be identified and punished in future retaliation attacks by the out-group. In-group sanctions for opportunistic behaviour are also not likely because since the opportunists are outsiders to local community, sanctions against them can be too costly. Outsiders are not embedded in local social relations and sanctions imposed by local leaders on their immediate constituencies have few implications for them.

In-group Policing, Credible Commitment, and Intergroup Pacts

Effective in-group policing has dual importance. First, it keeps political or ethnic groups under control of their leaders and second, it signals about commitment to the terms of agreement.

Commitment problem is one of the most serious problems in the process of peace negotiations cited by the scholars of civil wars (Fearon 1998; Lake and Rothchild 1998; Walter 1999, 2009). Bargaining problems, which include the problem of credible commitments along with information problems, uncertainty, and indivisibility of stakes, are key factors that prevent combatants to reach a negotiated settlement (Walter 2009). Reaching pacted agreements is difficult where competing parties have difficulties to demonstrate credible commitments. These are usually countries with weak political institutions, deep cleavages, and fast-changing demographics (ibid., 258). These characteristics also have strong implications for understanding the micro-scale violence in southern Kyrgyzstan. Leaders in ethnically segregated neighbourhoods with weak local social institutions and fast-changing demographic composition with high residential instability had major difficulties in conducting self-policing and therefore to implement terms of pacted agreements.

Thus, power shifts are an important factor that may trigger problem of credible commitment. Yet, as I already suggest in the previous sections, power shifts can also help to achieve peace or convince reluctant and radical forces to negotiate and to moderate their demands. This research demonstrates that the stronger group or radical fraction within the stronger group concedes its radical demands, if the recent power shift does not favour them. The events in southern Kyrgyzstan highlight the importance of rumours and contingent events and their effect on de-escalation.

Some types of political settlements such as power-sharing agreements provide formal institutional mechanisms for conflict resolution. However, during the 2010 conflict in southern Kyrgyzstan, such mechanisms were not available to the local-level ethnic community leaders. In the absence of such mechanisms, what other mechanisms did community leaders use to demonstrate their commitment to interneighbourhood pacts? In localities, community leaders relied on their authority to restrain their communities from participating in violence. Visible in-group sanctions against culprits became a mechanism signalling to ethnic communities about the level of commitment to peace.

As this study shows, when it concerns micro-scale conflicts between small groups such as ethnic communities at a town or neighbourhood level, institutional distribution of power is not an option of bargaining simply because these groups are too small to influence changes in national-level institutions. Under circumstances of intense ongoing violence, these small groups' main interest is physical safety which can be negotiated through the use of informal mechanisms. This involves different types of commitments. In the context of violence at town- and neighbourhood-level ethnic communities and when institutional and state guarantees are absent, nonaggression pacts are effective only if they are backed by strong in-group policing that becomes the main mechanism that signals about credible commitments.

In-group Policing from Other Fields

In criminology and policing studies, the role of outsiders among police forces and protesters is one of the key characteristics that affect disorder in communities (Waddington 1989, 148–9). In many cases, disorder resulted from the actions of the police who were deployed to the protest sites from outside areas. Several protests in the UK escalated into violent riots due to the lack of community commitment from external police contingents sent as reinforcements to local police. External police officers implemented unjustifiably harsh attitudes toward protesters: "The involvement of outside forces, lacking any commitment to long-term community relations, would help to explain allegations of indiscriminate arrests and the excessive use of force" (ibid., 137).

On the other hand, negotiated pacts highly increase chances for nonviolent outcomes in large-scale protest demonstrations even in an atmosphere of little trust between police authorities and protest organizers. Negotiation process often involve mediators and interlocutors who help to reduce mutual mistrust (della Porta and Reiter 2006).

Wahlström and Oskarsson (2006) provide insightful accounts for the importance of the linkage between intergroup negotiated agreements and intragroup monitoring for the protest policing. Drawing on Ostrom's (1990, 42–5) analytical criteria for the solution of social dilemmas, they distinguish three key preconditions for pacted negotiations between the police and protest leaders that could help to sustaining public order during mass protests. For making pacts effective, the negotiating sides need: (1) an agreed set of rules accepted by all involved parties; (2) the credible commitment of each party to the negotiated set of rules that form part of the pacted agreement, and; (3) monitoring or the ability to conduct in-group control and to sanction violators of the agreement (Wahlström and Oskarsson 2006, 117–18). If the first and the third preconditions respectively refer to the terms of negotiated agreement and to the concept of in-group control, "[t]he notion of 'credible commitment' of the negotiating parties can be interpreted as the level of trust ... based on experiences from past interactions, [and it] will strongly influence all stages of negotiation, but especially the parties' willingness to enter negotiations" (ibid., 119).

As Ostrom and Wahlström and Oskarsson argue, these three preconditions are highly interrelated as the absence of one precondition deprives the validity of the other two preconditions, since without one the other two cannot be realized. Without intragroup control and sanctions there is no credible commitment and without credible commitment there is no sense to enter negotiations (Ostrom 1990, 45; Wahlström and Oskarsson 2006, 119). Trust/credible commitment is important not only for entering negotiations but also for reaching pacted agreements (Wahlström and Oskarsson 2006,

130), while effective in-group control and monitoring and sanctions against violators of an agreement signal about credible commitment.

In addition, there are some constraints that hinder initiation of pacts and undermine their efficiency. A comparative study of transnational protests in Copenhagen and Gothenburg conducted by the same authors identify two more factors constraining negotiation of pacts between police and protesters. One is asymmetric power relations between police and protesters with their respectively unequal legal powers and access to information that limit opportunities for successful pacted agreement (ibid., 140). This factor closely relates to the problem of asymmetric distribution of power that I discussed in the previous sections. However, protesters can sanction police for not respecting the conditions of a pact by drawing media attention to the police's abuses, discrediting the police, and so on. Another constraining factor is the lack of authority of negotiators within each group. The decisions about agreement can be overridden by outsiders within the police hierarchical structure, such as superior police officers, or by marginal/peripheral groups within a protest network (ibid., 140–1). In transnational protests, local activists have little power and authority over outsider groups. The lack of authority within each side creates suspicions between police and protesters as both sides know about this problem. This leads to mutual mistrust and the problem of credible commitment.

The last point highlights the importance of outsiders as a variable that can undermine intragroup policing activities, especially among protesters. Organizers of protest demonstrations self-police their members but they often cannot control demonstrators and events outside their organization (ibid., 131). The overall argument is that pacts between police and protesters and in-group policing provide opportunities for de-escalation of violence.

The strong linkage between intergroup pacts and in-group control is evident in O'Donnell's (1986) analysis of transitional pacts in Latin America that underlines scope conditions of self-policing. He explains the infrequency of formal intergroup pacts in the Latin American transitions by the absence of requisite conditions for elite-negotiated agreements which is the lack of intragroup policing and weak socio-political control by the opposition party leaders over their constituencies.

Strong political networks and parties that can conduct effective in-group control are key to negotiating pacts in political transitions. This can be complemented by one prerequisite – the level of civil society's development. O'Donnell (ibid.) explains the probability of the occurrence of formal and explicit pacts during regime transitions in Latin America by two conditions: (1) weakly organized and politically inactive civil society, or (2) high social and political organization of the political representative party system/leadership. According to him (ibid., 12), "The first condition is conducive to narrow and exclusive elitist agreements, undisturbed by 'demagogic' eruptions. The second in principle allows more comprehensive compromises to be worked out and implemented by institutionalized actors." He further argues that if parties representing a socially and politically active popular sector are not able to control it, then it makes the implementation of elitist pacts difficult.

O'Donnell's assumptions about the linkage between pacts and party leadership's control over its political constituencies have direct theoretical implications for the importance of the linkage between intercommunal pacts and in-group policing in ethnic politics. This logic applies to interethnic pacts between neighbourhood-based communal leaders in southern Kyrgyzstan explaining the absence or presence of intercommunal pacts between some neighbourhoods. First, in the context of southern Kyrgyzstan, with weak intercommunal social ties between two communities, pacts between communal leaders became a key solution to mitigate violence and intercommunal distrust. Second, if local brokers have low social legitimacy and weak in-group social control, then informal pacts cannot be effectively implemented due to the credible commitment problem and inability of leaders to control radicals who can create substantial "noise" in intergroup interactions (Fearon and Laitin 2011). Third, strong intercommunal ties in a few mixed unsegregated neighbourhoods allowed local residents to cooperate directly negotiating pacts without the need to rely on community leaders.

If O'Donnell highlights the significance of the level of civil society's development for the intergroup elite pacts and intragroup policing, it is the level of interethnic civic ties that plays important role in ethnically divided and residentially segregated societies (Varshney 2002). As O'Donnell (1986, 12) puts it: "[T]he political and social presence (at various levels and modes of organization) of a quite active and organized popular sector, as well as of parties claiming to represent this sector (but often unable to control it), makes the realization of such pacts difficult." The implication is straightforward: leaders who speak on behalf of their constituencies, but are unable to control them in reality, cannot enforce the realization of pacts. An agreement between leaders with limited authority cannot guarantee its reliable implementation. This factor partly explains why some pacts fail.

O'Donnell (ibid. 12) suggests that the conducive conditions for pact-making are the existence of party or strong partisan identities with organizational networks representing the popular sector and able to exert control over it. The relations between party leaders and a popular sector in respect to intragroup policing in transitional politics correspond to the similar patterns in intracommunal relations in ethnic politics. Organizational networks are strong in Uzbek residential areas (mahallas) or Kyrgyz individual unit house neighbourhoods with their communal leaders being socially embedded in the local neighbourhood constituency and exercising strong social control over it. Social authority and strong connection with local population favours communal leaders in such neighbourhoods to conduct effective in-group policing, which, in turn, increases chances for the success of intercommunal pacts.

This chapter showed that theoretical assumptions discussed in relation to violence and peacemaking mechanisms from such diverse fields as IR, security studies, democratization studies, ethnic politics, and policing studies could be directly applied to explain communal conflicts and micro-scale urban violence through the analysis of in-group policing and pact-making. This approach especially suits to account for variations in violence and meso-level group behaviour. Although most of the literature mainly refers to actors and groups operating at the national level, the analysis of empirical cases in this book suggests that the theoretical mechanisms from studies engaged in state- or national-level analysis are also, with some reservations, relevant for the micro-scale analysis of small groups operating at the neighbourhood-level. The main distinction is that different scales affect the context in which interactions of between groups develop. For small groups such as neighbourhood-level communities, it is mostly physical survival rather than struggle for power or economic resources is the main driver that influence their decisions and responses to uncertainty and violence.

Based on the theoretical discussion in this chapter, and corroborated by the empirical evidence from the next chapters, I suggest that the following theoretical observations display the linkage between in-group policing and pacts:[2]

1. Communal leaders provide compliance of community residents with the terms of a pact in exchange for communal security.
2. Leaders' initiative to conduct intragroup policing in respective communities to comply with pact conditions derives from fear of possible spiral escalation of violence.

3. To ensure compliance, leaders must be deeply socially embedded in and have strong social authority among neighbourhood-based constituencies.
4. Commitment to a pact requires in-group control and sanctions: Leaders must be capable of punishing violators who do not comply with a pact.
5. Leaders without real connections to local community and neighbourhoods with weak social organization will likely have difficulties in organizing intercommunal pacts, controlling locals, and persuading them to comply with a pact.
6. Intercommunal pacts tend to be negotiated among a narrow set of leaders, in isolation from the involvement of wider constituencies, to limit radicals' negative influence on the negotiation process.
7. This last observation is rather factual, but provides an interesting point. Some pacts in Kyrgyzstan were negotiated when the violent phase of conflict was over. Perception of the future threats to the interethnic peace may explain the post-conflict pacts – peace declarations during *dastorhon* feast festivities sponsored by local authorities. Such pacts had declarative nature intended to rebuild minimal trust between communities.

Another distinction is that, in studies engaged in the national level analysis, spatial factors are very rarely taken into consideration when analyzing intergroup peacemaking interactions and violent dynamics. But in urban settings, environmental factors such as the impact of space and the built environment play a key role in understanding the dynamics and variation in violence. In this chapter, I did not discuss theoretical implications of space. I do it in chapter 5 in which I conduct comparative analysis of spatial factors' impact on two neighbourhoods in Osh with divergent outcomes. I assume this integrated way of presentation better illustrates the theoretical significance of spatial analysis.

In the next chapters, I discuss how the above theoretical implications for intergroup pacts and in-group policing work on empirical ground in the context of urban communal warfare.

PART TWO

Historical Context and the Dynamics of Violence in Osh

3

Structural-Historical Context and the Onset of Violence

Conflict Background

The events leading to the ethnic violence developed according to the scenario of ethnic security dilemma (Fearon 1998; Lake and Rothchild 1998; Posen 1993; Walter and Snyder 1999). The sudden breakdown of the state on 7 April 2010 because of a popular uprising against the dictatorial and corrupt rule of President Bakiev has important implications for the ethnic violence in June 2010 in southern Kyrgyzstan. One implication was that the regime breakdown caused a power vacuum, institutional chaos, and emerging anarchy. The events described below in more detail show that state institutions such as police were demoralized by the loss of legitimacy on 7 April 2010, after they shot dead eighty-nine demonstrators in the central square in Bishkek and were consequently attacked and beaten by the same protesters. The interim government could not reassert state control in some regions, especially in the south – the stronghold of the overthrown president. The ethnic tensions both in the south and in the north of Kyrgyzstan that followed the regime change and the resulting power vacuum clearly demonstrated the weakness of the new central state and its inability to establish order. Ethnic entrepreneurs used the power vacuum to instigate ethnic violence. In the north, the state was initially unable to protect Meskhetian Turks against violent ethnic opportunists. However, as the interim government's control was stronger in the north, it soon managed to reassert control there. In the south, short violent clashes erupted: in Jalalabat in May 2010, first between the pro- and the anti-Bakiev forces and then between local Kyrgyz and Uzbek communities. These clashes produced uncertainty and fear among the two ethnic communities and triggered ethnic mobilization and escalation of tensions at the national level nurtured by ethnic entrepreneurs.

SHORT HISTORICAL BACKGROUND

Kyrgyzstan is the post-Soviet Central Asian republic with more than 90 per cent of its territory covered by mountains. The bulk of the population is concentrated in a few valleys. The mountains naturally divide the territory of Kyrgyzstan into its northern and southern parts. This condition has, to some extent, determined regional divisions in the state, in terms of economic welfare and regional politics and identities.

Kyrgyzstan is an ethnically diverse country of more than six million people, and the largest ethnic group are Kyrgyz (comprising 60 per cent to 65 per cent of the population), Uzbeks (14 per cent to 20 per cent), and Russians (10 per cent to 14 per cent), depending on the estimates. The Russians are concentrated in the northern part, mainly in the capital Bishkek and the Chui valley, while the Uzbeks live in the oblasts (provinces) of southern Kyrgyzstan: Osh, Jalalabat, and Batken. Geographically, these southern oblasts are a part of the Fergana valley that contains substantial territorial parts of three Central Asian states: Tajikistan, Uzbekistan, and Kyrgyzstan. It was one of the most densely populated regions in the Soviet Union and, today, the total population of the valley exceeds 20 million people, most of them ethnic Uzbeks.

When the Russians conquered Central Asia and colonized the region in the second half of the nineteenth century, the mountainous territories and some valleys of modern Kyrgyzstan were mostly populated by Kyrgyz nomadic tribes. These tribes did not constitute one state or a political union at that time. Instead, they were subordinated by the Kokand khanate (kingdom),[1] one of the three khanates of the Central Asian region in the nineteenth century.

All Kyrgyz tribes were connected by a common language and a shared genealogy. Historically, each Kyrgyz tribe was located in a genealogical structure that continued until relatively recently. A shared genealogy allowed Kyrgyz nomadic tribes to remain in close contact and to "imagine" themselves as one ethnic group.[2] *Kurultai* was another institution that enabled the Kyrgyz and other nomadic peoples of the Eurasian region (mainly of Turkic and Mongol origin) to maintain their shared identity as distinct. In essence, kurultai was an informal political council which facilitated interaction between tribes. Representative of tribes used kurultai to meet and to make collective decisions regarding political and diplomatic issues, resolution of problems at the intertribal level, distribution of pastures and roamed territo-

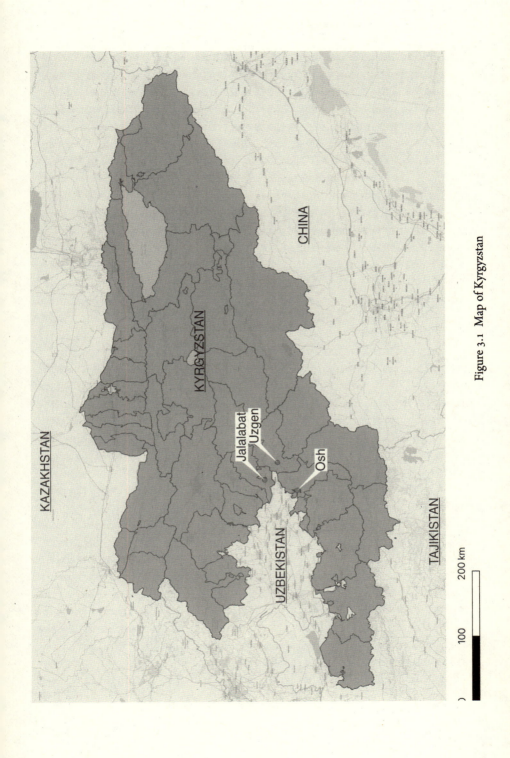

Figure 3.1 Map of Kyrgyzstan

ries among tribes, elections of political leaders (*khans*), collective military actions against common enemies, and so on. The nomadic style of life prevented the Kyrgyz from mixing with other regional sedentary ethnolinguistic groups. Cultural and linguistic influence of sedentary populations upon the Kyrgyz was minimal because nomads and sedentary populations were mainly isolated from each other geographically. The former roamed in mountainous landscapes while the latter resided in the fertile oases of the Fergana valley. The two populations made contact only on rare occasions, mainly during trading transactions.

Unlike the Kyrgyz nomads, the sedentary population of the Fergana valley did not identify itself with a particular ethnic group. It was a diverse and fragmented population with mixed and contested identities. These identities were rather based on territorial, religious, professional, tribal, or some other grounds, and were not built along distinct ethnic boundaries. People spoke various dialects of Turkic or Iranian languages. Later, exactly this population of the Fergana valley constituted the core of the newly created Uzbek nationality (Fierman 1991).

Kyrgyz referred to the sedentary people of the Fergana valley as "sart," a pejorative term used by nomads in respect of Iranian- and Turkic-speaking traders and farmers of the valley. In modern days, the term "sart" is still used in a negative sense by the nationalist Kyrgyz regarding the Uzbeks and the Tajiks. This provides a rationale for some local historians to explain the communal conflict in primordial terms by tracing contemporary interethnic tensions to the history of the nomad-sedentary conflicts of the nineteenth and earlier centuries.

After the Russian colonization of Central Asia in the second half of the nineteenth century, the Tsarist administration established Turkestan's general governorship over significant parts of territories of today's Central Asian states. The colonial administration developed different attitudes toward nomads and the sedentary people. The Russians regarded the lands inhabited by nomads as "empty spaces" and nomads as "noisy" tribes that could threaten stability of the colonial rule. The Tsarist administration encouraged the migration of landless Russian peasants to the Central Asian region and allocated land plots to them, mainly in the territories used as pastures by Kyrgyz and Kazakh nomads. This territorial-colonialist expansion resulted in a mass rebellion of the Kyrgyz in 1916 and the subsequent Russian genocide of the Kyrgyz nomads. On the other hand, the Russian colonial administration did not interfere much in the affairs of the local sedentary population in the Fergana valley. It never settled Russian peasants to this region and granted local nobility a great deal of autonomy. The valley was the main source of cotton for the Russian empire and so long as taxation and the cotton supply were secure, the Russian governor-general did not alter existing socioeconomic settings.

In 1924, the Soviets conducted territorial and administrative reforms in Central Asia. As a result of these reforms, the Turkestan Autonomious Soviet Socialist Republic was reorganized into several administrative units, such as the Kyrgyz Autonomous Oblast, the Uzbekistan Soviet Socialist Republic, the Tajikistan Autonomous Socialist Republic, and the Turkmenistan Soviet Socialist Republic. The delimitation process was accompanied by ethnic categorization of the Central Asian population.

Initially, the Soviet nationality policy consistently promoted linguistic and ethnic categories at the institutional level. The 1920s and 1930s were a period of ethnic category creation through the census and the introduction of passports. Each ethnic category approved by Moscow was added in the census lists of nationalities and the nationality graph was introduced in all Soviet passports. Thus, those categories which were not included in the official census lists ceased to exist for all intents and purposes, at least at the official level. For instance, the category of sarts, one of the largest groups of that time, were not officially approved by Moscow as a nationality. Recognition at the institutional level had very important consequences because the officially recognized nationalities could benefit all advantages of the Soviet nationality policy.

When the Soviets first introduced passports, individuals could choose their nationality, although the choices were limited based on their knowledge of languages, the region of residence, and some other characteristics. Thus one could choose, for example, Ukrainian nationality if he or she spoke the Ukrainian language, was of European appearance, of Ukrainian descent, and/or was a resident of Ukraine (Martin 2001). Once passports were introduced, the citizens of the Soviet Union were no longer able to change their nationalities.

As for nomadic groups, such as the Kazakhs, Turkmens, and Kyrgyz, it was easier for ethnographers to distinguish them as distinct ethnic groups as they had already had a relatively strong sense of ethnic identity based on common genealogies and shared myths of a collective lineage. The main problem emerged regarding sedentary populations. Because the population of Fergana valley represented a mixture of groups not necessarily based on ethnic identities, the Russians could barely identify them. Soviet policymakers employed ethnographers to distinguish these groups and create ethnic categories. Eventually, the Turkic-speaking population became, more or less the core of Uzbek nationality and Iranian-speaking groups constituted the core of Tajik nationality (Hirsch 2005). The introduction of literary and standardized language grammar in the secondary-school curriculum produced, over generations, homogenizing effects on development of national identity, especially with regard to local sedentary groups later known as Uzbeks and Tajiks. One implication of the Soviet delimitation of administrative borders among Soviet republics in Central Asia – nowadays widely criticized by modern Central Asian regimes for its clumsiness – was that it left large Uzbek communities within Kyrgyzstan's borders, thus, creating the largest ethnic minority in southern Kyrgyzstan.

THE COMMUNAL CONFLICT IN JUNE 1990

The first ethnic clashes between the Uzbeks and Kyrgyz took place in 1990, on the eve of the Soviet Union's collapse. The late years of the USSR were marked by increasing ethnic mobilization and a growing number of nationalist movements that spread across the national republics. The nationalist movements put forward various political demands, which varied from demands of recognition of national languages to demands for full state independence. As a late riser to the nationalist mobilization, Kyrgyzstan faced violent outbreaks of ethnic nationalism (Beissinger 2002).[3] The emergence of nationalist movements in Kyrgyzstan was denoted by the establishment of nationalist organizations including two clearly ethnic organizations – the Uzbek organization Adolat (Justice) and the Kyrgyz organization Osh Aymagy (the Osh region), both based in the southern regions. These two nationalist organizations played a crucial role in instigation of ethnic violence in June 1990. Adolat was created by the Jalalabat Uzbeks in 1989, but its influence soon extended to the Osh Uzbeks as well. Reportedly, Adolat's membership had reached 400,000 (Lubin et al. 1999, 47).

In May 1990, Adolat sent a petition to the Soviet government in Moscow, in which it demanded preservation of Uzbek traditions and culture, and recognition of an Uzbek autonomous republic in Kyrgyzstan. This action was perceived by the Kyrgyz population as clear evidence of the separatist intentions of the Uzbek minority. The consequences of that move were profoundly serious. It generated outrage among the Kyrgyz population and also established long-lasting suspicions among the Kyrgyz regarding Uzbek separatist aspirations. The Kyrgyz implicitly and then explicitly perceived the

Uzbek mobilization in 2010 as secessionist, with the Kyrgyz nationalist politicians actively playing this card for their own political interests.

Osh Aymagy was created in May 1990 with the intention of assisting unemployed and landless Kyrgyz. It set a task to provide the landless Kyrgyz people with plots for the construction of houses. The organization quickly became popular as many Kyrgyz youth felt deprived. In the Osh city, the Uzbeks dominated the trade sector and had better job opportunities. For example, they constituted 79 per cent of taxi drivers,[4] 84 per cent of workers in the commercial sector of manufactured goods, 75 per cent in public food chains, and 71 per cent in trade and retailing (Gaziyev 2008, 298; Lubin et al. 1999, 47). The established economic infrastructure in many southern cities favoured the economic interests of the Uzbek community and made it difficult for many ethnic Kyrgyz, especially from rural areas, to find decently paying jobs. Access to the trade sector, catering business, and agricultural market dominated by Uzbek business networks was extremely difficult to penetrate for individuals from outside groups. Uzbeks enjoyed overwhelming access to agricultural lands around Osh.

The residential patterns in southern regions reinforced social and economic segregation and horizontal ethnic inequality. Uzbek ethnic groups prevailed in urban areas of major cities and towns, especially in Osh province,[5] while the Kyrgyz lived in surrounding villages. Only 15 per cent of the Kyrgyz population in the southern regions lived in urban areas (Gaziyev 2008, 299–300). The mountainous districts such as Alai, Chon Alai, and Kara-Kulja, with difficult life conditions and less-developed infrastructure, were monoethnically Kyrgyz. Even nowadays, this pattern is largely the same. A share of Uzbeks in the towns of Uzgen, Karasuu, Nookat, and Aravan – the administrative centers of respective districts – varies from 65 per cent to 90 per cent (Kyrgyzstan census 2009). During Soviet times migration of rural Kyrgyz to urban areas was strongly prevented by the system of *propiska*.[6]

Such residential and social divisions and institutional barriers to migration only contributed to Kyrgyz perceptions of an unjust distribution of public goods. The Uzbeks were seen as being at the top of the economic and residential pile, enjoying comfort and the many infrastructural advantages of urban life. On the other hand, local government and administrative positions were dominated by the Russians and the Kyrgyz. The Uzbeks felt that they were highly underrepresented in power structures and were therefore discriminated against for political reasons. Being at least 29 per cent of the overall population in the region, Uzbeks constituted only 4 per cent of communist party first and second secretaries and 11 per cent of the heads of the municipal and district (raion) executive committees in southern Kyrgyzstan (Lubin et al. 1999, 47). Many of the features described above, such as a lack of balance in political, social, and economic arenas and communal segregation, have been effective till the very present. Paradoxically, the relative deprivation was instrumental for mobilization of both ethnic communities in 1990 and to some extent in 2010.

There is little documented evidence available on the 1990 conflict. Besides criminal investigations conducted by security services, there only few studies that sought detailed factual reconstruction of the events of June 1990. Due to the lack of fine-grained evidence, it is practically impossible to establish reliable comparisons in spatial variations and historical controls between the 1990 and the 2010 communal violence at the neighbourhood level. What is known about the 1990 violence is only the general course of events. The 1990 ethnic riots started as a conflict over land distribution and by official estimates left in their wake 318 individuals dead and 31 individuals claimed as lost; among them 93 Kyrgyz, 220 Uzbeks, and 36 other nationalities. More than 1,000 people were wounded. Several hundred houses and buildings were burned and looted. 331 individuals were convicted, among them 225 Kyrgyz, 72 Uzbeks, and 19 Russians (Joint Working Group 2012). Despite its high mortality rate, participants in that conflict did not engage in full-scale firearm combats. The conflict started in Osh but then diffused to and predominantly affected the city of Uzgen and also some villages surrounding these cities. In 2010, however, Uzgen managed to stay peaceful thanks to extraordinary efforts of local mediators.[7] The most active phase of the conflict in 1990 lasted from 4 to 6 June, with skirmishes and ethnic aggressions in subsequent days through to early August. The ethnic violence in the end was stopped by the intervention of Soviet troops. The government declared a state of emergency, including a curfew which was lifted in November of the same year.

The dynamics of the conflagration in 1990 was in many respects repeated during ethnic violence in 2010. Therefore, it is critical to reconstruct the events of 1990 at least in general lines. The tensions between the Uzbek and Kyrgyz communities accelerated after Adolat sent a petition to the Kremlin in May 1990, demanding administrative autonomy for the Uzbeks in Kyrgyzstan. The petition engendered huge outrage among the Kyrgyz. The spring of 1990 was characterized by repeated large demonstrations by Kyrgyz youth who lived in Bishkek and Osh. At the time, Bishkek was a predominantly Russian city where the Kyrgyz composed not more than one-fifth of the city's population. Only in one out of more than sixty schools the language of instruction was Kyrgyz.

A similar situation was observed in Osh. Many young Kyrgyz who came to Bishkek and Osh to work or study lived in rented apartments and student's and worker's dormitories. The social problems with housing and unemployment of the rural youth were ignored by local authorities for years. Neither did they seek to solve the problems in rural areas to reduce internal migration. Many of the same problems preceded the 2010 communal violence. The young Kyrgyz from rural areas constituted the core of land movements and organizations like Osh Aymagy.

In the Osh city, on 17 May, Osh Aymagy demanded distribution of land plots from the local authorities for the landless Kyrgyz who lived in Osh, threatening otherwise to squat at available land plots starting from 17 June. After the regional authorities ignored this demand, 5,000 Kyrgyz youth gathered in Osh on the plots of arable land of the Lenin kolkhoz (collective farm) that belonged to Uzbek farmers. On 30 May, Osh Aymagy demanded that the problems with housing, unemployment, and *propiska* are addressed for internal migrants in the Osh city. A parallel Uzbek meeting took place, attended by a group of ministers and municipal officials of Uzbek origin. Uzbek protesters decided to appeal to the Kyrgyzstan government about creation of Uzbek autonomy with a deadline set to 4 June. In response, Osh Aymagy set a deadline for the resolution of its demands also to 4 June (Fergana.ru 2010). The next day, Uzbek bakers "stopped selling bread to Kyrgyz in the city and Uzbek flat-owners, in an unprecedent action, expelled 1,500 Kyrgyz tenants from their rented flats. Local KGB sources reported that that action had only added more Kyrgyz supporters to the ranks of Osh Aymagy" (Gaziyev 2008, 281). Although, in the end, the republican commission agreed to allocate few land lots for construction of private housing in other areas in Osh surroundings, the radical wing of Osh Aymagy refused to accept that deal.

As the deadline for the demands of both Adolat and Osh Aymagy approached, it became clear that the supporters of both organizations were going to confront each other. On the evening of 4 June, two crowds – about 1,500 Kyrgyz and about 10,000 Uzbeks – gathered on the fields of the Lenin collective farm, separated by a thin line of the police officers. Uzbek supporters from districts of Namangan, Andijan, and Fergana in Uzbekistan joined local Uzbeks in Osh (Fergana.ru 2010; Gaziyev 2008, 282). Reportedly, the Uzbek crowd attempted to attack the Kyrgyz by breaking police lines. Clashes between the police and the Uzbek crowd broke out. The police fired live bullets. Instead of dispersing, the Uzbeks rushed toward the downtown, burning cars and municipal transportation and destroying Kyrgyz property on its way. The Kyrgyz crowd, following this example, began to target Uzbek houses (Fergana.ru 2010). In the following days, Uzbeks attacked several police stations. Violence erupted but diminished by 6 June:

> As the clashes between the two groups escalated, a state of emergency, including a curfew, was declared in Osh. The centre of Osh city eventually became quiet when troops blocked roads into the city to prevent opposing groups from entering. However, the violence spilled beyond Osh city into the surrounding countryside. The first day of violence in Osh city left 11 people dead and 210 injured. With the arrival of additional troops of the Army on 6 June, the situation improved and violence subsided. But the city was totally isolated. Rumours spread fast, and those reaching adjacent villages prompted many Kyrgyz villagers to travel en masse to support their people in the Osh city. Fortunately, most of them were prevented from entering the city by the military, which was crucial in cordoning off Osh city and warding off agitated young Kyrgyz and Uzbek people from adjacent areas to aggravate the situation further (Gaziyev 2008, 284).

However, in the time it was subsiding in Osh, a more intense violence had spread to the city of Uzgen on 5 June. As Uzgen was predominantly an Uzbek city with more than 90 per cent of the population being Uzbek, the riots took the form of clashes between the Uzbeks from the Uzgen community and the Kyrgyz from surrounding villages. The Kyrgyz participating in clashes were aided by their ethnic fellows from the mountainous districts of Alai and Kara-Kulja. Many of them arrived in Uzgen riding horses armed with metallic bars, sticks, and knives. The clashes in Uzgen resulted in pogroms and burning of Uzbek houses; however, the entrances to the rest of the city were barricaded preventing further violence. The city was besieged by the Kyrgyz from surrounding and remote territories. The local authorities tried to evacuate the Kyrgyz minority in Uzgen, however, those who left in the city were assaulted by the local Uzbeks. In some villages surrounding Uzgen – notably in Mirza Aki – local Kyrgyz residents attacked local Uzbek minority with consequent killings, sexual violence, and looting. In Mirza Aki village, "19 people were assaulted on 5–7 June, 10 women were raped and 188 houses were destroyed and property looted" (Tishkov 1995, 136). The violence in Uzgen largely stopped on 8 June when the military troops entered the city. The communal clashes in the district of Uzgen became the most violent and left approximately 200 deaths and several hundred houses burnt (Gaziyev 2008, 286). In addition, violent incidents, killings, and riots also took place in several locations in the districts of Karasuu, Aravan, and Nookat. In Uzbekistan, 15,000 Uzbeks attempted to break through the Uzbek-Kyrgyz border to the city of Osh. Ethnic Kyrgyz in Uzbekistan were assaulted and beaten up by Uzbeks and as a result several thousand Kyrgyz fled to Kyrgyzstan as refugees. Tensions emerged in the areas where the refugees were concentrated.

KYRGYZSTAN'S ETHNIC POLITICS, 1991–2005

The communal conflict in 1990 was followed by twenty years of rather stable intercommunal relations. In the initial stage, the ethnic policy of the first president, Askar Akaev, was relatively balanced. While promoting the national identity of the Kyrgyz, the president reassured the ethnic minorities of continued state support and security. He proclaimed "Kyrgyzstan is our common home" as a slogan for his civic policy of accommodation of ethnic minorities into Kyrgyzstan's political community. At the same time, "at an institutional level the creation of the Assembly of the People of Kyrgyzstan provided a venue to discuss the concerns of minority communities—although in a carefully structured and limited fashion" (Melvin 2011, 9).

The Uzbek minority of Kyrgyzstan distanced itself from Kyrgyzstan's political arena by adopting a neutral stance; however, in the electoral arena it supported political parties and forces affiliated with Akaev's personal rule. This loyalty to Akaev's regime was reinforced as some opposition leaders from the southern regions relied more on nationalist rhetoric in their electoral campaigns against Akaev's leadership. Akaev's main political opposition in the 1990s was in the south, where his principal opponent, Apsamat Masaliev, a former communist leader of Kyrgyzstan during the 1990 conflict and perestroika times, had great support among the local Kyrgyz population. Masaliev lost the first presidential elections to Akaev that were held a few months later following the ethnic violence in Osh in June 1990. One reason of the communists' defeat was that the latter failed to undertake any meaningful action to smooth over the negative consequences of the conflict (HRW 2010; KIC 2011). Being originally from the north, Akaev did not have good political connections with the Kyrgyz population in the south. The president's unpopularity in the south was displayed in the 1995 presidential elections, when Akaev's main challenger Masaliev, himself from the south, received a majority of his votes from the southern constituencies. At the same time, the Uzbeks voted in favour of Akaev. To balance a lack of support in the south, the president increasingly relied on support of the Uzbek community and its ethnic leaders and manipulated it against southern opposition leaders. Neil Melvin (2011, 10) accurately depicts the nature of these relations between Akaev's regime and the Uzbek leaders:

> In return, the Uzbek community was largely left alone, notably to promote business interests and the Uzbek language as the de facto working language in southern urban centers and areas with large Uzbek populations. Representatives of the Uzbek community were present in the national parliament and even on occasion in government. Akaev cultivated a loyal Uzbek leadership – while at the same time ensuring that there was no single figurehead or unified Uzbek movement that might be able to promote stronger claims. He advanced symbolic projects, such as the Uzbek-Kyrgyz University in Osh, which also supported key allies in the Uzbek community. In this way, interethnic relations in the south became interlinked with the struggle for power in Kyrgyzstan through an interaction of north-south, rural-urban, patronage (clan) and ethno-political elements. The informal balancing of Kyrgyz and Uzbek communities practiced under Akaev was not a static system and was affected by the country's broader politics. The longer that Akaev stayed in power the greater grew the political struggle around him, which was essentially confined to an inter-Kyrgyz struggle. At the elite level, the Akaev regime became reliant on the president's family, relatives, friends, and representatives of his home region in the north. The opposition looked to mobilize local connections and groups to challenge the Akaev regime, notably in the south.

Akaev's regime started as truly democratic but gradually eroded into a corrupted neopatrimonial rule where all important decisions were made on the level of the president's family members. By the end of his second term, Akaev had turned increasingly authoritarian. After jailing some of his main political opponents from the north, Akaev faced his main political challenge from southern politicians including Kurmanbek Bakiev, who would become the next president. In 2005, Akaev's neopatrimonial and corrupt regime was deposed in a popular uprising, called the Tulip Revolution. Bakiev emerged as a new oppositional leader, becoming the new president but his rule, as it turned out later, had disastrous consequences for the country and interethnic relations in the south.

By 2010, Bakiev's regime had become highly repressive and unpopular, quickly approaching the standards of brutal repression practised by the neighbouring Central Asian regimes in Uzbekistan and Tajikistan. Under Bakiev's rule, Kyrgyzstan, for the first time in its history, was ranked as "non-free" by Freedom House. The intimidation, jailing, blackmailing, and assassination of political opponents, journalists, and political activists became a common practice. Many oppositional figures were forced to leave the country, fearing arrests on political grounds or an assassination by security services.[8]

Bakiev's clan aggressively monopolized the political and economic arenas of the country. The president's brothers and his cronies composed a narrow circle of his neopatrimonial rule. The various spheres of political power and the Kyrgyz economy were assigned among his brothers and sons. One of president's brothers, Akhmat, became an informal boss of the whole Jalalabat province, a native land of Bakiev's family. In Jalalabat, Akhmat had shaken economic interests of some Uzbek elite, including prominent Uzbek leader Kadyrjan Batyrov. This also had far-reaching repercussions on ethnic relations in the south of Kyrgyzstan.

On 7 April 2010, a brutal dictatorial regime of Kurmanbek Bakiev was overthrown by popular uprising in the capital city, Bishkek. That day, people gathered in the central square to peacefully protest against the dictatorship and the government's sweeping corruption. However, Bakiev, in contrast to Akaev, decided not to give up his power without fight. He ordered security services to open fire against demonstrators. Eighty-nine peaceful demonstrators were killed and 1,500 wounded by snipers and the police forces, in a similar scene that the world saw in Kiev during the Euromaidan in 2014. This brutal attempt to frighten away people backfired on the regime. Contrary to Bakiev's expectations, fearless protesters in the central square did not retreat, clashed with the police, and stormed the Government House (also known as the White House), forcing Bakiev to flee to his native village in Jalalabat province. There, Bakiev's clan tried to raise the southerners against the new government playing the regionalist card. The cynical attempt failed when Bakiev and his escort were expelled from the Osh city by ordinary citizens where he had arrived seeking to consolidate his power. Several days later, Bakiev left Kyrgyzstan and found refuge in Belarus at the invitation of President Alyaksandr Lukashenka.

The regime transition proved to be a difficult period for the newly formed interim government. It was accompanied by waves of social and political disorder and chaos especially in the first weeks after the regime change. Like during the previous regime change in 2005, the police were demoralized and completely disappeared from the scene shortly after this regime change occurred on 7 April. The same night and the following days, when the widespread looting of supermarkets and shops started in the streets of Bishkek, no policeman arrived to prevent the looting and disorders. Upon returning to the streets sometime later, the police were reluctant to act decisively, as they faced multiple challenges emerging from the vacuum of power.

The interim government, fragmented however by internal rivalries and contradicting interests and political backgrounds, acted indecisively and ambiguously. While the reformist members of the government pushed heavily on with political and constitutional reforms, they completely ignored sharply deteriorating interethnic relations in the south and in the northern province of Chuy. On 19 April, several hundred land squatters, mainly ethnic Kyrgyz from rural areas and the outskirts of Bishkek, mobilized by ethnic entrepreneurs and provocateurs, attacked the village of Maevka in the vicinity of Bishkek. The village was inhabited by an ethnically diverse population, but the targets were mainly the Meskhetian Turks. The land squatters claiming the land plots and houses that belonged to the Turks set fire to several houses. Violent clashes ensued which left five people dead and several dozen wounded. Twenty-eight houses of Turks were targeted, some of them burned and looted (Trilling 2010). Among the 120 people arrested on charges of murder, arson, and looting, only five were sentenced while the rest were released. A decision to release the majority of arrested rioters can be explained by the government's fear of generating discontent among nationalist groups in the Kyrgyz population. Besides arresting "scapegoats," the authorities did not attempt to find the real organizers of the attacks. Neither did they seek to understand the causes of the riots. These riots also signalled the government's weakness and its willingness to tolerate ethnic violence.

ETHNIC MOBILIZATION AND GROWING TENSIONS IN 2010

The disorders in Bishkek that followed the regime change of 7 April induced escalation of tensions between the Uzbek and Kyrgyz communities in southern Kyrgyzstan. Tensions had been accumulating throughout April, and especially in May and the beginning of June, and then ultimately resulted in a communal warfare during 11–15 June. The growing tensions between the communities triggered mobilization along ethnic lines mainly in Osh and Jalalabat, the largest cities in the south, and their surrounding villages. The ethnic mobilization showed itself in creation and proliferation of vigilante and self-defence groups, mass ethnic rallies, and the political activities of ethnic entrepreneurs. Prominent Uzbek leaders attempted to politically mobilize Uzbek communities across the southern regions. This mobilization occurred in the context of intra-Kyrgyz struggle between supporters and opponents of the interim government and was accompanied by many violent incidents such as ethnic brawls, street fights, attacks on cars and the beating of car passengers or passersby in Osh, the largest city in southern Kyrgyzstan. This section provides descriptive accounts of the events that preceded the communal violence of 11 to 15 June.

Events in Jalalabat in May

On 13 May, Bakiev loyalists attempted to take power in various southern areas of Kyrgyzstan. Organized by some key figures of Bakiev's regime, this attempted coup sought to restore Bakiev's power in the south. Armed with sticks, pro-Bakiev forces stormed and occupied the governor's provincial administrations in three provincial centers: Batken, Osh, and Jalalabat. Attempted takeovers in the first two locations quickly failed but in Jalalabat, the native province of Bakiev, a violent confrontation between supporters of the interim government and Bakiev loyalists followed. The interim government lacked political support in the south as the majority of its members were originally from the northern regions. Its control of the southern regions was nominal.

In these circumstances, some members of the interim government negotiated with Kadyrjan Batyrov, one of the most influential Uzbek political figures in the south and the leader of Jalalabat Uzbeks, seeking his help to suppress the revolt by expelling the Bakiev loyalists from the provincial administration buildings. Batyrov, who was also a leader of the ethnic Uzbek party Vatan (Motherland) and a deputy head of the Uzbek National Cultural Center in Jalalabat, agreed to mobilize his local Uzbek constituency. Armed with sticks and some firearms, his group converged on the streets with Kyrgyz supporters of the interim government. Accounting for about 3,000 activists, the joint Kyrgyz-Uzbek group drove out Bakiev's adherents from the city center and government buildings. The clash, accompanied by gunfire, left two people dead and fifty injured (ICG 2010, 8).

The same night, after expelling Bakiev loyalists from the city center, the supporters of the interim government went to Bakiev's native village in Jalalabat suburbs. The group attacked and torched several houses of the Bakiev family. Batyrov and his followers took an active part in the burning and looting of Bakiev's houses. Although Kyrgyz activists also participated in the march to Bakiev's native village, led by Batyrov (KIC 2011, 14), the arson generated a backlash among many Kyrgyz. They suspected Batyrov, and the Uzbeks in general, of attempting to assault the Kyrgyz and their ethnic symbols.[9] The incident convinced the Kyrgyz that "the Uzbeks had been planning their revenge since 1990, hiding weapons in their mosques, just waiting for the time to strike" (ICG 2010, 10). Batyrov's further political activities in the following days enforced these suspicions among the Kyrgyz.

On 15 May, Batyrov organized a political rally at his university in Jalalabat city attended by the Uzbek communities from various villages and towns of Jalalabat province, but also by the Uzbek leaders from the Osh city (Memorial 2012, 20). During the rally, Batyrov and his associates made certain political demands. He denigrated the role of the Kyrgyz activists and emphasized the importance of the Uzbek community in restoration of order. Batyrov also accused the police and security services of incapability and called for creation of "people patrols" in order to save the order in the streets of Jalalabat city.

The demands and content of Batyrov's speeches at the rally sparked fears among the Kyrgyz population and convinced them about growing Uzbek mobilization. In the words of Bektur Asanov (KIC 2011, 15), a governor of Jalalabat province, "no radical demands were made by Batyrov, but that the tone of the speeches expressed intense frustration and inspired the Uzbeks to be bolder in their aspirations." Another account by a Kyrgyz journalist based in Osh shows the growth of ethnic fears among Kyrgyz who perceived Batyrov's rallies as aggressive Uzbek mobilization:

> He talked about democracy, the Interim Government, corruption, the Bakiev regime ... At no point did they openly talk about Uzbek autonomy or make any kind of illegal encouragements. But the words had a hidden meaning. The call to "gain conscience," what's that all about? When you read the transcription, that's one thing, but when you see it on TV it is something completely different. When Batyrov talked about establishing volunteer groups, he listed areas: People are coming to us from Osh,

Uzgen, Aravan, and Nookat [towns in Osh province]. This was interpreted as mobilization of the Uzbek population. And another encouragement: We have been quiet for 20 years, now the time has come to take our rights. In the evening, when the TV program had just ended, everyone started calling each other, asking: "Did you see it? What's going to happen?" From that moment on, different rumours started spreading, and populist nationalism increased sharply (Memorial 2012, 22).

After this rally, the events of the next several days unfolded with greater violence. Some local Kyrgyz nationalist officials, closely linked to Bakiev, established a camp at the local hippodrome which became a focal point for Kyrgyz ethnic mobilization from rural areas. By 19 May, the crowd at the hippodrome had accumulated about 5,000–6,000 people who demanded "an immediate criminal prosecution of Batyrov and the management of Osh TV and Mezon TV for 'incitement of interethnic hatred.' Rumours about the demands for autonomy by Uzbeks gained strength" (KIC 2011, 16). On 19 May, the crowd marched to the city center and attacked Batyrov's university. The security services failed to curb the violence which erupted with intensive gunfire. The clashes – in which both sides were armed – claimed four Kyrgyz and two Uzbek lives, and left seventy-two individuals wounded. Batyrov, along with five other Uzbek leaders, fled the country after they were charged by the general prosecutor as being instigators of ethnic clashes. A curfew and a state of emergency were introduced in the city of Jalalabat and Suzak district from 19 May to 1 June (ibid., 16).

Tensions in Osh

The authors of the Memorial report identify three waves of ethnic tensions in the Osh city that preceded the communal conflict. Each new wave was associated with increasing frequency and intensified violence in interethnic incidents. The first tension in the Osh city started in late April. The first documented evidence points out that on 29 April, there was a fight at the Osh-3 railway station between two members of a Kyrgyz criminal gang and Uzbek businessmen who imported used cars from South Korea. The fight had repercussions as ethnically framed news about it quickly spread across the town. Subsequently, small fights and brawls in the streets took place on regular basis.

Although the first stage of the conflict – late April to early May – was not characterized by open violent clashes, both ethnic communities developed mechanisms of quick mobilization. This was especially evident among the Uzbek communities. The Uzbeks did not trust local authorities or the police and their respective ability to provide communal safety in the environment of growing ethnic tensions and activation of criminal gangs (Memorial 2012, 20). The response of the Uzbek community was to create vigilant "self-defence" groups and patrols in the mahallas – the traditional Uzbek neighbourhoods. At the same time, small-scale mobilization of Uzbeks was observed in various parts of the city and suburban areas. People gathered in groups of 50–250, and sometimes 500–800 people. The larger crowds usually gathered during meetings with the Uzbek leaders Salakhutdinov, Batyrov, and Abdurasulov.

The quotation from one of the local newspapers cited in the Memorial report (2012, 17) illustrates proliferation of vigilante groups and the state of panic spreading in one of the days among residents of Osh:

> The residents in the city were in a state of panic all weekend. They called each other, saying that wandering groups of young Uzbeks armed with sticks and pistols were gathering to attack ethnic Kyrgyz, and vice versa. Some spoke of shooting. People from the Uzbek population started organizing groups of young people to protect their areas, yelling "The Kyrgyz are coming." Others organized brigades to keep order.

The second wave of tensions in Osh, according to Memorial (2012, 19), with the reference to the police reports, took place during 16–21 May. This wave was touched off by events in Jalalabat city, when, on 13 May, supporters of the former president Bakiev attempted to seize power in the south, and there was political mobilization of the Jalalabat Uzbeks led by Batyrov. Although the Uzbek communities in Osh did not participate directly in Jalalabat events, the disorders in Jalalabat fuelled tensions between Kyrgyz and Uzbeks in Osh and induced further ethnic mobilization and the spread of ethnic fears and rumours.

One of my key informants, Rahman (a pseudonym), is an ethnic Uzbek, a human rights activist, and a community leader from Turan – an Uzbek-dominated district in Osh. His evidence and accounts of the events were highly reliable and later were corroborated by investigative reports of the international missions. In an interview that I conducted in July 2010 – in the immediate aftermath of the conflict – Rahman described how things were getting tense in Osh:

Rahman: On 1 May, during the night, there was a car accident. One taxi minivan with an Uzbek driver and a BMW automobile with a Kyrgyz driver crashed. Of course, there were and are and will be such incidents which can never be shown in [police] data. But that day then I saw in an Uzbek neighbourhood, next to *domkom* [the head of a residential quarter or an apartment block], around 200–300 of young Uzbeks supporting the Uzbek taxi van driver; they all surrounded the Kyrgyz young driver and lynched [*samosud*] him. And a week before there had been an opposite case, again interethnic conflict when the Kyrgyz young men were trying to punish an Uzbek violator. Then I approached the domkom and asked him why he hadn't called the district police, the traffic police to solve the problem in a legal way. Then they were called and were investigating the case in the domkom's living place, meanwhile outside the crowd was getting out of control. And I could see 3–4 young men in that crowd with the guns – automatic rifles. I came close enough to speak to them and asked whether they were police; they said no. They were Uzbeks. Later I made some informal inquiries and realized that they were bodyguards of Inom Abdurasulov (one of the Osh Uzbek leaders).

Joldon: Who is he?

Rahman: He is an ex-MP of Jogorku Kenesh [parliament]. Although he is an Uighur, he considers himself an Uzbek leader … Then I said to them it is not good to walk around armed since they are not law-enforcement people. I asked whether they have licence. They were strong and militant [*boevoi*] young men and asked me to leave them alone and forced me out of the crowd. Then I approached the policemen and said that there were civilians [*grajdanskiy baldar*] with the guns. The police replied that they cannot go to the crowd which is big and may destroy them [the police].

He observed similar incidents in other parts of the city with spontaneous street mobilization of people from both ethnic groups and involvement. Despite that he signalled about these incidents to high-profile officials in Bishkek, the latter failed to take meaningful preventive measures. The speech by Batyrov at the rally in Jalalabat was constantly played in the Uzbek language TV channels, Mezon TV and Osh TV. The continuous TV translations of the rally in Jalalabat affected the interethnic relations in Osh by inciting fear among the Kyrgyz population. Batyrov's speech obviously had negative effect on the Kyrgyz's perceptions of the Uzbek's "insurgent" political activities. Memorial (2012, 21) states that: "Almost all sources mentioned the extremely distressed reaction of the Kyrgyz population to the video recordings of the demonstration in Jalalabat on 15 May that were shown on Osh TV and Mezon TV, both based in Osh, and especially to the speech by Batyrov."

The number of incidents with brawls and street-group fights increased considerably at those days. Otherwise, everyday routine quarrels turned to the focal points for quick ethnic mobilization. The regular traffic brawls unusually attracted ethnically divided large crowds of 100–200 people. In such cases, the rapid ethnic mobilization was going on through the phone calls to their friends and acquaintances by witnesses of the incidents. The police records show at least nine instances of interethnic group fights and beatings. "In all registered incidents, the victims were recognized as being Kyrgyz or persons who had been mistaken for Kyrgyz by the attackers" (ibid., 23).

The rise of vigilantism in Uzbek mahallas contributed to the further escalation of interethnic relations in the city. Some of the regular stop-and-searches of passing cars conducted by militant "self-defence" groups ended with violent incidents. On several occasions, vigilante groups formed in the Uzbek mahallas attacked several cars that looked, from their perspectives, suspicious; the Kyrgyz passengers in these cars were taken out and beaten. Some evidence indicates that such vigilante groups escalated tensions between the ethnic communities in the city. One report suggests that "[o]n 21 May, the Head of UVD [police department] in the Osh city, Kursan Asanov, demanded an end to checks of cars carried out by volunteer groups established by Uzbek territorial councils in Osh (especially in the Turan and Sheyit-Dobo Microdistricts and on 8 March Street), and that such groups should patrol only in cooperation with local police inspectors. On this background, one may assume that some of the conflicts taking place were connected to the actions of officially formed 'people's watch groups'" (ibid., 24).

This case also suggests that before the violence broke out on 10 June, there had been the proliferation in the numbers of Uzbek vigilante groups. In the second interview with Rahman in 2012 – who was monitoring the situation on the Uzbek side – he told me the following:

> One could feel that interethnic conflict was inevitable. Because here [in Osh] Kadyrjan Batyrov started to organize self-defence groups while from the other side the Kyrgyz youth had gatherings and some clashes. Then we

knew that there could well be interethnic conflict but of course we could never know its scale and did not expect it would end up like this ... We felt that both sides were preparing for something. When I went to Jalaldin Salakhutdinov's [head of republican-level Uzbek National Cultural Center] office I saw around 70 young sportsmen of different sports – sambo, wrestling, boxing, etc. I asked why he was gathering them together and he replied that he was told by the mayor's office that they wanted each of the quarters – *kvartal* – to prepare its own district with a self-defence group [*otryad samooborony*] to be ready to protect themselves. He said that those sportsmen were his district's self-defence group. Similar self-defence groups were established in the Kyrgyz communities as well.

In the context of Osh, the police-civilian relations have ethnic dimensions. It is considered that police officers tend to be predominantly ethnic Kyrgyz. According to the NGO, For Interethnic Tolerance, among 627 police officers in the Osh city 86 were ethnic Uzbek and of 550 police officers in Osh province (the locations outside the Osh city), 30 were ethnic Uzbek (Memorial 2012, 19). For prevention of violence, the Osh police placed a special emphasis on cooperation with influential representatives of the Uzbek community. In the course of preventive actions, the police met with the leaders of the Uzbek population and trainers at local sports clubs belonging to different ethnic groups, led similar meetings with representatives of such institutions as the city council, neighbourhood committees, territorial councils, and *aksakal* (elders) courts, who probably could provide a realistic evaluation of the situation. On the evening of 19 May 2010, sportspersons were asked by the authorities to carry out night-time patrolling of the streets alongside law enforcement officials. The authorities demanded that the leaders of the Uzbek population in Osh province make public statements on television including criticism of Kadyrzhan Batyrov and calls for the Uzbek population not to give in to provocations. The chairman of the Republican Uzbek National Cultural Center [hereafter UNCC], Zhalaldin Salakhutdinov, was warned by the head of UVD [the city police department] that he would be held personally responsible for any demonstration or attempt at organizing gatherings among the Uzbek population (Memorial ibid., 24–5). Subsequently, such patrols and public order brigades proliferated in virtually every Uzbek neighbourhood. As discussed earlier, the aggressive behaviour of these volunteer squads, de facto vigilante groups, contributed more to escalation rather than to de-escalation of ethnic tensions. At the city entrances, the police set up ten roadblocks and eight mobile teams of police special forces, each comprising five policemen. Upon emergence of rumours about gathering of crowds of ethnic youth, police officers would drive to the alleged locations of ethnic mobilization to monitor the situation. In some cases, when in response to some rumours or street incidents small-scale mobilizations were observed in Uzbek mahallas, the police worked together with the leaders of local Uzbek communities who tried to persuade people to disperse (ibid., 16). The authors of the Memorial report also point out that little is known about similar cooperative activities in Kyrgyz neighbourhoods.

There were also some problems in cooperation between the police and the leaders of the Uzbek community. Some of the rank-and-file police officers were strongly embedded in the everyday discourse of the tensions and routine nationalism between the members of Kyrgyz and Uzbek ethnic communities. This factor posed an obstacle to interethnic trust and cooperation between the Kyrgyz policemen and civilian Uzbeks. This distrust revealed itself during the ethnic violence. In many cases, the police and other law enforcement troops considered Uzbeks as enemies and mahallas as hostile territories. In the same way, the Uzbeks distrusted the police as for them the policemen were just the same Kyrgyz who support their ethnic fellows.

The third wave of ethnic tensions took place on 9 and 10 June. The culmination of this wave, the Uzbek ethnic mobilization near the Alai Hotel in Osh downtown on 10 June, became the onset and a trigger event for subsequent violent ethnic riots erupted. Practically all investigative reports agree that the onset of the riots started with emerging rumours and increasing tensions in the streets of Osh reportedly characterized by brawls, stabbings, indiscriminate beatings, and mass attacks against the Kyrgyz. Aggressive Uzbek mobs conducted stop-and-search of cars, and dragged Kyrgyz passengers out of their cars and beat them (HRW 2010; KIC 2011; Memorial 2012). On 10 June, these violent acts against Kyrgyz took place at the same time in several locations in Osh: in the city center, in Furkat village (the eastern entrance to Osh), and in Nurdar (the neighbourhood on the way to the airport), where Uzbek mobs indiscriminately attacked, beat, and stabbed random Kyrgyz.

Ethnic and Community Leaders

In general, two sets of ethnic leaders were identifiable during violent events in June 2010 – national- or regional-level leaders at the first level and community leaders at the lower level. Local-level community leaders played a key role in influencing micro-outcomes. Their efforts to contain violence caused aggregate outcomes in certain neighbourhoods, districts, and even towns. In chapters 6 and 7, I provide detailed accounts of community-policing activities of community-level leaders (kvartkoms and domkoms). In self-policing local communities, traditional leaders strongly rely on the power of local social norms. However, not all leaders enjoyed power in among their constituencies. Kyrgyz community leaders in multi-storey building complexes with a high concentration of the residentially unstable migrant population were generally weak. Their authority was not recognized by the majority of local residents. To be influential, local leaders need long-life and stable residential communities that share common social norms.

The role of the Kyrgyz national leaders was ambiguous. Some of nationalist leaders were seen actively mitigating aggression among Kyrgyz groups and in some cases even preventing crowds from attacking Uzbek mahallas (Matveeva, Savin, and Faizullaev 2012, 32).

Bakiev's regional clients were involved in storming of local government buildings in Osh, Jalalabat, and Batken in May 2010. They put active efforts to sabotage the new regime. It is not clear whether regional leaders from Bakiev's southerner network tried to organize spontaneous violent mobilization. Some of Bakiev's most active supporters were sent on the helicopter to pacify the Kyrgyz crowd in Furkat. Gayipkulov, a former minister from Bakiev's network, was a key figure who prevented violence in Aravan and brokered a nonaggression pact between local Uzbek and Kyrgyz communities (Khamidov, Megoran, and Heathershaw 2017). A leader of Kyrgyz neighbourhood of Uchar, in my interview with him, positioned himself as an ethnic nationalist. However, he played a crucial role in negotiating peace with Uzbeks in Turan. He actively assisted in providing humanitarian aid to Turan. However, the above examples do not suggest that all national-level leaders and other lower-level networks behaved in the same way. Some of them probably turned a blind eye to, silently encouraged, or even actively helped to organize the violent mobilization. Since, I do not have any direct evidence, I suggest that more research should be taken to investigate leaders involved in the mobilization.

The role of religious leaders in containing violence was rather marginal. I have not observed their active involvement on brokering peace between conflicting communities during the most violent phase of the conflict. According to my observations, religious mediating was mostly visible in highly religious Uzgen district. Their involvement increased at the later stages of the conflict and in post-conflict reconciliation activities.

Uzbek Ethnic Actors and Entrepreneurs

Evidence suggests that those days, Batyrov travelled extensively to the Osh city and its neighbouring towns and villages trying to mobilize local Uzbek communities. In their turn, the Uzbek leaders of Osh participated in meetings organized by Batyrov in Jalalabat.

In the days preceding the June violence, the Uzbek leaders conducted remarkably high number of activities with the local Uzbek communities including political rallies and meetings in the Uzbek neighbourhoods. According to the police records, from April to 10 June, the leaders of the Uzbek National Cultural Center (UNCCs,[10] and particularly Batyrov, Salakhutdinov, Abdurasulov, Abdullaeva, and Davron Sabirov conducted more than twenty-five meetings and gatherings with the Uzbeks in the Osh city and its surroundings. During these meetings, the Uzbek leaders and the participants discussed the issues of interethnic relations. At the same time, the Uzbek leaders established the headquarters and public order and "self-defence" groups for the purported purpose of providing safety in the neighbourhoods and urban districts with a predominantly ethnic Uzbek population (National Commission 2011). It is not clear here, what is meant by a term "headquarters," however. It can be inferred that such "headquarters" facilitated fast mobilization of the members of "self-defence" groups in case of confrontations with outsiders. As noted earlier, such vigilante groups conducted stop-and-search of cars and passersby. The stop-and-search actions were from time to time accompanied by beatings of car passengers of ethnic Kyrgyz background and random interrogation of allegedly suspicious individuals who accidentally found themselves in the Uzbek mahallas.

Notably, among the abovementioned top Uzbek leaders, Batyrov was the only representative of the Uzbek community from Jalalabat. The fact that he was actively involved in the organization of political meetings with local Uzbek communities in Osh region was very unusual given that the Uzbek leaders usually confined their political influence within the scope of their local constituencies. Since the communal violence of 1990, Uzbek leaders had restrained themselves from political activities that could be considered an open challenge to the dominant Kyrgyz political establishment. The meeting organized in May 2010 in Jalalabat was only the second Uzbek political event after 1990. The first political rally was organized in May 2006, also by Batyrov, in which the participants of the meeting demanded greater representation of Uzbeks in political and law enforcement bodies and to recognize the Uzbek language as a state language (Khamidov 2006; KIC 2011, 17). Batyrov's active involvement in political mobilization of the Uzbeks in Osh province, therefore, displayed his apparent aspirations to become a nationally-acknowledged leader of the Uzbeks in Kyrgyzstan. He used his Vatan party to promote his influence and embrace and unify the otherwise fragmented prominent Uzbek leadership of Osh, in the framework of his party. Essentially, this was the first serious attempt to unite the Uzbek leaders of Osh and Jalalabat.

However, not all segments of the Uzbek elite supported the brand of political activism energetically promoted by Batyrov and his supporters from Osh. The leaders of the city-level Osh UNCC held a position traditional to the Uzbek minority, aimed at supporting the central government and restraining the Uzbek community from political activism at the national level. They cooperated in establishing an institution called a public council and created the board of aksakals[11] under the Osh UNCC. Such boards of aksakals were created in various territorial districts in the Osh city. The task of the public council was to gather community leaders from various boards of aksakals to establish a common line in addressing diverse social issues – for example, fighting corruption.

The position proposed by the Osh UNCC and some community leaders closely linked to this organization was not to put political demands on the agenda until the legal government was elected. In situation when there was no legitimate elected government and a project of the new constitution had not yet been adopted, they clearly opposed to the political activism, at the time being produced by national Uzbek leaders like Batyrov. To preclude from hazardous ethnic mobilization, activists of the Osh UNCC went to various districts, large mahallas and neighbourhoods, schools, and other places to convince local residents not to participate in mobilization promoted by Batyrov, Salakhitdinov, and Abdurasulov. The Osh UNCC had disagreements and political fights with the republican UNCC, which marked political and ideological divisions between the Uzbek leaders at the national (the republican UNCC) and the Osh city (the Osh UNCC) levels. In my interview with Sheraly, one of the most active and senior members of the Osh UNCC and a member of the public council and the board of aksakals in the city of Osh, describes me the position of the center before the June conflict:

> Then, in April and May, the situation was so tense in Osh, full of various events. We were protesting opposing Kadyrjan Batyrov and his supporters [*Batyrovtar*] to participate in rallies. We said we didn't want to get involved in politics, we were taking a neutral position, we had lots of fights [with the national-level UNCC]. Our Center [the Osh UNCC] had a position not to get involved, the board of aksakals determined this solution. We decided to leave them [politicians] to fight it out over the portfolios and then to work with those who were left [laughing]. We were in a neutral position, there were meetings in 2–3 places in Osh coming from Jalalabat that of Abdrasulov's. We didn't allow any of our active members to take part in any of them. We did our best to prevent any unrest. We held gatherings with the active members in different places in microdistricts telling them not to participate in protests, "don't allow your children to go out," not to get mixed up with them. At that young age they might be keen to be involved. Otherwise, we had lots of pressure from different parts to take part in the protests in the square. They [various competing Kyrgyz political factions] wanted to see Uzbeks as well in this and that group. But we were standing against all this and didn't want to get involved in it ... So more than half of us were against the meetings, about 90 per cent were against such dirty protests. And now what? That has happened, the fact is done (interview, Osh, August 2012).

In my interview with another community leader, Rahman, he blames Batyrov for bringing militants to the city of Osh who were destructive for social cohesion of local Uzbek communities.

> Rahman: Eventually those in black shirts were those sportsmen of Inom Abdurasulov and Kadyrjan Batyrov, I think.
> (another Uzbek man sitting next to Rahman): Mainly they were exported from other regions.
> Rahman: The beginning of the conflict has started in Jalalabat. You know it. Kadyrjan Batyrov's property was being taken out by Bakiev's brothers. And Kadyrjan Batyrov was not able to stand against the Bakievs and began engaging ordinary Jalalabat people, the Uzbeks into the process. When the Uzbeks didn't support, he started political demands ... then he said that the Constitutional Advisory Board did not accept

our suggestions. So, the main figure who escalated the situation between Uzbeks and Kyrgyz was Kadyrjan Batyrov (interview, Osh, August 2012).

Some phrases from Batyrov's speech indicate that the situation unfolding after the 7 April, was characterized by the weak and fragmented interim government, the demoralized police, and open confrontation between various political groups and clans within Kyrgyzstan's political arena distinctive with its prevalence by ethnic Kyrgyz actors, and was perceived by him as a "window of opportunity" for making political claims on behalf of all Kyrgyzstani Uzbeks. The phrases such as "we have been expecting this moment for twenty years"; "Uzbeks have been waiting this moment for long time"; "the time has come for the active participation in the political life of the country"; "if the Interim Government is not able to restore order and justify people's trust then ..." and so on (see Joint Working Group 2012), point at his growing ambitions to speak in the name of the whole Uzbek community. The speech by Batyrov during the Uzbek political rally in Jalalabat on 15 May was interpreted differently by the Uzbek and the Kyrgyz communities. For Uzbeks, the speech signified the opening of new political opportunities prompted by regime change and breakdown of the central authority. The Kyrgyz population perceived it with fears of new Uzbek resurgence. Many Kyrgyz interpreted the content of Batyrov's speech as a sign of preparation for Uzbek violent mobilization. The Kyrgyz memories of the 1990 conflict suggested "a separatist scenario" of Uzbek political mobilization and aggression against the Kyrgyz. The law enforcement bodies interpreted the very speech as an instigation of the interethnic clashes – which followed few days later after the meeting in Jalalabat organized by Batyrov – and issued a warrant for Batyrov's arrest.

Despite the multiple interethnic violent incidents ethnic tensions and street fights did not escalate into deadly ethnic violence until 10 June 2010. However, the events preceding 11–15 June show high ethnic mobilization of the Uzbeks in Osh and Jalalabat. This dynamic of ethnic mobilization presented itself in multiple street fights, group beatings, and vigilante violence (the latter mostly by Uzbek "self-defence" groups), with its culmination on the night of 10 June when several thousand Uzbeks took over the streets in the downtown Osh, setting fire to the shops of the ethnic Kyrgyz, crashing windows, stopping cars, and beating the Kyrgyz. These dynamics were completely reversed in the subsequent days, when the rural Kyrgyz mobilized against the Osh Uzbeks. Ethnic violence was probably exacerbated by the absence of top Uzbek leaders on 10 June 2010. Many republican-level UNCC leaders went to Tajikistan to meet Batyrov and others were absent for other reasons. An Uzbek criminal leader "Black" Aibek was killed two days before the onset of violence. Aibek was embedded in Bakiev's patronage network and was Batyrov's main rival among Uzbek leaders. There were practically no key Uzbek figures to mediate the onset of violence.

4

Microdynamics and Patterns of Violence

Conflic Data and Flashpoints of Violence in Osh

Uncertainty, induced by the temporary breakdown of the state in June 2010, created a sense of insecurity – a necessary condition for actors' innovative repertoires that characterize many great transformative events (Sewell 1996, 867). As McAdam and Sewell (2001, 110) argue, "By increasing th[e] sense of uncertainty ... [transformative] events also fuel a dramatic escalation in the mobilization of emotion by all parties to the conflict."

In contrast to the previous chapter that discussed the role of structural, historical, and political factors in shaping this conflict, the first section of this chapter emphasizes the critical importance of contingency in determining outcomes across Osh's urban neighbourhoods[1] and identifies the main flashpoints and the varying trajectories of violence in Osh. It outlines the patterns of the escalation and diffusion of violence across neighbourhoods. The neighbourhood-based examination of violent events in the first section demonstrates the importance of local dynamics and highlights the conditions that led to location-specific forms of violence. The sections following it present descriptive statistics of this communal warfare and the research methodology of this study.

The first outbreak of violence in southern Kyrgyzstan produced uneven effects across various locations. The scope, forms, and intensity of violence changed under the influence of critical events, local conditions, and actors' interactions. Given the complexity and different forms of violence in this conflict, this section carefully traces the diffusion of violence across the city of Osh and its neighbourhoods to provide an accurate overview of the patterns of violence in urban settings. It demonstrates how contingency causes the escalation of violence from the street mobilization into violent riots and then into large-scale communal violence and urban warfare. In most cases, riots escalated into communal violence and intensive armed combats. In locations where local Uzbek groups were defeated, armed combats transformed into pogrom-like violence. Contagious effects of the communal warfare were unevenly distributed across locations being influenced by local conditions and impacted local intra- and intergroup balances of power at the neighbourhood level.

Defining the June 2010 events as anti-Uzbek pogroms – as many scholars and external observers did (ICG, KIC, and others) – renders too simplistic accounts of this episode of ethnic violence. This violent conflict was a more complex event. Forms of violence varied across locations and events. Transformative power of unfolding events can change the dynamics of contention in one location while local structural conditions, demonstrational effects, and institutional constraints can alter actors' repertoires and convert one form of contention into another in other locations (Beissinger 2002, 2007).

The main common pattern of violence in the cities of Osh, Jalalabat, and other major sites of ethnic violence had the following sequence. In the first phase, there was evident increasing ethnic sensitivity and growing mobilization of Uzbek communities, beatings and attacks against Kyrgyz, eruption of violent riots initiated and dominated by Uzbek groups, and the first assassinations of Kyrgyz. The second phase was characterized by countermobilization of rural Kyrgyz from neighbouring villages but also from remote mountainous districts, rumours of extermination of urban Kyrgyz by Uzbeks, and large-scale communal violence and property destruction in Uzbek mahallas. The third phase was de-escalation of violence characterized by exhaustion of combatants and increasing role of the state in containing violence. In Osh, an additional factor was a mass panic flight of Kyrgyz militants after the spread of rumours about an invasion by Uzbekistan's army. The de-escalation phase was marked by a sharply decreased rate of mortality in the conflict but an increasing rate of hostage-taking.

As the previous chapter shows, the trigger to ethnic violence, to a large extent, resulted from the accumulation of the preceding marginal forms of violence such as multiple street brawls and vigilante violence exercised by the local Uzbek "self-defence" groups. The trigger event was preceded by growing Uzbek mobilization. At this stage, two events were important for the escalation of violence: (1) an attempted assault on the female student dormitory by an Uzbek crowd, and (2) the police's violent dispersion and shooting of the Uzbek protesters. The first event produced a very powerful rumour about mass rape of Kyrgyz female students. This rumour had a crucial mobilizational effect on the Kyrgyz from rural areas. The second event produced an escalating effect as a game-changer that produced first killings. Violent clashes erupted after these killings. This signified the shift to the new level of violence.

Similar transformative events also occurred at later stages such as a violent standoff at the roundabout in Furkat and the rumour about Uzbekistani troops invasion (see detailed accounts of these events later in this chapter). Such transformative events had escalating or de-escalating effects. However, these effects were uneven across locations being influenced by local conditions. As McAdam and Sewell (2001, 107) put it, "contingent sequences of actions and purely local causes help to produce surprising, significant, and enduring effect." One important implication of such transformative events was that they not only produced a cascade of other significant events but also influenced local intra- and intergroup balances of power at the neighbourhood level. At final stages of this conflict on 14 and 15 June, violence de-escalated into sporadic attacks and skirmishes. However, marginal forms of violence in the form of hostage-taking came to predominate even after the active phase of this ethnic conflict (i.e., after 15 June).[2]

COMMUNAL WARFARE IN OSH, JUNE 2010

In general, all investigative reports converge on identification of the initial outbreaks of violence. The difference in the number of these hotspots can be attributed to the levels of violence, conceptual definition of violence, and the spatial/geographical scale of aggregation in the analysis. Major reports and witness accounts almost fully converge in identifying the main hotspots of violence, except for some minor discrepancies.

The trigger event, which entailed the main impetus to the escalation of violence, took place in the city's downtown, near the Alai Hotel. It started as an ordinary scuffle between several Kyrgyz and Uzbek youths in a small casino. What otherwise would be a routine brawl, it quickly mobilized the Uzbeks from neighbouring communities in Sheit Tepe, Majrimtal, and Kyzyl-Kyshtak, all located along Navoi street. The rumours about the Kyrgyz "beating" Uzbeks quickly spread across Uzbek mahallas of the city. The Uzbek mob quickly grew to around 3,000 people "who were highly prepared to mobilize" (Memorial 2012, 36).

As the crowd became more aggressive, it rejected the police's mediating attempts "by throwing stones and chanting anti-Kyrgyz slogans ... The roads to the City Police Office had been locked by the crowds. Police were injured. Police vehicles were burnt" (KIC 2011, 27). The crowd went out of control and used stones to attack the dormitory of the Osh State University where mainly Kyrgyz students including female students from rural areas were accommodated. The students in the dormitory barricaded its entrances while female students hid on the roof of the building (Memorial 2012, 40). Later they were evacuated by law enforcement troops. The Uzbek mob started destroying public buildings and burning shops that belonged to ethnic Kyrgyz and attack passersby and cars driven by ethnic Kyrgyz.

The assault on the female dormitory had very serious consequences for the development of violence. The news about the assault, in its distorted versions, quickly reached the Kyrgyz population. An informational vacuum engendered by the absence of credible media coverage and inability of the authorities to provide timely reports about unfolding events generated a horrible and very powerful rumour about Uzbeks attacking the dormitory, and raping and killing Kyrgyz female students spread across the country. The rumour triggered huge outrage among the Kyrgyz. Vengeance became one of the strongest motives that moved hundreds of Kyrgyz from rural areas against Uzbek mahallas during the violent events. It became a strong mobilizational factor for ethnic Kyrgyz who justified their attacks in terms of revenge.

The police used gunfire against the Uzbek crowd after the latter torched nearby shops and public buildings and wounded several police officers. An armoured personnel carrier (APC) with riot police, that initially stayed neutral between Kyrgyz and Uzbeks, lost control and started indiscriminate fire at people standing along the street. The police's gunfire killed several and wounded dozens of Uzbeks. The crowd dispersed and retreated to the mahallas to the north of the Alai Hotel. An unjustifiably violent response by the police and the military introduced the new wave of escalation of the conflict. Thus, the first deaths were resulted not from the actions of riotous crowd but from the uncontrolled mortal shootings from the police. These killings crucially affected the dynamics and level of interethnic violence in the subsequent days by turning the disorder at the Alai Hotel into a flashpoint of deadly violence. The authors of the Memorial report (Memorial 2012, 54) similarly characterize the trigger event as a key moment which determined the highly violent course of the consequent events:

> The unjustified use of assault weapons and the dispersion of civilians from the night-time streets, many of whom were in a state of shock, led to

a further destabilization of the situation in the city. Some of the youth saw what had happened as a change in the "rules of the game," according to which the conflicting sides had formerly tried to avoid actions that could lead to deaths among the population. The public speech of the Mayor of Osh on local television at 4:40 AM calling for calm could not influence the situation in any way.

First riots followed by both Uzbeks and Kyrgyz. However, Uzbek groups dominated the streets of the city till the morning of 11 June. Ethnic mobilization occurred almost at the same moment near several Uzbek neighbourhoods in the city. Several flashpoints emerged after the trigger event at the Alai Hotel. According to the investigative reports, the military was inexperienced and unprepared to deal with emerging violence and riots when compared with those of the police officers. On the other hand, the police were often ethnically biased. During the riots, police officers in some cases provided unbalanced treatment toward Uzbek residents and incorrect judgment toward the operative situation. Inadequate behaviour of the military often led to the escalation rather than de-escalation of violence.

The Memorial report (ibid., 2012, 82) characterizes overall situation in first hours of riots as follows:

> In spite of the presence of extremist groups on both sides, the level of violence and mutual attempts at worsening the situation was far lower than what would be the case during the next days. Violent confrontations were often brief and many of those who were caught by the crowds and beaten up were released soon after. In terms of the standoffs of hundreds or thousands of people, the participants were merely trying to prevent violence being carried out by the other side. Both Uzbeks and Kyrgyz in different parts of the city went out on the street in order to prevent pogroms [property destruction] and looting near their own houses or to secure the safety of their friends or relatives. The exaggerated rumours of violence in other parts of the city played a destabilizing role. The process of ethnic mobilization became large scale, including armed criminal groups.

However, according to the KIC (2011, 28), already then, communal groups perceived the emerging of violence as an onset of war: "witnesses anticipated not simply violence, but war. An azan (call to prayer) called, irregularly, from at least 4 mosques at about 2 am and warned people to take care. Uzbek men travelling in cars in the mahallas shouted that the war had begun. The same message was conveyed in innumerable telephone calls. Immediately following the trigger incident at the Hotel Alai, an expectation of Kyrgyz attack on the mahallas was shared by the Uzbeks, Kyrgyz and the Government."

The dynamics of violence sharply changed by the morning of 11 June when many neighbourhoods in Osh physically isolated from each other by erecting barricades and roadblocks, turning themselves into self-contained zones. As opposed to the night fights, the Uzbek crowds stopped roaming in the streets and concentrated their efforts on defence of their neighbourhoods. In Uzbek neighbourhoods, local residents drew large signs saying "help" and "SOS," making them visible for aviation and satellite pictures. The below excerpt from the Memorial report (Memorial 2012, 83) summarizes different phases of violence. It demonstrates how the violent disorders first transformed into an armed conflict and then de-escalated into sporadic violence.

> The peak of violence in Osh came between 11 and 12 June, in spite of a state of emergency having been introduced the night before. Looting and torching of private homes and businesses began already on the morning of 11 June, and was soon taking place on a massive scale. Hundreds of residents of the city were killed, thousands were wounded. Tens of thousands left their homes and fled to the border with Uzbekistan. The use of armoured vehicles and automatic weapons against the self-defence forces in the Uzbek mahallas also indicated that the conflict had entered a significantly new level. The relocation of forces from other regions in the country and the rumours spreading on 12 June that Russian and Uzbekistani forces may be brought to the region eventually helped curb the level of violence. Kyrgyz youth arriving from village districts to participate in "the war" started leaving the city. On 13 and 14 June, the pogroms continued, but the intensity of the conflict became markedly lower. Only separate torchings and local incidents were reported on 15 June.

On 11 June, when thousands of furious Kyrgyz from rural districts forced through the roadblocks into the city, the authorities lost control over the situation. Kyrgyz rioters enraged by rumours and real facts of violence stormed several large Uzbek neighbourhoods. From 11 June onward, the main sites of intense attacks on Uzbek mahallas were the villages of Furkat and Shark along Pamirskaia-Monueva street and Amir Timur ward in the eastern part of the city; Cheremushki and Kyzyl-Kyshtak mahallas in the western part; and

Sheit Tepe, Teshik-Tash, and Majrimtal mahallas along Alisher Navoi street adjacent to the grand bazaar in the downtown. In the central-northern part (Alymbek Datka, Manas-Ata, and Jiydalik), the clashes were still intense, but their pattern was different from those of the formerly mentioned neighbourhoods. In the latter, violence and property destruction took place in both Uzbek and Kyrgyz neighbourhoods with concentration of the gunfire in the territory of multistorey apartment complexes inhabited mainly by ethnic Kyrgyz. Both sides made iterative inroads to the "enemy" zones. The southern districts, however, experienced no riots or managed to quickly contain escalating violence. Figure 4.1 presents a map of Osh with the names and locations of those neighbourhoods that appear most frequently throughout the book as case studies and areas where most important events took place.

The attacks on Uzbek mahallas usually followed the same pattern depicted in the investigative reports and corroborated by my own field research. Initially unarmed Kyrgyz crowds conducted repetitive attacks on fortified Uzbek mahallas. They usually retreated after receiving gunfire from the barricades. Being unable to overcome the defence, Kyrgyz would attack the barricades again after gaining automatic weapons, including three APCs that became available for the Kyrgyz after they stormed several military depots and attacked some military convoys. The iterative attacks on mahallas were sustained through "[b]oth random civilians and armed men, most likely from the criminal underworld, who acted as local leaders, participated in the attacks. These leaders inspired or put pressure on others to go forward when they were too scared or too tired to continue. The attacks subsided every so often, but then would recommence with fresh arrivals from the countryside. Late at night the attacks mostly stopped" (Matveeva, Savin, and Faizullaev 2012, 24).

At the same time, the Uzbeks also used lethal weapons, including Kalashnikovs and armoured trucks. With the latter, they successfully counteracted the actions of APCs in a number of cases. In many instances, the military deliberately removed the barricades erected by the defenders of mahallas fulfilling orders from the military commanders. According to the HRW (2010, 28): "Law enforcement officials also referred to information about the taking of hostages in Uzbek neighbourhoods, among other acts, as grounds to remove barricades and disarm the Uzbeks." However, by removing the barricades the military rarely ensured the security of local residents, leaving the mahallas vulnerable to the attacks from combatants to opportunistic behaviour, including gang rapes, mass looting, torture of victims, and arson of residential houses.

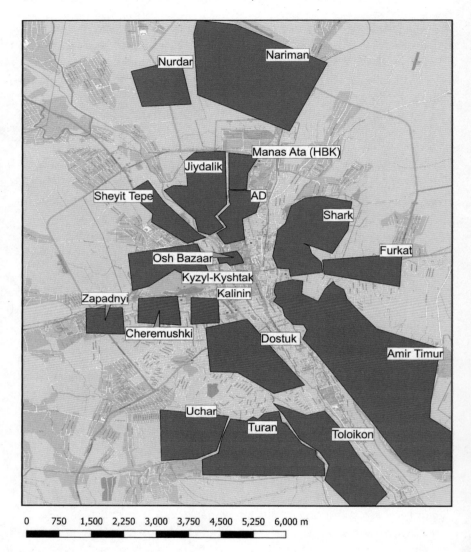

Figure 4.1 Osh city and its neighbourhoods

More than 2,000 houses were totally destroyed by the mass arson. Opportunism and retaliation were also pertinent to the defenders of mahallas. Some Kyrgyz residents, who lived in Uzbek-dominated mahallas, were attacked and killed. Some women were gang-raped and killed while others were taken hostage. Those caught on looting site were severely beaten and killed.

Western Part

To have a full grasp of the violence that broke out in the western Uzbek mahallas we must take into account the Kyrgyz rural mobilization that took place in Zapadnyi,[3] a neighbourhood of multistorey apartment complexes inhabited mainly by Kyrgyz and few Russians. Upon hearing news and rumours about what happened in Osh the previous night hundreds of Kyrgyz arrived from rural areas. Spatial proximity to the interregional road that connects Osh with rural districts to its west and south, made Zapadnyi one of main focal points for the Kyrgyz mobilization. Being located in the western outskirts of the city, it has a strategic location: the western entrance roads leading to the city from the rural districts of Nookat and Aravan and also from the province of Batken, all pass through this neighbourhood. However, to enter the city's downtown from its western outskirts, one must proceed through Uzbek-populated mahallas in Cheremushki and Kyzyl-Kyshtak, located respectively on the southern and northern foots of the Sulaiman Mountain.

Kyrgyz mobilization at the Zapadnyi district became crucial for the dynamics of violence. Being a focal point for rural mobilization because of its strategic location at the intersection of roads connecting Osh with rural districts, Zapadnyi facilitated the main attacks by the Kyrgyz on Cheremushki and Kyzyl-Kyshtak mahallas. The directions of attacks were shaped by the city's road infrastructure and geographical landscape.

Around 2,000 rural people, who were outsiders to Zapadnyi, dominated the neighbourhood, while the local residents remained passive observers. The main entrance street to the neighbourhood was barricaded and patrolled, mainly by rural outsiders and probably by a few local residents. Residents and elders did not intervene in the activities of outsiders even when some opportunists looted a local shop and a café owned by a Kyrgyz. This non-interference was due to fear of outsiders, lack of community cohesion in the neighbourhood and because residents viewed the utility of rural mobilization as a guarantee for the security of their neighbourhood against retaliatory attacks of Uzbek groups, shaped by perceptions of a common "enemy." The availability of a bazaar and small cafes, right there in the neighbourhood, made it possible to sustain a crowd of several hundred people. The Kyrgyz who arrived at Zapadnyi from rural districts found the neighbourhood a convenient place to stay as they could find relatively easy sources of board and sometimes lodging.

Attacks from Zapadnyi on Cheremushi and Kyzyl-Kyshtak Neighbourhoods

Escalation of the situation in Zapadnyi neighbourhood occurred after Kyrgyz refugees from other neighbourhoods were evacuated into Zapadnyi. That created fears among local Kyrgyz who saw this as direct evidence of the Uzbeks' belligerency. Another precipitant emerged when the Uzbeks in Cheremushki blocked the central street to the city center and preventively fired guns against a group of rural men who were trying to get access to the city center. Both events exacerbated a sense of threat coming from another side.

The below excerpt from Memorial (2012, 115) summarizes the nature of attacks on Cheremushki neighbourhood:

> In general, and as seen from the accounts of witnesses, the "success" of the attack on Cheremushki by groups of Kyrgyz youth on the day of 11 June was ensured by their domination in terms of weapons (those seized from the military and also those they had received from unknown sources). The estimated number of people armed with automatic weapons while carrying out pogroms varies from 30 to 60 persons. The fact that they were supported in the first period by armoured vehicles from the government forces, who were acting against the self-defence groups in Uzbek areas under the pretext of clearing barricades from the street and ending disturbances, also played an important role both in the military sense as well as the psychological. However, on the second day, the attackers were unable to expand the territory they controlled in any noticeable sense, there being pockets of resistance located inside this territory. After the losses they had suffered during previous shoot-outs, many of those arriving to carry out pogroms were scared of entering smaller streets inside the mahallas. Only very brief visits to these streets were made, often under the cover of armed support.

Two main implications from this passage can be drawn. First, successful attacks of Kyrgyz militants in Cheremushki were secured by their predominance in firearms and irresponsible actions by government APCs. Firearms obtained by the Kyrgyz changed the local intergroup balance of power. Second, combatants could not extend the territory of property destruction because of local resistance. Many militants were reluctant to enter small streets fearing gunshots or counterattacks. Some were killed or wounded during such inroads. These two patterns were inherent to many other violent locations.

At first, Kyrgyz groups in Cheremushki as well as in other neighbourhoods were weakly armed, mainly with sticks. Having faced armed defence at the barricades, they initially retreated. In the first day of clashes, the firearm response by the Uzbek self-defence groups was unnecessary, and even counterproductive and sometimes provocative, as we can see what happened in Furkat neighbourhood later in this chapter. The aggressive response radicalized Kyrgyz participants and made them think that Uzbeks were armed and well prepared for this conflict and without firearms it would be impossible to resist Uzbeks. As a result, some groups were compelled to acquire firearms by storming military warehouses. Now having advantage in firearms, the Kyrgyz managed to overpower Uzbek defence groups. This was a common pattern in the development of armed conflict in virtually every major place affected by violence in Osh. The use of firearms spiralled the violence to a much higher level, transforming these ethnic riots into a full-scale armed combat with a very high mortality rate.

Evidence shows that most of the early weapon seizures had non-premediated nature and were mostly a reaction of Kyrgyz participants to the initial unfavourable balance in firearms vis-à-vis Uzbek groups. Soldiers were usually beaten up before crowds seized weapons. In Jalalabat, the military shot dead two and wounded five Kyrgyz assailants on the military depot (Kylym Shamy 2011). In some cases, the military managed to transfer lethal weapons to safe destinations before crowds attacked the military depots (interview with a military officer from Jalalabat, July 2010). On 11 June, most attacks on military depots occurred after Kyrgyz groups suffered losses in early violent encounters with Uzbek groups that had predominance in terms of weapons. This convinced Kyrgyz to storm military depots to change the unfavourable situation. In Jalalabat province, weapons seizures took place on 13 June when violence diffused there from Osh (see chapter 7). However, the initial advantage of Uzbeks in firearms was not prevailing. To my best knowledge, there were no attacks on military warehouses from the Uzbek side, besides one seizure from police officers in Furkat. Weapons were most likely stockpiled in small amounts in local Uzbek communities. But even a small number of automatic weapons and other types of firearms was enough to deter Kyrgyz in an initial stage of violence. General intergroup balance of power shifted toward Kyrgyz when they acquired weapons from military depots.

The main destruction zone in Cheremushki was confined to several blocks along several streets. This was among the most densely concentrated and violent destruction clusters. In total, 341 buildings were destroyed in Cheremushki as a result of communal violence (Memorial 2012, 115). In comparison with Cheremushki, clusters of violence and arson in other areas were less densely concentrated and stretched along principal roads (except Shavkat Rahman area in Shark). In those areas, combatants did not risk going deep inside the mahallas. One possible explanation for why the destruction in Cheremushki was so heavily concentrated in one area is that being a centrally-located mahalla, it was crossed by several principal streets which made it easier for attackers to penetrate blocks from different directions. In another destruction cluster – Kyzyl-Kyshtak – 422 buildings were destroyed (ibid., 100).

De-escalation; Panic in Western Neighbourhoods

All reports highlight the role of rumours about invasion by Uzbekistan's and sometimes of the Russian army in the de-escalation of violence. The rumours triggered de-mobilization of Kyrgyz rural youths, chiefly, in the western part of the city where this rumour was intensely circulated. However, the process of de-escalation began even before the rumours about the invasion actively spread in the city. In Cheremushki, attempts to negotiate a nonaggression pact by local Uzbeks with moderate Kyrgyz leaders on 12 June eventually failed.

The same night, rumours about invasion by Uzbek troops produced strong effects on the de-escalation of violence. The rumours were taken seriously at the highest level of the administration as they came through intelligence service channels. The Kyrgyz intelligence service detected twenty flights landing in the neighbouring city of Andizhan in Uzbekistan, with the Uzbek troops allegedly led by the notorious Uzbek commander Khudayberdiev – a rebellious general from the Tajik civil war of 1992–97, who later defected to Uzbekistan (ibid., 120). The military commandant of the southern region gave an order to the military units in Osh to prepare for defence against foreign invasion. There were top-level meetings held among officials and the military that discussed the defence plans for the city.

However, the rumour spread unevenly across various neighbourhoods. It affected mainly the western neighbourhoods. In Zapadnyi, local residents could hear a loudspeaker warning people about invasion of the Uzbek army.

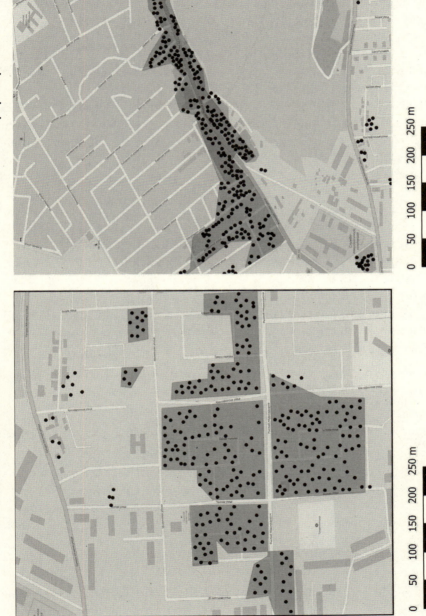

Figure 4.2 Property damage clusters in Cheremushki and Kyzyl-Kyshtak

According to the rumour, an early morning azan (a call to ritual prayer) would be used as a signal for Uzbek troops. The high military commanders ordered mobilization of Kyrgyz military forces and distribution of automatic weapons first among the military forces and then among Kyrgyz civilians willing to participate in the defence. The mayor of Osh ordered the organization of self-defence groups and evacuation of women and children. The order forbade males to leave the city. Kyrgyz military troops were advanced closer to the border with Uzbekistan. A Kyrgyz resident in a multistorey apartment block in Cheremushki, through a phone conversation, received confirmation about the invasion from a security officer who advised him to climb on the roof of his house and prepare petrol bombs to use against Uzbek tanks (interview with a local resident, July 2010).

According to Memorial (2012, 124):

Concluding the summary of night-time events in the western part of Osh, we would also note that the dispersal of large crowds of people carrying out pogroms in the Zapadnyi Microdistrict due to rumours of the arrival of Russian and Uzbekistani forces, indirectly confirms that the situation was characterized by impunity and a lack of willingness by the army and the law enforcement agencies of Kyrgyzstan to use force to stabilize the situation on 11 and 12 June, and that these were important factors in the escalation of violence in the parts of the city that were exposed to large-scale destruction.

Despite many combatants leaving the city on the night of 12–13 June, the violence continued in Cheremushki on 13 and 14 June, though on much smaller scale. By this time, the military and the police had received reinforcements from Bishkek and had taken greater control over situation and intervened in clashes more decisively. Violence subsided into small separate skirmishes. Forms of violence changed from full-scale fights that recalled quasi-military combat – with intense killings, use of firearms, and mass arson – to hostage-taking. Some Kyrgyz looters who were caught looting on the spot were tortured and killed by Uzbek self-defence groups. Others were exchanged for Uzbek hostages. Mediators, and sometimes local councils, actively facilitated such exchanges. On the other hand, some police officers and criminal gangs were engaged in the hostage exchanges, making a profit out of this process. Criminals took hostages to exchange them for ransom. Allegedly they offered their "services" to the victims' families. It is not clear to what extent police officers were involved in the hostage exchanges or in the ransom business. Presumably some of them offered themselves as commercial intermediaries. Two police officers were killed in Cheremushki during such operations. They were beaten and stabbed by an Uzbek crowd from the damaged area. Another "business" practice was when police officers offered safe evacuation to rich Uzbek families from the distressed areas. Such facts have been highlighted in several international and human rights investigative reports. Violence stopped in Cheremushki and Kyzyl-Kyshtak on 15 June but sporadic instances of violence including hostage-taking continued for several more days. Uzbek and some Kyrgyz neighbourhoods remained barricaded till forced opening of barricades by government forces.

The Escalation of Violence in the Eastern Part

When the disorders started in the Osh city on 11 June, the Uzbek residents barricaded the eastern entrance and partly the western entrance (where the road passes through Uzbek neighbourhoods). Residents of Nurdar neighbourhood in Nariman district blocked the road from the airport. Furkat, the eastern entrance to the city, was one of the first locations to undergo deadly ethnic clashes. By the morning of 11 June, it became "one of the three the most dangerous zones, where confrontations between large groups of Uzbek and Kyrgyz youth were reported near the roundabout" (ibid., 124). Blocking of the city entrances and the highly violent behaviour of Uzbek groups against unarmed Kyrgyz at the road blocks in Furkat proved to be a counterproductive strategy as it led to radicalization of Kyrgyz groups and to a sharp escalation of violence.

Eastern Entrance to the City: Furkat and Shark

The first Kyrgyz who arrived in Osh after hearing about the ethnic riots and rumours about killings of Kyrgyz and rapes of Kyrgyz female students gathered at the roundabout road at Furkat, an eastern neighbourhood of Osh Initially, the crowd was composed of people who were going to Osh to rescue their children and relatives who had been studying or working in Osh. According to HRW (2010, 27), "Many had relatives who studied at one of Osh's universities, and the rumours about horrific acts of violence committed by Uzbeks compelled them to go to Osh to bring their relatives home to safety." However, when they reached this ill-fated roundabout road at the neighbourhood of Furkat, they found that the entrance to the city was blocked by makeshift barricades constructed by local Uzbeks. With accumulation of the Kyrgyz mainly from the *raions* (districts) of Alai, Chon Alai, and Uzgen at the roundabout, tensions grew gradually that eventually resulted in clashes between Kyrgyz and Uzbeks. According to one witness: "When we got to Furkat, there were about 1,000 to 1,500 Uzbeks there. They did not let us through. We moved a bit closer to them and we started throwing rocks at each other. At around 10 a.m., however, the Uzbeks opened fire on us. Three people fell right in front of me. I was hit as well, in my hand" (ibid., 27).

As the tensions grew, people in the Kyrgyz crowd tried to break through the barricades but were stopped with gunfire. When the Kyrgyz saw the wounded people and damaged cars arriving from the city, that convinced them about the aggressive intentions of the Uzbeks. A brutal and demonstrative public murder of two Kyrgyz men by Uzbeks, where they killed and then burned them as the rest of the Kyrgyz group was watching, induced retaliatory behaviour on the Kyrgyz. The report by Human Rights Watch (HRW 2010, 28) seems to confirm this dynamic: "Rumours and evidence of brutal killings and hostage-taking rapidly escalated the tense situation. The sight of the charred remains of two Kyrgyz men behind the Uzbek barricades in Furkat, for example, enraged the crowd. The younger Kyrgyz men, in particular, became "uncontrollable" and started to torch Uzbek houses as they moved into the city."

A witness story narrated by Memorial indicates that between midday and 1 p.m., when the Uzbek group using sickles killed two more Kyrgyz men whom they had caught earlier, no firearms were yet possessed by the Kyrgyz. The dead bodies were soaked with gasoline and torched. The killers placed Kyrgyz national headwear on the dead bodies to demonstratively humiliate the Kyrgyz, who were helplessly watching this act of cruel violence. The witness' recollections are telling: "Everything took place in the middle of the road, demonstratively, right in front of both Uzbeks and Kyrgyz. There were no weapons, so we could not do anything" (Memorial 2012, 129). This episode refutes the widespread claims that first Kyrgyz coming to Osh were initially armed and organized.

This moment drastically changed behaviour. Previous clashes had never involved acts of killing and now the Kyrgyz considered this event no longer the kind of brawl that had been in fact fairly common in the period before the conflict. Eight were killed and about hundred wounded, all of them Kyrgyz, in this face-off confrontation at the Furkat roundabout (HRW 2010, 24). For

Kyrgyz, that was now an open declaration of war. Only after the Kyrgyz attacked the military convoy and took one APC and automatic rifles from the soldiers accompanying the convoy, could they break through the makeshift barriers and break down the armed lines of a local Uzbeks group.

The violence in Furkat involved more and more radicals on both sides. Radical Kyrgyz youth arrived at the spot from Alai, Uzgen, and other raions, reaching a total number of about 3,000, and becoming a decisive factor in the interethnic violence and, particularly, in the eastern part of the city. According to many witness accounts from both sides, precisely this group was actively engaged in street fights and attacks against fortified mahallas.

> [S]everal thousand people from the Alay district went to Osh immediately upon hearing about the violence ... [A respondent's] claims were supported by several other people interviewed by Human Rights Watch both in Gulcha and in Osh. People from Kara-Suu, Kara-Kulja and Chong-Alay districts in the Osh province also reportedly went to the city in response to the outbreak of violence. Several Kyrgyz villagers who descended upon Osh told Human Rights Watch that they initially went there to rescue their relatives or family members. Many had relatives who studied at one of Osh's universities, and the rumours about horrific acts of violence committed by Uzbeks compelled them to go to Osh to bring their relatives home to safety (HRW 2010, 27).

Having acquired an APC and automatic rifles, the balance of power between two groups turned toward the Kyrgyz. What followed this violent standoff was disastrous. Furious Kyrgyz attacked the Uzbeks in Furkat and other mahallas along the entry road to Osh.

The consequences of the violent standoff at the roundabout were catastrophic, especially for those Uzbek communities living in the suburb districts of Furkat and Shark, and the Uzbek neighbourhoods in Ak-Buura and Amir Timur districts. After the roundabout standoff violence, the Kyrgyz crowds moved to the city along the Pamirskaia-Monueva street,[4] a principal road and a part of the Bishkek-Osh highway. The highway connects northern and southern regions of Kyrgyzstan and the towns of Jalalabat and Uzgen and mountainous regions of Alai, Chon Alai, and Kara-Kulja with the city of Osh. It also links Furkat and Shark with Osh's downtown. Being the only highway that connects the Osh city with the northern regions and most of the raions and districts of the southern region, this area spatially presented itself as a conducive place for a violent flashpoint. Blocking this road brought tensions and killing arriving people who wanted enter the city sparked and escalated violence.

Figure 4.3 shows that the main clusters of house destruction in the eastern part of the city lie along Pamirskaia-Monueva street. Three out of seven large clusters of property destruction identified by United Nations Operational Satellite Applications Program (UNOSAT) (UNITAR/UNOSAT 2010) fall in this area. According to the UNOSAT map, the houses were burned along a 3.5 km stretch of Pamirskaia-Monueva street. Destruction did not penetrate very deep into the mahallas except the area of Shavkat Rahman street, in front of the provincial hospital (the map in the left in figure 4.3). Memorial (2012, 146–7) carefully summarizes the scope of destruction in the eastern part of the city shown by figure 4.3: "According to the satellite images, 107 residential houses were completely destroyed along a 1 kilometer stretch of Furkat village ... In residential blocks between Furkat and the area near the Provincial Hospital, the destruction went up to Pamirskaya Street ... 155 buildings were completely destroyed ... The greatest destruction was in the area near the Provincial Hospital, where 357 buildings were completely destroyed ... [T]he total number of residential houses destroyed during the mass unrest between 11 and 14 June in the eastern part of the conflict zone is 650."

Toward the night of 11 June, more Kyrgyz people arrived in Furkat from rural regions. According to the Memorial report (ibid., 137), several thousand Kyrgyz spent the night in the village discussing plans to attack Amir Timur district where many Uzbek militants and peaceful residents of Furkat had fled. The next day, early on the morning of 12 June, Kyrgyz groups undertook fierce attacks on Shark and on Amir Timur, a big monoethnic microdistrict located on the hills of the eastern part of the city with an almost exclusively Uzbek population of about 40,000 residents. Additionally, in those days, it sheltered up to 15,000 displaced persons from other Uzbek neighbourhoods. To break through the barricades, the Kyrgyz used a captured APC. Uzbeks reportedly used lorries fully armoured with steel shields in customary way. Both sides increasingly used automatic and other firearm weapons.

While the Kyrgyz attacks of 11 June can be characterized as spontaneous and marked by strong emotions, their attacks of 12 June took a more organized and planned shape. The strategy of the Uzbek defence of mahallas also changed. Before, the crowds of Uzbek rioters roamed the streets of the city attacking Kyrgyz residents, on 12 June, the Uzbeks contained themselves in

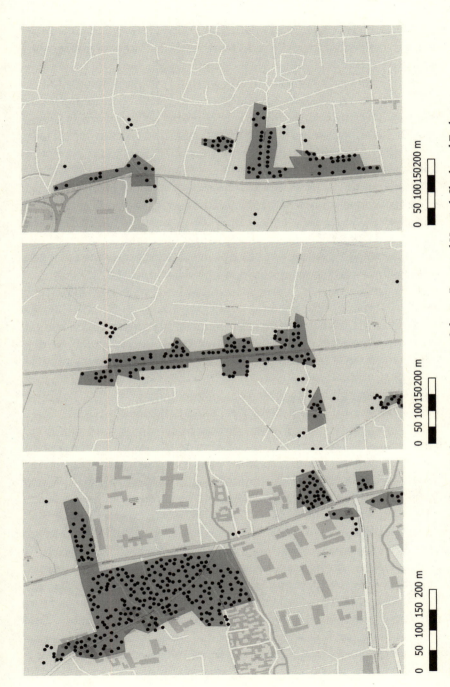

Figure 4.3 Three property damage clusters in the eastern entrance to Osh city: Provincial Hospital, Shark, and Furkat

mahallas and fully concentrated on defence (Matveeva, Savin, and Faizullaev 2012, 24). This pattern was pertinent to the whole picture of violence in Osh that day.

The escalation phase in this area (Furkat, Shark, Amir Timur, and the provincial hospital) falls within 11–13 June. On 14 June, de-escalation of violence took place with isolated instances of arsons till 15 June. The rumour about Uzbek army invasion did not affect this area, so no mass panic exodus of the local Kyrgyz as a result of the rumour about the Uzbekistan's army invasion was observed in this area.

The map in figure 4.4 shows that the main clusters of property damage were concentrated in the western and eastern parts of Osh with large clusters of damage around the city's grand bazaar. The location of these clusters can be explained by spatial factors such as the road infrastructure. Main clusters of property damage lie along two principal roads leading from the city's western and eastern entrances that converge in the city center.

Although main clusters of property damage largely coincide with clusters of violence, violent fights also broke out in other parts of the city. The next two chapters cover urban warfare in the southern, central, and northern parts of the city in presented empirical case studies allowing us to more clearly evaluate the interactions between local Kyrgyz and Uzbek groups and their responses to uncertainty.

CONFLICT STATISTICS

In this section, I provide descriptive statistics on ethnic distribution of population by Kyrgyz and Uzbek groups and number of deaths during communal warfare in June 2010. Table 4.1 shows ethnodemographic data on the size of Kyrgyz and Uzbek groups and their distribution in three southern provinces and the cities of Osh and Jalalabat. These three provinces (oblasts) include substantial Uzbek communities. As of 2009, the smallest Uzbek minority was in the Batken province – only 11 per cent. This probably partly explains the absence of violent Uzbek mobilization in this province. However, it does not imply the absence of intercommunal tensions in June 2010. Uzbek communities in the Batken province are chiefly concentrated in several small towns and villages. Isfana is the only town in the Batken province where Uzbeks comprise the majority of the population – 76 per cent. The Uzbek community in Isfana faced same challenges as many other Uzbek communities in Osh and Jalalabat provinces. One problem with the official statistics is that it

Figure 4.4 The distribution of the damage clusters in Osh city

Table 4.1
Ethnic distribution in urban and rural areas in southern regions of Kyrgyzstan (by Kyrgyz and Uzbek populations)

Region	Ethnicity	Urban	%	Rural	%	Total	%
Osh city	Kyrgyz	100,000	47%	23,500	94%	123,000	52%
	Uzbeks	112,000	53%	1,500	6%	114,000	48%
Osh province	Kyrgyz	15,000	18%	743,000	76%	758,000	71%
(without Osh city)	Uzbeks	70,000	82%	239,000	24%	309,000	29%
Jalalabat city	Kyrgyz	49,000	59%	N/A	N/A	49,000	59%
	Uzbeks	34,000	41%	N/A	N/A	34,000	41%
Jalalabat province	Kyrgyz	166,000	78%	560,000	73%	726,000	74%
(with Jalalabat city)	Uzbeks	47,000	22%	204,000	27%	251,000	26%
Batken province	Kyrgyz	66,000	64%	262,000	80%	328,000	84%
	Uzbeks	27,000	26%	36,000	11%	63,000	16%

Source: National Census of Kyrgyz Republic, 2009.
Note: The percentage figures in this table indicate shares of local Kyrgyz and Uzbek groups relatively to each other but not relatively to the overall population of the provinces and cities. See more disaggregated data on ethnic distribution by raions (districts) in table 4.1.

does not show the real demographic picture in the cities of Osh and Jalalabat. Official figures showing the size of Uzbek and Kyrgyz groups do not count for non-registered residents of these cities. Furthermore, the statistics do not count the suburban population that had an important role in violent dynamics in these cities.

Tables 4.2 to 4.5 show the distribution of deaths by dates, nationality, gender, age, and mortal wounds. The majority of deaths occurred in the Osh province. About 84 per cent of all killings committed during the ethnic conflict in 2010 occurred in the Osh city and its surroundings. According to Kylym Shamy (2010), a human rights NGO that conducted a careful investigation of homicides in the morgues of the southern cities and examined destroyed houses and properties, the number of deaths in the Osh province including the Osh city was 355, and 68 in the Jalalabat province (including Jalalabat city). The total number of deaths in both provinces was 423.[5] There were also 36 missing individuals, mostly Kyrgyz. Of them, 32 were in the Osh province. The exact numbers of deaths by town, city district, and village are not available. There are also two reports on the number of deaths produced by the Ministry of Health and the prosecutor general's office. The estimate of deaths (418 deaths in total) made by the Ministry of Health relies on data from hospitals, morgues, and exhumations. The estimate (444

Table 4.2
Number of deaths by dates and nationality

Date	Osh province				Jalalabat province				Total
	Kyrgyz	Uzbeks	Others	Total	Kyrgyz	Uzbeks	Others	Total	
11.06.2010	22	85	2	109	0	0	0	0	109
12.06.2010	16	114	0	130	6	1	0	7	137
13.06.2010	13	16	0	29	9	29	1	39	68
14.06.2010	4	4	1	9	6	6	0	12	21
15.06.2010 and after (or not determined)	27	51	0	78	4	6	0	10	88
Total	82	270	3	355	25	42	1	68	423

Source: Kylym Shamy NGO.

Table 4.3
Number of deaths by gender

Date	Osh province			Jalalabat province			Total
	Male	Female	Total	Male	Female	Total	
11.06.2010	103	6	109	0	0	0	109
12.06.2010	117	13	130	5	2	7	137
13.06.2010	27	2	29	38	1	39	68
14.06.2010	9	0	9	11	1	12	21
15.06.2010 and after (or not determined)	61	17	78	8	2	10	88
Total	317	38	355	62	6	68	423

Source: Kylym Shamy NGO.

deaths in total) from the prosecutor general's office is based on data from criminal cases. The three reports have some discrepancies in number of deaths, but the range of difference is not high. The low rate of discrepancies gives us the ground to suggest that estimates made by these three organizations are reliable.

The data presented in tables 4.2–4.5 shows that the most active phase of the violence in the Osh province took place in the first two days – 11 and 12 June (109 and 130 deaths respectively). They account for 67 per cent while the events on 13 and 14 June (which saw 29 and 9 people killed, respectively) account for only about 11 per cent of the total number of deaths. In terms

Table 4.4
Number of deaths by age

#	Age	Osh province	Jalalabat province	Total
1	0–7	3	0	3
2	8–14	5	0	5
3	15–20	38	4	42
4	21–30	86	24	110
5	31–40	69	15	84
6	41–50	77	16	93
7	51–60	38	7	45
8	61–70	10	1	11
9	71 and above	12	1	13
10	not determined	17	0	17
	Total	355	68	423

Source: Kylym Shamy NGO.

of ethnic distribution of deaths by nationality, three-quarters of the aggregate deaths in the Osh province were ethnic Uzbeks. Lack of ethnic balance in the number of deaths is evident on 11 June, and especially on 12 June. Nearly a half of all Uzbeks killed during the June riots died on 12 June.

Table 4.3 shows that a majority of those killed were males. Males were direct participants in riots and interethnic clashes. Women had a much lower mortality rate; however, they were the main targets for sexual violence. The data on sexual violence is barely available. The existing data is not reliable because victims of sexual violence in many cases do not report crimes committed against them for different reasons. The main reason, however, is desire to hide a fact of rape and humiliation from a conservative and traditional community environment. Disclosure of the rape may have very negative consequences for women exposed to sexual violence.

Table 4.4 indicates that the victims of the ethnic violence represent all age categories. Among victims, there were small children, teenagers, and old people over 70 years of age. However, the highest concentration of deaths lies in age category between 20 and 50.

Table 4.5 demonstrates that the most frequent type of mortal wound is gunshot. People killed from gunshot account for 67 per cent, or two-thirds, of total deaths in Osh and Jalalabat provinces. Such a high rate of killings resulted from gunshots clearly validates my proposition of the 2010 ethnic violence's strong resemblance to a civil war, as discussed in the introductory chapter. It was an armed violent conflict of high intensity.

Table 4.5
Number of deaths by nationality and type of mortal wound

#	Type of mortal wound	Osh province				Jalalabat province				Total
		Kyrgyz	Uzbeks	Others	Total	Kyrgyz	Uzbeks	Others	Total	
1	Gunshot	39	195	2	236	16	31	1	48	284
2	Cerebral injury	9	19	0	28	1	3	0	4	32
3	Stab wounds	14	15	0	29	4	2	0	6	35
4	Thermal burns	7	25	1	33	0	2	0	2	35
5	Other	13	16	0	29	4	4	0	8	37
	Total	**82**	**270**	**3**	**355**	**25**	**42**	**1**	**68**	**423**

Source: Kylym Shamy NGO.

Additionally, hundreds of buildings were destroyed by arson. They include residential houses, commercial facilities, and public buildings. A great majority of destroyed buildings were houses belonging to ethnic Uzbeks. UNITAR/UNOSAT (2010) reports: "Almost all affected buildings appear to have been residential or situated within residential neighbourhoods, however there are a few cases of destroyed or severely damaged industrial warehouses or commercial / government facilities. No damages have been observed to the transportation network (e.g. roads, bridges) or other key infrastructure sites within the city." According to UNOSAT, the total number of buildings destroyed and severely damaged was 2,843. Of the total number of buildings affected by arson, 2,067 were identified within the city of Osh and its surroundings, 330 in the city of Jalalabat, and 446 in Bazar-Korgon village, Jalalabat province. However, Kylym Shamy NGO gives other figures. According to Kylym Shamy (Fergana News 2010), 1,721 buildings in total were destroyed by arson. 1,265 houses were destroyed in Osh province. Of them, 673 in the Osh city itself and 592 in the surrounding villages. 177 houses were destroyed in the city of Jalalabat and 137 in the Bazar-Korgon village.

According to the Kyrgyz government, more than 1,000 hostages – both Uzbeks and Kyrgyz – were taken during the violence (Comments 2011, 11). In segregated Osh, ethnically homogenous neighbourhoods contain small populations distinct from the prevailing ethnic group. During the clashes many of those who were not able or did not want to leave their homes found themselves as hostages or were attacked, killed, or beaten.

During the conflict, ten policemen and one military representative of the Ministry of Defence were killed. 172 policemen were wounded. Twelve wounds from firearms were received and over 50 soldiers were victims of bodily harm of various kinds. The Kyrgyz government claims that all these victims and all the wounds happened precisely because the police and the military were not merely observers. Law enforcement and military personnel aimed at preventing clashes between the parties and localizing the conflict (ibid., 11).

RESEARCH DESIGN

This is a comparative design research. I compare violent and nonviolent neighbourhoods in the Osh city across different dimensions in relation to ethnic violence, which are: (1) the effect of self-policing and strength of informal authority in neighbourhoods; (2) the effect of intercommunal pacts; and; (3) the effect of spatial differentiation, the built environment, and spatial mobility of combatants, police, refugees, and residents. Based on observations during my ethnographic fieldwork, I identified the above three dimensions as the most valid determinants of urban communal violence at the neighbourhood level.

The analysis in this research is based on 111 semi-structured interviews – mainly with community leaders, but also with police and military officers, journalists, human rights activists, and ordinary residents – and spatial observation data collected during a total of nine months of my ethnographic fieldwork between 2010 and 2014. To reconstruct the conflict events and identify and describe spatial variations in violence, in addition to interviews, I used investigative reports produced by various governmental and international commissions and human rights organizations as well as media resources, census, and geo-referenced data available on websites. In addition, I relied on multiple everyday informal conversations with local people from diverse backgrounds. These conversations became a great source of valuable information that allowed me to get important nuances and contextual data. Everyday conversations also helped me corroborate information that I was receiving from formal interviews. Another valuable source of information for this study was spatial data collected through my visual exploration of neighbourhoods and their built environment, spatial structures and spatial differentiation, landscape, type and density of housing, identification of the sociodemographic composition of neighbourhoods (in

Table 4.6
Violent and nonviolent towns in 1990 and 2010

	Osh	Jalalabat	Uzgen
1990	Violent	Nonviolent	Violent
2010	Violent	Violent	Nonviolent

Source: Based on the author's own research.

addition to census data and city maps). To get familiarized with urban environment, I made repeated visits to almost all neighbourhoods in Osh and Jalalabat city mostly by walking or sometimes by passing through urban neighbourhoods on public transportation.

As noted in the previous section, I use the number of deaths and property destruction as quantifiable indicators of violence. The spatial distribution of killings and property destruction across neighbourhoods is evidently verified in the investigative reports produced by human rights organizations and satellite pictures and maps of property destruction created by the UNOSAT/UNITAR research center. Additionally, I rely on incomplete lists of wounded people and information about instances of ethnic clashes documented in investigative reports and interviews.

Another important observation is that when we control for city-level outcomes in violence between the 1990 and the 2010 communal violence among three largest southern towns, table 4.6 shows that the recurrence of violence occurs only in the city of Osh while the other two cities alternate their outcomes across these two episodes of communal violence. Since Osh is the city that experienced the most intense outbreak of violence in 2010, it became my main focus of fieldwork research. However, I also spent considerable time in Jalalabat and Uzgen.

DATA COLLECTION

My fieldwork consisted of interviews, spatial and participant observations, and analysis of investigative reports and official documents produced by international inquiry missions, human rights organizations, and governmental bodies.

My main method of data collection is semi-structured interviews. I consider interviews as the main component of my ethnographic research.[6] Semi-structured interviews are especially useful for investigating short violent events that are weakly covered by mass media outlets. My main purpose was to reconstruct the events, mechanisms, and dynamics of violence during the communal warfare of 2010 through semi-structured interviews that were the most suitable method in given circumstances. However, one weakness of this method is that after violent events interview respondents may give unreliable information biased by rumours, political interests, ethnic affiliation, psychological shock, and so on.

To address this challenge, I cross-checked and corroborated the reliability of evidence collected in semi-structured interviews by triangulating these interviews with other methods such as participant observation, and through engaging in informal conversations with locals, and tracing the events through the reports produced by various investigative commissions and human rights organizations. By asking different respondents from both sides of the conflict about the same event I tried to verify the reliability of information given by informants during interviews. Additionally, I attempted to achieve higher level of reliability of information through repeated visits to the same respondent, especially with key informants. As suggested by Stefan Malthaner (in a personal conversation 2012) and Jones Luong (2002), to achieve better reliability results, it is advisable to interview the same person in different environmental settings. In this sense, interviewing the same person in both formal and informal environment allows us to check the consistency of information and strengthen the reliability of interview data given by a respondent. I followed this suggestion by conducting a second interview with some of my key respondents.

In my interview sampling, I used two approaches: the snowball sampling and territorially representative sampling methods.[7] The snowball sampling method is an effective way of finding contacts. The main advantage of snowball sampling was that I was introduced to respondents through trusted networks. In the initial stages, journalists, experts, human rights activists, and teachers helped me in finding key informants. The disadvantage of this method is obvious: snowball sampling may involve contacts from the same network, location, and social and professional group, which makes the interview sample potentially non-representative of the broader population. However, for the study of small-size town-districts, snowball sampling might be not a big problem because population in this type of location is densely located and my interviews targeted mainly local community leaders. They are well known among local population and interconnected in the same networks.

However, for the larger territorial units snowball sampling should be supplemented by additional sampling techniques. To eliminate the shortcomings of random selection of respondents, I tried to make contacts among groups which were underrepresented in my snowball sampling. To make my sample geographically representative, I used town hall lists containing neighbourhood-committee-leaders' names and contact information, including a phone number. This practice proved to be a good strategy because heads of territorial districts and neighbourhood committees, usually called domkom or kvartkom,[8] tend to be informal community leaders in their neighbourhoods, especially in southern cities like Osh. While a head of territorial council/district is normally appointed by a local mayor, heads of neighbourhood committees are usually informally elected by the neighbourhood's residents during improvised meetings conducted in a district office or even in an open street. I interviewed local leaders in all twelve territorial councils (urban districts) in the Osh city and in all four territorial councils in Jalalabat. In some territorial councils/districts in both cities, I interviewed leaders of different neighbourhood committees within one district.

Additionally, in geographically sampling my respondents, I relied on the list of a network of local mediators from "Yntymak Jarchylary" project coordinated by Iret NGO and the regional office of the Organization for Security and Co-operation in Europe (OSCE). The project was created in 2011, after the communal conflict, as a part of post-conflict reconstruction and conflict prevention activities, and it facilitated the work of mediators from local community leaders to bring them into one network. The network encompasses all raions in the Jalalabat and Osh oblasts, which were primary sites for my fieldwork. Overall, I conducted interviews with approximately equal number of respondents from both sides of the conflict. This included only formal interviews, which continued from forty minutes to three hours, with most of them lasting between one and two hours. All interviews were held in Kyrgyz, Uzbek, mixed Kyrgyz-Uzbek, and Russian languages (many residents of Osh and other southern cities are bilingual or trilingual). Before each interview, I followed a short formal procedure by introducing myself and the aims of my research, and promised not to reveal their real names and identity. I asked my respondents to choose the language that they would prefer to speak. Each time I asked permission to use the digital recorder during interviews however, in many cases, to improve the reliability of respondents' answers, I deliberately did not use a recorder and wrote down notes instead.

Interviews in post-conflict settings is another important issue. The challenge is to get reliable information from respondents. Individuals are often reluctant to speak to researchers and provide honest answers for various reasons such as post-conflict traumas, fears of retaliation, and unwillingness to reveal committed crimes. Furthermore, my interviews were exacerbated by state repressions, mainly against Uzbek participants in violence. In addition, the reliability of information drawn from my interviews could have been compromised by the fact that my ethnic background has affiliation with one of the conflicting sides. Being a Kyrgyz, I was easily recognized by my facial features and other ethnic characteristics.

As discussed above, I tried to minimize some potential drawbacks by using the snowball techniques of sampling. This method was especially helpful for me in overcoming distrust in interviews with Uzbek informants. I was introduced to new respondents through recommendations of their trusted persons and networks.

Two other factors helped me to establish more trustful relations with Uzbek respondents. One was that I was originally from Bishkek (northern Kyrgyzstan), which is considered by local Uzbeks as more neutral and less ethnically biased and less nationalist in local interethnic relations. Another was my affiliation with the European University Institute where I was doing my PhD program – that gave me more credibility as an unbiased and non-aligned person coming from the neutral European/western context. In the wake of the conflict, many international NGOs rushed to help local communities, especially Uzbek ones. Many of these NGOs employed ethnically Kyrgyz staff from Bishkek who made genuine and meaningful efforts to facilitate post-conflict recovery among exposed communities, therefore earning trust and recognition among Uzbek residents also. Obviously, not all interviews went smoothly. Some respondents when giving their accounts of conflict events simply reproduced existing ethnic biases, popular myths, and template analyses of a conspiratorial nature from the Russian TV channels and tabloids. Others did not want to fully share their experiences. Yet, in most interviews, I received invaluably informative and reliable accounts.

During first interviews, I quickly realized that straightforward questions related to the recent conflict sometimes caused negative reaction and suspicions among some interviewees. They would then restrain themselves from giving me detailed accounts of the events and processes and details of their personal involvement in the events providing general and uninformative answers. I immediately changed my strategy presenting my research to respondents in more general terms as a study on local communities and local (communal) self-governance. I instantly felt that the quality of the interviews improved after I changed my approach. During interviews, my respondents, having discussed the issues of local self-governance and communal social organization, would themselves eventually turn to the issue of the June 2010 ethnic violence. This was a suitable moment for me to ask important questions about local communities' reaction to the ethnic violence and communal group behaviour. Yet, to some local leaders – especially with those actively involved in the OSCE's "Yntymak Jarchylary" (literally "Heralds of Peace") mediators' network activities or in other local peacebuilding and human rights initiatives – I could ask more straightforward questions. On the other hand, I tried to avoid pushing my respondents too far. For example, I never asked them if they were personally implicated in violence. I would change the topic whenever I saw my respondents feeling uncomfortable with my questions.

In general, I did not have significant problems with getting access to Kyrgyz respondents. However, on very few occasions they either refused or were suspicious of my research. In Uzgen, one Kyrgyz mediator designated me as an al-Qaeda member when he felt that I was interested in interethnic relations. He abruptly stopped the interview by asking me about who was the then al-Qaeda leader. Since bin Laden had already been killed in Pakistan by the US special forces in 2011, I honestly told him that I did not know who the next leader was. He asked me, "Why don't you know? You must know because you work for the CIA." According to him, only the CIA was interested in studying interethnic relations and al-Qaeda was simply the CIA's project and its tool to instigate ethnic conflicts around the world.

In Osh, another Kyrgyz leader refused to give me an interview after I had introduced myself as a researcher from the European institution. He was a well-known former official. Together with his Uzbek counterparts, he established an interethnic team of mediators that tried to reconcile raging crowds amid ethnic violence in the streets. However, in the immediate afterwards of the communal conflict, many western-based organizations and media outlets one-sidedly blamed aggression on the Kyrgyz side without going into accurate investigation of the conflict. This caused outrage among many Kyrgyz including those who were actively involved in peacemaking activities. Consequently, this respondent did not trust westerners and did not want to play into hands of those who wanted to unfairly discredit Kyrgyz people. In my presence, he phoned to the Uzbek mediator – his longstanding former colleague from the Soviet times – who recommended him (this Kyrgyz mediator) to me for the interview. He warned the Uzbek mediator to be wary of "suspicious" researchers like me.

After these failures, I became more cautious about how to introduce myself and my research to respondents. To my Uzbek respondents, I usually highlighted the European University Institute as my institutional affiliation and Bishkek as my regional origin. To the Kyrgyz respondents, I introduced myself as a researcher from Bishkek. This seemed to work in most cases barring a few exceptions.

In addition to the interviews, I employed participant observation. The method of participant observation is most useful for observing current dynamics and unfolding actions, whereas my research focuses on causes of ethnic violence which cannot be observed directly by this method. A participant-observer's main focus is on "detailed accounts of people, places, interactions, and events that the researcher experiences as a participant-observer" (Lichterman 2002, 121). However, because the term "participant" sounds ambiguous in my research, as I studied past events, I refer this as empirical or spatial observations. While I could not directly observe past events and interactions between main actors, nevertheless I was able to make spatial observations in towns and neighbourhoods of my interest. Observations of places helped me to decipher the geographical, spatial, ethnical, and infrastructural environment in particular neighbourhoods or locations and identify some crucial conditions and structural factors which could possibly drive key actors into the conflict and violence.

These kinds of observations are especially relevant for analyzing the causes of violence and nonviolence at the city, village, and neighbourhood levels. I examined such factors as geographical terrain, and strategic roads and hills; territorial distribution of ethnic communities and the extent of territorial segregation within a town or a neighbourhood; geographical dynamics of violent events; location specifications; strategic objects such as the location of bazaars, private business objects, universities and whether they tend to concentrate in violent or peaceful locations; and economic, social, and security systems in the locations. Geographical observations are required for identifying territorial characteristics of violent and peaceful locations. I closely investigate the sites with different outcomes in violence.

To measure violence, I used killings and property destruction data as indicators. Violence is a "thick" concept which needs to be operationalized. "Unpacking a thick concept, exploring its dimensionality, and translating it into quantitative indicators can be seen as a process of discovering more of the observable implications of a theory and therefore of rendering it more testable" (Coppedge 1999, 469). In the case of communal violence, violence has several dimensions and observable implications such as killings, bullet, knife, and club wounds, property damages, looting, and sexual violence (i.e., rape). These dimensions can serve as quantifiable indicators of violence which can also measure the extent of violence. Among these dimensions, sexual violence is not a fully reliable indicator because for many reasons, including "rape victim blame" (see Murthi 2009), victims prefer not to report to police or even tell their close relatives about what happened to them (Ataeva, Belomestnov, and Jusupjan 2011). Therefore, instances of sexual violence tend to be undercounted in official documents. "Looting" is also a problematic indicator. Looting is often an integral part of riots; however, it is difficult to identify if looting is a part or a consequence of violence. In this research, I mainly consider homicides and property damage as indicators of ethnic violence. Death is the most reliable and unambiguous indicator which is easy for measurement of violence (Kalyvas 2006, 20). Property damage is also easily countable. The data for both deaths and property damage are available and therefore, I use these two indicators to measure the spatial variation in violence and peace.

Investigative Reports

My analysis of the conflict events, especially in chapters 3 and 4, is based on several reports produced by various international and local investigative missions. I reconstructed the onset of the conflict and its main events essentially by relying on the report jointly produced by the Memorial Human Rights Center (Russia), the Norwegian Helsinki Committee (Norway), and Freedom House (USA) (hereafter referred to as the Memorial report, or simply Memorial). Of other similar several reports, the Memorial report is the most detailed and reliable source for reconstruction of violent events in Kyrgyzstan in 2010. Its accounts are based on more than 300 interviews, 550 videotapes, 300 photos,[9] and hundreds of live chat messages from popular national websites (Memorial 2012, 4). Basically, the report cautiously and rigorously investigated and reconstructed the violent events in Osh. By doing this, it saved me an enormous amount of time from carrying out several additional months of intensive fieldwork. For this, I am grateful to the mission's team of researchers. In the analysis of violent events, I draw heavily on the report's documented evidence. This report was published later than other reports.

The members of the mission had opportunity to compare the information, factual events, and their interpretations cross-checked through different sources. It devoted a lot of attention to factual analysis of the events and the cross-checking data. Unfortunately, Memorial did not produce a similar report on the violent events in Jalalabat.

Other reports, produced by both international and local mission teams, were mainly preoccupied with normative judgements and political, ethnic, and ideological biases, and provided an insufficient amount of factual information despite having collected a huge amount of evidence. For example, the Kyrgyzstan Inquiry Commission mission alone conducted 750 interviews and collected 700 documents and several thousand photographs and video extracts (KIC 2011) but was not able to produce a completely reliable and unbiased report. The factual information that appears in this report is not supported by credible references and, in many instances, contains many errors, non-existent events, unchecked information, and normative but poorly-grounded judgements.[10] Yet, despite these shortcomings it contains some valuable information. In addition, some researchers from the KIC team later produced their own independent report "Tragedy in the South" (Matveeva, Savin, and Faizullaev 2012) which contains much more reliable and detailed factual information that I used intensively in this study.

My interviews uncovered information which the investigative report overlooked due to various reasons. I cross-checked the information that I obtained from my respondents with the information from various reports, particularly with those produced by the Memorial and Matveeva et al.

The conflict was initially analyzed by international investigative missions (KIC), international organizations (International Crisis Group), human rights organizations (Human Rights Watch, or HRW; Memorial; Kylym Shamy), state law enforcement institutions and commissions (parliamentary commission, police, and some experts). Some of these investigations, especially those conducted by state institutions and by some international missions shed little light or produced partial information (KIC, International Crisis Group) on the problem as these investigations have been afflicted by political or/and ethnic bias. They tend to put blame on one or another side in the conflict without seriously attempting to identify mechanisms, conditions, and drivers of the conflict. Their reports are full of political, partisan, and normative judgements weakly and manipulatively supported with superficial factual analyses.[11] Investigations produced by human rights organizations (HRW, Kylym Shamy, and especially by Memorial) stand out in this sense and are much more reliable. They give invaluably rich factual accounts of the events and insights on the dynamics of the violence.[12] Despite the factual richness of these reports, they are still descriptive and do not engage in scholarly analysis of the events and, indeed, this was not the main aim of these reports. Therefore, my main aim in this book is to fill gap in academic analysis of this significant episode of communal violence.

There is dearth of mass media reporting on the conflict. Most reports about the events are produced retrospectively and biased by post-conflict interpretations. Weak presence of international and national newspaper journalists on the ground in the Osh and Jalalabat areas during the communal conflict makes it difficult to reconstruct conflict events in detail (through examination of publications in mass media outlets). The local media outlets were paralyzed during the conflict, due to security reasons. Therefore, until the Memorial (2012) produced its own report, we had little knowledge about what really happened in Osh during 11–15 June. The report by the Memorial is the most comprehensive and reliable, and significantly filled the informational gap by objectively documenting conflict events.

PART THREE

Neighbourhood-Level Comparisons

5

Spatial Security during Communal Violence in Osh

How Spatial Factors and the Built Environment Affect the Local Dynamics of Violence and Neighbourhood Security

The role of space and the built environment has rarely been applied to explain outcomes and the local dynamics of ethnic conflicts and has never been analyzed in the context of the June 2010 ethnic violence in southern Kyrgyzstan.[1] As this volume demonstrates, space significantly shaped the behaviour of the main actors in this conflict. Given the general neglect of spatiality and its impact on the local dynamics of violence in the literature, this chapter aims to shed light on this gap by bringing attention to the role of spatiality and the built environment in the analysis of political violence and ethnic conflict.

This chapter analyzes the spatial dynamics of violence during the June 2010 ethnic conflict among the Kyrgyz and Uzbeks in the city of Osh. Spatial categories such as the built environment of neighbourhoods provide favourable conditions for occurrence or non-occurrence of violence. These spatial conditions affect the local dynamics of violence and facilitate or hinder security measures conducted by ethnic community leaders and brokers. To measure the impact of spatial conditions on the local dynamics of ethnic violence and to identify the degree of availability of neighbourhood security options for local ethnic community leaders, I compare two typical neighbourhoods in Osh, one violent and the other nonviolent. Different spatial structures and the built environments in these two neighbourhoods facilitated violent mass mobilization and hindered conflict management initiatives in one neighbourhood and provided relevant security options for the ethnic leaders to contain the violence in the other neighbourhood. The findings of this study are based on the ethnographic fieldwork carried out by me between 2010 and 2014.

In evaluating spatial aspects of security, this chapter follows a call for disaggregation of empirical evidence (Weidmann, Rød, and Cederman 2010). I analyze the spatial categories that affected the level of security of local ethnic subgroup communities at a disaggregated level. The main analysis will focus on meso-level responses by local communities in ethnically mixed and segregated neighbourhoods. Studying violent ethnic conflict at the neighbourhood scale is an important methodological innovation which points at a potential area, where disciplines that are usually pertinent to a certain level of aggregation can mutually benefit from each other. Examples include the theoretical insights that urban sociology can gain from studies analyzing ethnic violence at higher levels of aggregation, and vice versa.

I argue that among other factors, a particular type of urban space provides favourable conditions for occurrence or non-occurrence of violence. For example, in Osh, such places as areas around the central bazaar and densely populated multistorey building complexes were especially prone to violent outbreaks. By contrast, residential areas with individual unit houses and low residential mobility represented spaces with easier riot control and were more favourable for in-group policing. In addition, some residential areas implemented actual strategies as physical self-isolation to avoid the violence and contacts with external groups. By restricting freedom of movement and erecting improvised barricades, the residents of such neighbourhoods created a temporally new space with its own rules and interethnic cooperation. In some instances, spatial brokers played a key role in this temporal reconfiguration of the neighbourhood's built environment. In this chapter, I do not imply spatial determinism, but rather point out how different types of space/places in interaction with spatial agency can affect the efficiency of community policing and local social norms creating (un)favourable conditions for violent mobilization.

SPACE AND ETHNIC CONFLICT

The concept of space is becoming increasingly important in the social sciences to explain how it shapes and constrains human agency. In studies of contentious politics, however, the category of space has long been understudied (Sewell 2001). Spatial aspects of security during violent armed conflicts have been insufficiently addressed in the relevant literature on ethnic conflicts and civil wars. Auyero (2006, 568) maintains that "the absence of attention to the geographic structuring of collective action remains a significant gap." (See also Martin and Miller 2003.) Only much recently has some systematic research been carried out on the interaction between the two (Dhattiwala 2016, 2019; Madueke 2018, 2019). In this chapter, I build on Sewell's spatial concepts and categories to explain the spatial dimensions of the 2010 ethnic violence in Osh.

So, here I regard space as place, territory, and the physical (built) environment. Wong (2006, 535) argues that "features of a place can matter to political behaviour because of ecological characteristics or social characteristics." In his famous article, Gieryn (2000) disaggregates the concept of place into three dimensions: (1) a geographical location; (2) a material form; and (3) a constructed space. I demonstrate that all three dimensions are relevant for the analysis of spatial security in the urban neighbourhoods of Osh. These dimensions appear in different stages of the analysis as spatial contexts, causes and effects of the contingent events revealing the importance of spatial factors for the dynamics of violence.

Space can be considered as both independent and intermediary variable but also as a dependent variable. The interplay between place and action exemplifies the dialectics of structure and agency (Thernborn 2006, 512). Place can thus affect political action, provide the context for action, and can also be an outcome of such action. This chapter presents space mostly as an intermediary variable; that is, how spatial categories provide context for actions and contingent events. However, it shows as well that space also affects and becomes an outcome of actions. Space shapes, constrains, and provides opportunities for mobilization and behaviour of actors. As Sewell (2001, 55) argues, contentious events are "shaped and constrained by the spatial environments in which they take place, but are significant agents in the production of new spatial structures and relations." (See also Auyero 2006, 569, for a similar argument.)

This chapter makes two important contributions to the literature – theoretical and methodological. First, it analyzes the impact of spatial categories on the dynamics of violence. This dimension has been largely ignored in the literature on ethnic conflicts. Second, it explores the problem at the neighbourhood scale. This level of (dis)aggregation has rarely been implemented in the analysis of ethnic conflicts. This methodological contribution has great potential to enrich the literature by scaling down the comparative analysis on the communal ethnic conflicts to the cross-neighbourhood level.

Scholars studying ethnic conflicts and civil wars made some arguments about the impact of geography, territory, and landscape on the causes and duration of violent conflicts. Fearon and Laitin (2003) observed that rough mountainous terrain provides opportunities for rebels to fight against the government. Similarly, Weidmann (2009) argues that geography produces motivation and opportunity for ethnic conflict.

One spatially related argument that was developed by Toft (2002, 2006) and Wiedmann (2009) can be particularly applicable to the context of the Kyrgyz-Uzbek violence. As this chapter analyzes Osh – a segregated city with strong ethnic concentrations in certain neighbourhoods – the following discussion of the literature on civil wars and ethnic conflicts can shed some light on the dynamics of ethnic violence in Osh.

Settlement patterns matter and they are important for explaining conflict occurrence. According to Toft (2002, 2006), group identity issues afford certain territories an indivisible stake in the territorial disputes between majority and minority ethnic groups within one state. She asserts that whether an ethnic group is spatially dispersed or concentrated affects its decision to fight for independence or negotiate greater autonomy. Geographically concentrated groups are more willing to fight for "their" territory.

Weidmann (2009) suggests possible mechanisms to explain why geographically concentrated groups face a higher risk of conflict. He argues that "concentrated groups face fewer difficulties in overcoming the collective action problem, and might therefore be more likely to successfully mobilize for conflict" (ibid., 530). Basically, "geographic concentration facilitates conflict because people are located close to each other and can get together quickly" (ibid., 532). On the other hand, concentrated territory gives a group a strategic advantage. Spatial proximity of population is important as strategic geographical concentration can bring certain advantages such as better group mobilization. It can also bring disadvantages such as being an easily identifiable target for attacks.

While many aspects of these mechanisms are relevant for the argument in this chapter, Toft's and Wiedmann's respective hypotheses do not fully account for the spatial opportunities that the territory provides for mobilization at micro-spatial scales of analysis. As both authors discuss an ethnic conflict at aggregated group level, they do not explain how territorial and population concentrations work among ethnic subgroups and at smaller spatial scales. Neither do they explain the cross-neighbourhood variations in violence in Osh and Jalalabat. Indeed, evidence from the 11–14 June 2010 violence shows that mainly neighbourhoods with a high concentration of one ethnic group were involved in violence. This observation supports the "territorial concentration" hypothesis. However, not all ethnic subgroups concentrated in the residentially segregated neighbourhoods participated in violence. That the violence disproportionately took place in ethnically segregated neighbourhoods is by itself unsurprising. Such neighbourhoods constitute the majority in Osh and they provided favourable grounds for begetting violence or became easy targets for ethnic attacks in June 2010. What the ethnic concentration hypothesis does not explain is the reason why only some of these ethnically concentrated neighbourhoods were involved in or became the targets of ethnic violence. In this chapter, I provide accounts of the micro-spatial effects of the built environment and territory on the dynamics of violence in Osh.

The examination of the micro-spatial effects brings us to the discussion of the level of aggregation in the analysis of violent ethnic conflicts. As I noted before, here I propose to focus at the cross-neighbourhood level of analysis of ethno-communal conflicts. Although neighbourhood-level analysis lies within the methodological traditions of urban sociology (Sampson and Wikstrom 2008), this chapter shows that this disaggregated scale of analysis can also be applicable to studies of civil wars and ethnic conflicts.

The focus on neighbourhood allows us to identify mechanisms and conditions that usually remain invisible in the studies with larger-scale aggregation. The research that deals with the neighbourhood scale can identify environmental effects at the small-scale level. For example, neighbourhood effects on local-level crime, collective efficacy, and social control and disorder have been discussed in many studies conducted by urban sociologists, particularly by Sampson and his collaborators (Morenoff, Sampson, and Raudenbush 2001; Sampson, Morenoff, and Gannon-Rowley 2002; Sampson and Wikstrom 2008). These studies make important observations of neighbourhood-based mechanisms and effects that affect the dynamics of violence, its level of intensity, and its spatial distributions that studies at higher level of aggregation were not able to identify and therefore, not able to take into account.

Although most of the literature on armed conflicts discusses interstate and civil war type of large-scale violent conflicts, its theoretical implications can apply to lower-level forms of violence and to smaller and disaggregated spatial scales. Settlement patterns, urban landscape, and the built environment in urban neighbourhoods also affect the spatial distribution of violence in smaller-scale conflicts such as ethnic riots. So far, this kind of analysis has been undertaken mainly by scholars of contentious politics who study urban riots and street protests. Yet, the lowest level of aggregation that studies on violent ethnic conflicts employed to explain spatial variations has been at the level of district and town. Important influential studies on violent ethnic riots have been undertaken by Varshney (2002) and Wilkinson (2006). While Varshney conducts cross-town-level paired comparisons of Hindu-Muslim violence, Wilkinson makes comparisons of the same ethnic conflict at both town and state (provincial) levels. Similarly, Straus (2008, 2010) analyzes spatial variations in violence across districts during the Rwandan genocide of 1994.

The studies that analyze violence at neighbourhood level usually deal with non-extreme riots that result in non-lethal street clashes and looting, but no deaths. An exception is the study done by Brass (2003) who explains the variation in violence between Hindus and Muslims in the city of Aligarh, however without engaging in systematic cross-neighbourhood comparisons and explanations of variations. (See also the volume edited Waddington, Jobard, and King 2009.)

It is important to emphasize that, in those days, trust between members of the two ethnic groups was to great extent shattered by increasing/continuing ethnic violence. Even the residents who would normally have felt little prejudice and no hostility toward "the other" ethnic group felt insecure about possible aggressive acts by the neighbouring "confronting" ethnic residential communities, and also by opportunistically behaving rioters and looters. This produced a so-called security dilemma (Lake and Rothchild 1996; Posen 1993;) among the peaceful city dwellers, who undertook security measures by constructing barricades in their streets and neighbourhoods; creating patrol and vigilante groups; and arming themselves with firearms, sticks and clubs, cold steel, and Molotov cocktails. According to a report produced by KIC (2011), after the trigger incident at the Alai Hotel, "witnesses anticipated not simply violence, but war." The azan (call to prayer) was heard at an unusual time (2 a.m.) in the mosques in at least four Uzbek neighbourhoods. "Uzbek men travelling in cars in the mahallas shouted that the war had begun" (ibid., 28).

The onset of violence rapidly (and unexpectedly) changed the built environment of many southern towns. In Osh, the city's spatial structures were transformed overnight. Communications infrastructures and the built environment in urban neighbourhoods were reshaped according to the interests of the main actors involved in this conflict. These spatial changes were enabled by human agency – local residents built the barricades across streets and neighbourhoods. They altered the whole landscape of the city converting it into multiple spatially isolated and self-regulated entities. These spatial entities/units often corresponded with the ethnic boundaries of residentially segregated neighbourhoods. In just one night, residents in many neighbourhoods built barricades in the streets, blocking access to their neighbourhoods. Barricades and roadblocks both constrained and shaped the actions and movements of residents, refugees, combatants, looters, and police.

The spatial/geographical location of the neighbourhoods also matters. Some neighbourhoods suffered violence simply because of unfavourable contingency. Such unfortunate neighbourhoods fell victims to spatially contingent events and spillover effects but also because the transport and communications infrastructures channelled the flows of militants, emotional mobs, or revengeful refugees to these particular neighbourhoods. For instance, Cheremushki – a neighbourhood in the western-central part of Osh that suffered one of the highest levels of ethnic violence during the conflict – underwent attacks from intruders who were advancing from the western part toward the central area of the city. In Nariman – a district in the northern outskirts of Osh – initially strong local social control and self-policing by local community leaders were undermined by the vengeful actions of refugees. Nariman village, which connects Osh with Uzbekistan's border was forced to accept hundreds of returning male refugees who had been denied passage to Uzbekistan. As chapter 6 shows, embittered radicals among these refugees openly challenged local social order and overpowered the traditional authority of local community leaders, forcing moderates to join them in a fight against their ethnic enemies (Fearon and Laitin 2011; Lemarchand 1996, 2009; Straus 2006; Wilkinson 2006). Their actions resulted in violent disorder and infamous assassinations of police mediators, one of whom was the chief of district police. Other neighbourhoods experienced spillover effects from violence-prone areas. One such violence-prone area is around the grand bazaar in Osh. Weak social control in this territory was exacerbated by the grand bazaar's status as a focal transit point for local trade and transport communications. Local trade businesses attracted looters. Militants who arrived at the area of the grand bazaar from the town outskirts and rural areas were naturally directed there by communication roads. Looting, violence, and the accumulation of belligerents in the bazaar area resulted in attacks and disorders in the adjacent neighbourhoods of Tajrimal and Teshik-Tash.

Nevertheless, the residents in segregated neighbourhoods also developed their own security measures and community defence strategies. For instance, as chapter 6 shows, Kyrgyz and Uzbek ethnic communities in the southern district of Turan in Osh faced the same problems as in many other neighbourhoods in violent areas. However, in Turan and its adjacent neighbourhoods, they managed to turn local spatial structures and environmental conditions to their security advantage. Environmental conditions of Turan district in Osh enabled greater spatial control of the neighbourhood and more effective in-group policing of local residents by communal leaders.

In the next section, I present two cases of neighbourhoods with different outcomes of violence: the first is the Oshskii raion in the Alymbek Datka district, which was highly violent; the second is Kalinin in the Sulaiman-Too district, which was relatively peaceful (see the location of these two cases in figure 5.1, given later in the chapter).

THE OSHSKII RAION NEIGHBOURHOOD (ALYMBEK DATKA DISTRICT)

The Alymbek Datka district (hereafter AD) is located in the eastern part of the Osh city. The AD district was one of the first flashpoints in Osh where violence broke out. Virtually all the law enforcement and international investigative mission reports mention the main streets and mahallas of the AD district in connection with the riots and ethnic violence, including an infamous Café Nostalgie on Karasuiskaia Street, which was converted into a place where hostages were kept and sexually abused during the riots. However, most of the riots and violent actions took place in and around the Oshskii raion, an informal neighbourhood within the AD district. In this section I first provide a detailed description of violent dynamics that took place in the Oshskii raion, then, to understand why this neighbourhood was an active area for violent clashes, I show how Oshskii raion's *spatial configuration of built environment* (Zhao 2013) created favourable conditions for communal fights. That also enables us to draw parallels with other violent districts such as Manas-Ata (or HBK) and Ak-Buura which share many similar spatial, environmental, demographic, and social characteristics with the Oshskii raion, including their proximity to a grand bazaar. In this section on the AD district, I first reconstruct the violent dynamics that took place in there. Following that, I discuss the built environment in the AD district and particularly in the Oshskii raion and indicate how it contributed to the intense fighting in this neighbourhood.

The clashes involved some of the residents of the Uzbek mahallas located in Jim, Jiydalik, and Besh-Kuporok, and the Kyrgyz multistorey apartment complexes in the AD and HBK (Manas-Ata) districts. The local youths from

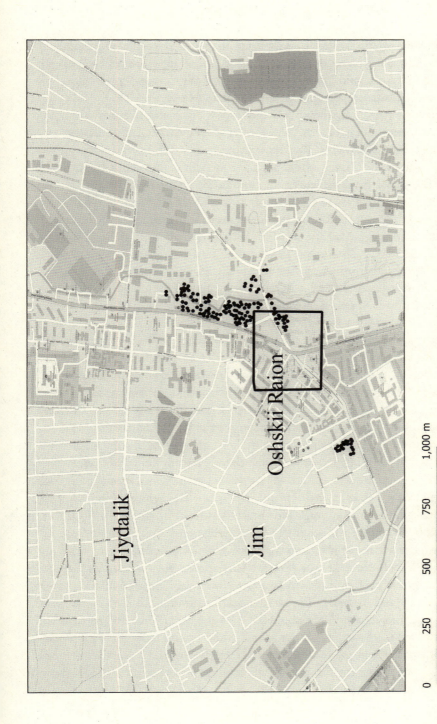

Figure 5.1 Central square and a damage cluster in Oshskii Raion. *Note:* The big rectangle indicates the location of the Oshskii raion's central square. The large damage cluster is the mahalla in Besh-Kuporok.

these apartment complexes and Uzbek mahallas were especially actively involved in the riots and violence Kyrgyz and Uzbek groups armed with metal bars, sticks, and hunting rifles clashed with each other as well as the military that occasionally intervened between the two crowds.

This site emerged as a hotspot because it was located at the main Masaliev-Razzakov street, between the Uzbek mahallas and the Kyrgyz multistorey buildings (see figure 5.1). Residents living in the dormitory-type of apartments around the bazaar probably played an active role on the Kyrgyz side, while the Uzbek groups drew young residents from the neighbouring mahallas (Memorial 2012, 151).

On 12 June the violence escalated. Two APCs captured by Kyrgyz individuals were used to destroy barricades and kill at least five people in Jiydalik (HRW 2010, 36; Memorial 2012, 154). According to the Fergana News Agency, a group of Kyrgyz from Chon Alai and other mountainous districts attacked various mahallas in several different parts of the city including an Uzbek mahalla in Besh-Kuporok (Fergana News 2010). This was the most violent attack in this area, in which 160 residential buildings were completely razed to the ground, making it one of the seven large destruction clusters in the Osh city. The streets leading from the Oshskii raion to mahallas in Shark and Jiydalik were barricaded with many Kyrgyz residents fleeing to more secure places and refugee camps in the Osh city suburbs (Memorial 2012, 156).

On 13 June, the violence suddenly de-escalated as many left the city after rumours about intervention of the Uzbekistani army that had been circulating the previous night. Heavy assaults with the support of APCs stopped and it is likely that by that time the military had already regained control over the lost APCs. However, the streets were still unsafe. As in many other parts of the city hostage-taking in the AD and HBK districts became widespread from 13 June. Criminal groups targeted single individuals passing in the streets. In the Manas-Ata district, several Kyrgyz were killed and taken hostage by Uzbeks from Jiydalik, who made sudden incursions in this Kyrgyz-dominated neighbourhood.[2]

Despite these clear signs of de-escalation, some rioters continued to maintain their domination of certain areas by impregnating the atmosphere with ethnic fears and hatred. A few of the local community leaders made some brave attempts to stop the violence. The Kyrgyz and Uzbek leaders from AD had met for the first time on the same central square to negotiate a nonaggression pact according to which they agreed to clamp down on these aggressive youngsters and to protect each other. On 13 and 14 June, and in fact even later, reconciliation actions were held between Kyrgyz community leaders of

AD and Uzbek elders of Jiydalik (interview with a Kyrgyz community leader, August 2013) and between leaders of HBK and Jiydalik (Memorial 2012, 156). However, these pacts came late and had little effect as sporadic hostage-taking continued for several days.

Space and the Built Environment of Oshskii Raion

One of the most densely populated residential areas in Osh, according to official accounts, the AD district has a population of around 26,000, but, according to the local territorial council, in reality, there are around 35,000 people living in this area. The difference between the official census and the data provided by the territorial council is represented by the number of unregistered or undocumented residents. Most of the unregistered residents are economic migrants who came to the Osh city from the poor rural and mountainous districts of Batken and Osh provinces[3] to find job opportunities in trade businesses related to the local grand bazaar – the largest employer in the city. After the collapse of the Kyrgyz economy in the 1990s, the proximity of the AD district to the bazaar and the availability of relatively cheap housing in bunk houses and dormitory-type apartments attracted thousands of distressed economic migrants to this district and its neighbouring districts of Manas-Ata (HBK) and Ak-Buura (Dom Byta).

Although both Uzbeks and Kyrgyz live in the AD district, urban planning and ethnic cultural housing preferences also contributed to create ethnic segregation here. There are more than 90 multistorey apartment buildings and 1,600 individual unit houses in this district. As in many other districts of the city, ethnic communities are residentially distributed according to the type of housing that has been built in particular neighbourhoods. The Uzbeks, who constitute 55 per cent of the AD district's population live in individual unit houses in mahallas, while the Kyrgyz and a few Russians, who form the other 45 per cent of the district's population, live in four- and five-storey apartment buildings, multiple dormitories, and bunk houses. According to the local neighbourhood committee, only one out of seven official neighbourhoods in the AD district is mixed, while the other six are ethnically homogenous. The AD district is also one of the three districts adjacent to the Osh grand bazaar. Clearly, its proximity to the bazaar greatly adds to the flow of transport and humans through this area.

The spatial location of the AD district in the city makes it a transit zone. Masaliev Street, which passes through the territory of the Oshskii raion, is one of the largest streets with very busy traffic. The street runs through the city's eastern half connecting its five eastern districts (HBK, AD, Ak-Buura, Kurmanjan Datka, and Amir Timur) and also the Shark district with the bazaar. It is full of cafes, teahouses, and private offices on both sides of the road. In addition, Razzakov Street (onto which Masaliev Street converges) connects the Osh city with the highly populated Nariman district on the northern outskirts of the city.

The built environment of the Oshskii raion, which is the main informal neighbourhood of the AD district, used to be rather different to what it is now. Since 2010, the city authorities and local territorial council with some assistance from international NGOs and foundations have considerably improved the local conditions and eliminated some of the factors that contributed to the spread of the violence to this particular area. However, before 2010, the spillover effects of the bazaar were already heavily contaminating the local social life and badly affecting the local criminal environment. As Gieryn (2000, 480) argues: "Place also plays a role in shaping rates of behaviour generally considered deviant or criminal no matter where they occur. Environmental criminologists suggest that the geographic location of various social activities and the architectural arrangements of spaces and building can promote or retard crime rates – mainly crimes against property."

Some of the AD district's neighbourhoods and streets were prestigious and exemplary during the late Soviet period, but gradually degraded over the 1990s and 2000s under the negative spillover effects of the continuously expanding bazaar. By 2010, some parts of the bazaar had expanded to the residential areas and, most notably, to the Oshskii raion's main public square. The rapid transition from welfare socialism to aggressive neoliberalism, corruption, and inefficient governance destroyed the local relatively vibrant civic life. Many longstanding residents left the area and the vacated residential space was quickly filled by rural migrants. Many of these new arrivals lived there in very poor conditions hardly making ends meet. The local city authorities did little to decently accommodate and improve the life conditions of economic migrants, and this meant that the problems related to the uncontrollable expansion of the bazaar with regard to residential space and the infrastructural collapse were dumped on local residents. Gieryn's (ibid., 474–5) remarks clearly identify such places as Oshskii raion: "Places reflect and reinforce hierarchy by extending or denying life-chances to groups located in salutary or detrimental spots. Most of the literature on ethnic enclaves has focused on segregated urban neighbourhoods whose physical, social, and cultural deterioration (whether due to exodus of middle-class minorities or to racist real-estate practices) has made it difficult for residents to better their conditions."

The poor social conditions in the neighbourhood can be characterized as "advanced marginality," a term utilized to explain the territorial stigmatization of residents in marginalized spaces such as ghettos, shantytowns, banlieues, and favelas. For some scholars, this kind of neighbourhoods demonstrates clear patterns of physical and social disorder that are "a manifestation of crime-relevant mechanisms" (Sampson and Raudenbush 1999, 614). The reason for the emergence of such advanced marginality can be explained by a declining welfare state under pressure from increasing neoliberal capitalism (Roy 2012, 692). Although in the pre-conflict period Oshskii raion could not be defined as a ghetto, it could still be considered as a "marginalized space," and, according to this, the main cause of spatial and human marginalization is a state's total negligence of helping to resolve difficulties experienced by poor economic migrants. In addition, many places in the AD district and others, especially neighbourhoods with multistorey apartment complexes in the period before 2010, could be defined as "unassigned public spaces" with high crime rates and anti-social behaviour and "with nobody interested enough to watch over them" (Gieryn 2000, 480). Such territories suffered from overwhelming violence. Altogether it represented the social configuration of the built environment in the Oshskii raion's multistorey apartment complexes and in other similar wards.

After the 2010 ethnic violence, the city authorities renovated the Oshskii raion's neglected central square, which had been the main arena of the clashes between Kyrgyz and Uzbek militants in June 2010. The renovation of this public space radically improved the neighbourhood, reducing the levels of criminality.

Some of the conditions listed below contributed to making the Oshskii raion conducive to violent mobilization. That is, they made the neighbourhood – and especially its large open spaces – the main arena of the interethnic clashes discussed above, and they facilitated violent mobilization when the conflict broke out. However, even before the conflict, the Oshskii raion had deteriorated into a site that attracted anti-social and opportunist behaviour.

As mentioned, the Oshskii raion's built environment engendered several of the conditions that were favourable for violent outbreaks. Particularly, five spatial factors, mostly related to the neighbourhood's built environment, location, and road communication structures, affected violent mobilization and full-scale armed combats in this specific area. These are: (1) spatial practices and routines; (2) spatial proximity and a high density of population; (3) population concentration and ethnic segregation; (4) the presence of a large open area in the intersection between segregated neighbourhoods; and (5) road communications structure and transit location within the city.

First, this large district's spatial practices and routines were not conducive for efficient community policing. The close vicinity of the central bazaar with its spillover effects impeded the development of local social control and the production of traditional power in multistorey building neighbourhoods. The combination of weak policing, low trust among the residents, and the almost-powerless community leaders produced favourable incentives for opportunistic behaviour during the conflict. The territory of the Oshskii raion, and particularly its large central square, was used by militants of both ethnic communities as an arena for clashes and after the violence escalated, as a focal point first for the Uzbek mobilization against Kyrgyz and then, when ethnic balance of power shifted, for the Kyrgyz mobilization.

Second, the high density of population ensured by the high concentration of dormitories, multistory buildings, and mahallas around the Oshskii raion facilitated a violent mobilization of both ethnic groups by making available a large number of people in a particular place – in this case, the main square in the Oshskii raion.

Third, the spatial residential segregation that was very evident and visible in the Oshskii raion made it more difficult to establish cooperation and communication between the two ethnic groups when violence broke out. The clear spatial division between the ethnic neighbourhoods and the absence of any bridging communication and contacts between the residents of the Kyrgyz and Uzbek neighbourhoods increased their perceptions and feelings of hostility, uncertainty, mistrust, and classification of the space as "ours" and "theirs" (Agnew and Oslender 2013, 124).

Fourth, the spatial configuration of the public square in the Oshskii raion made it a convenient place for violent mobilization and clashes. As figure 5.1 shows, the square is a large open space located in the intersection between several streets including the main Masaliev and Razzakov avenues. While large transit roads provide a natural connection with other parts of the city, medium and small streets all converge onto the large open area in the Oshskii raion, that leads to the central bazaar, Kyrgyz-dominated multistorey building complexes, and to the Uzbek mahallas of Jim, Jiydalik, Shark, and

Besh-Kopurok. It is therefore not surprising that the Oshskii raion emerged as one of the first flashpoints of ethnic violence in the city. Young Kyrgyz and Uzbek dwellers went to the large open area from local adjacent neighbourhoods with "the crowds arriving from different directions" (Memorial 2012, 74) and started throwing rocks at each other. At a later stage, when the violence escalated and Kyrgyz groups dominated the city, this open space was used as a springboard for attacks on the Uzbek mahalla in Besh-Kopurok described above as being the most damaged neighbourhood in the AD district. This mahalla was located along Razzakov avenue in the immediate vicinity of the open space and was therefore a convenient target for attacks.

Finally, the location of the Oshskii raion within the Osh city as a high transit zone, with its broad and heavily trafficked main Masaliev Street, made it easy and fast for violent mobs to travel from other parts of the city to reach this neighbourhood. Masaliev Street connects the districts and neighbourhoods that are directly located in the eastern part of the city and, in fact, militant groups from both sides used this road to travel to and clash in the central square in the Oshskii raion. In addition, Kyrgyz youths from the remote rural mountainous districts of Alai, Chon Alai, and Kara-Kulja who mobilized in response to the Uzbek-initiated violence, entered the city through its eastern entrance that eventually leads to the Masaliev Street and then on to the Oshskii raion.

THE KALININ NEIGHBOURHOOD (SULAIMAN-TOO DISTRICT)

During the June 2010 violence, the Kalinin neighbourhood remained peaceful. This case represents the strategy of self-isolation. Local residents made a decision to isolate the neighbourhood from the rest of the city. As a result, the neighbourhood avoided fights, mass killings, looting, and mass property destruction. This outcome seems striking if one takes into account that the Cheremushki neighbourhood, one of the most intensive flashpoints of ethnic violence in the Osh city, was located only a hundred metres away to the west from the Kalinin neighbourhood (see figure 5.2). In this section, based on the example of the Kalinin, I explain how the interaction between human agency and spatial structures changed the built environment of public space within a particular neighbourhood. Through strategic use of the new environment, local community leaders enabled and empowered their own agency and, at the same time, constrained the agency of the other actors. The case of Kalinin

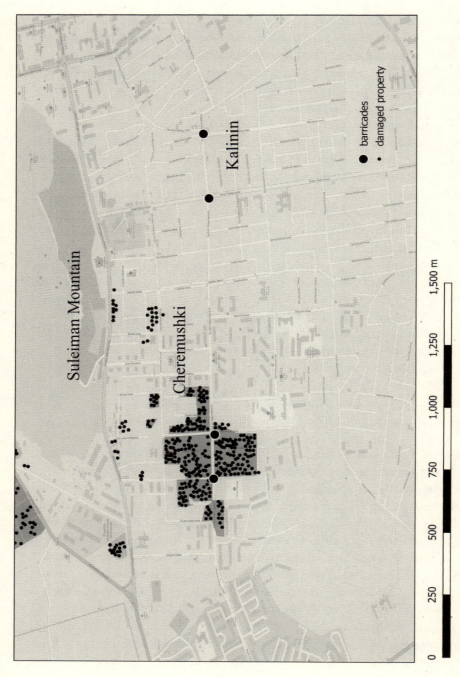

Figure 5.2 Cheremushki and Kalinin neighbourhoods

neighbourhood is interesting as many neighbourhoods in the cities of Osh and Jalalabat utilized the same strategy to avoid violence and mass property destruction. The spatial scale of such strategy is not limited to the neighbourhood level as the entire town of Uzgen, located between Osh and Jalalabat, isolated itself and implemented a special emergency regime in its territory.

The Kalinin neighbourhood is located in the center of Osh. It is the residential area of individual unit houses, mostly inhabited by Uzbeks but also by Kyrgyz who mainly live in several two-, three-, and four-storey apartment buildings. Car repair and service-related businesses, including a large open market of car parts and automobile accessories, is the main distinction of this neighbourhood. The Kalinin neighbourhood is where many of the city's motorists come to get their vehicles repaired for a reasonable price in the small repair shops located along the Amir Timur Street (formerly Kalinin Street). Many Uzbek repairmen have converted parts of their houses into car repair shops. On the northern side of the neighbourhood, there is a large market of car spares offered to customers for affordable prices. The eastern side of the neighbourhood adjoins the city's downtown area.

Violent events were quickly unfolding in neighbouring quarters in Cheremushki, right next to Kalinin. On the morning of 11 June, Uzbek residents in the Cheremushki neighbourhood blocked the main roads in Cheremushki and conducted stop-and-checks of passing cars. Uzbek self-defence groups did not let any Kyrgyz go through, beating the Kyrgyz motorists up. The Uzbek residents of Cheremushki constructed barricades in the main and secondary streets all over the neighbourhood. When Kyrgyz militants attacked the Cheremushki, they burned and looted hundreds of houses, and killing and beating up local Uzbeks who they found inside the houses. As described earlier in chapter 4, the scale of destruction in Cheremushki was considerable. Several blocks with around 350 residential houses mainly along the Abdykadyrov Street were completely destroyed. Around forty houses were destroyed along the eastern part of the Mominov Street. These two streets connect Cheremushki with Kalinin. Investigative reports (Memorial 2012, 114–15; UNITAR/UNOSAT 2010) outline how Kalinin's residents tried to protect the neighbourhood with barricades: "On the eastern part of Abdykadyrov Street and the crossing of Amir Temur Street, which were protected by barricades, 12 large written SOS were identified on the satellite images."

"Crucial to states' control over territory is policing – the surveillance or the activities of citizens and the use of coercion to enforce laws and maintain order" (Sewell 2001, 68). This quotation refers to state control and policing

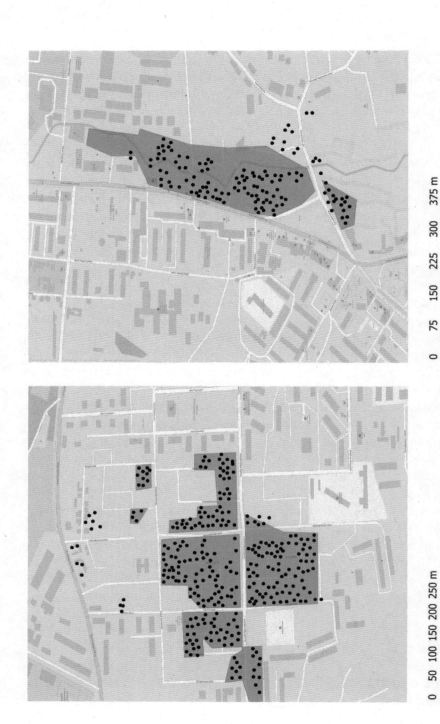

Figure 5.3 Patterns of property damage in Oshskii raion and Cheremushki

but in the absence of the state during the violence, some leaders temporally redesigned the built environment of their neighbourhoods in order to enforce their rules and maintain order. They did it by building barricades that enabled them to hold control over the territory and strengthen community policing.

When first violence broke out in Cheremushki and other neighbourhoods in the Osh city, the residents of the Kalinin neighbourhood followed the example of many other city neighbourhoods by constructing barricades. One aspect which distinguished Kalinin from other neighbourhoods was that the barricades here were erected all around the neighbourhood and not only in the direction of supposed attacks by militants. In addition, as Memorial's above observation suggests, the residents of the Kalinin neighbourhood wrote twelve large "SOS" distress signs[4] on the ground to make them visible for aviation. Local Uzbek elders proposed that a local Kyrgyz woman, Datka, take leadership and coordinate defensive measures in the neighbourhood. It was unusual for local informal authority to be granted to a woman in such critical moment in the local context; however, the Uzbek residents knew Datka as a person with informal links with the local police and as a neighbourhood activist. An established team of community leaders, mainly Uzbek elders, and activist women decided to block the streets with cargo container trucks from the car spares bazaar, thus encircling the whole neighbourhood with a chain of barricades.

Physical self-isolation of the neighbourhood allowed to Datka and other community leaders to impose greater social control and informal power over the territory. The neighbourhood was now turned into an isolated space with its own emergency rules and increased authority and power of local informal leaders. The first thing that Datka and other leaders did was to restrict freedom of movement within this isolated space. They prohibited local residents from leaving the territory and barred entry to and passage through the physically isolated neighbourhood to all outsiders. They even forced those local residents who wanted to flee to other areas within or outside the city to stay. A confined space made self-policing easier, as strangers and external instigators were denied access to the territory.

The next thing was that Datka stopped all activities in the local mosque and the mosque itself was temporally closed down. This happened after three people were killed at the entrance to the mosque by unidentified snipers from the hill of Sulaiman-Too, adjacent to the Kalinin from the northern side of the neighbourhood.[5] The closure of such a traditionally and religiously important public place as a mosque seems unbelievable, especially in an Uzbek-dominated community.[6] During the intense interethnic violence in June 2010, the mosques were still open for believers even in the distressed and violence-affected neighbourhoods in Uzbek and also in the Kyrgyz neighbourhoods in Osh, Jalalabat, and other towns. However, in the wake of the sniper shooting from the Sulaiman-Too and also because the self-isolation in the Kalinin increased the informal leaders' authority and power, local believers in general accepted the closure of the neighbourhood mosque.

The security regime in the confined territory also included regular monitoring of the neighbourhood's borders by community leaders and activist self-defence groups. In addition, the leaders took upon themselves responsibilities such as dispelling rumours, the distribution of humanitarian aid, and maintaining contacts with the police. One of the main aims of this special regime imposed on the residents by their leaders was to prevent any penetration of instigators, looters, and rumour-mongers who could considerably undermine the policing efforts in the local community. Despite the vigilant activists' watchful monitoring of the borders and protection of the neighbourhood from outsiders, a few instigators and looters did sneak into the guarded territory but they failed to instigate violence in this well-policed area. After several unsuccessful attempts to spread instigating rumours, they disappeared from the Kalinin. Some attempts at looting were also made but the residents caught these looters. In the interview with Datka, she did not want to reveal to me what happened to the looters in the end. They were most likely beaten and/or detained. However, the following short excerpt clearly demonstrates that the community leaders in the Kalinin had a sufficiently high level of control over the territory and that they enforced a strong self-policing of the community:

Joldon: Did looters come to your ward?
Datka: Looters came to my territory ... They got their punishment [giggling and looking at me ambiguously].
Joldon: Really? What kind of punishment they got?
Datka: Well, they were caught ... [then she stopped not willing to elaborate more on the fate of these individuals]
Joldon: They were caught, calmed down, and that's it?
Datka: Such things happen ... [still avoiding to clearly indicate the type of punishment they got] (interview with Datka, Osh August 2013).

Later on, during the same interview, she told me that she sometimes resorted to the assistance of "black guys" when dealing with especially non-compliant troublemakers in community policing. In the local context, this implies that when other sanctions did not have an effect, Datka asked local gangs or individuals with connections to the criminal underworld to threaten and calm down the violators of communal social order. In addition, for better community policing, she registered and conducted an interview with each newly arriving resident in her neighbourhood.

The Kalinin leaders also managed to counteract and dispel rumours. On the night between 12 and 13 June, a rumour about a military intervention by the army from neighbouring Uzbekistan spread through the city of Osh. Kyrgyz dwellers left the city in a great panic. However, no resident left the Kalinin neighbourhood. After the conflict was over, Datka became the most influential informal leader in the neighbourhood. According to her, since 2010, social control over the territory by community leaders increased as compared to the pre-conflict period.

The above description of the Kalinin neighbourhood shows that it managed to curb any potential violence and to keep peace within its territory. This points on several conditions. Most importantly, it indicates the significance of the neighbourhood's built environment in containing violence. In terms of spatial characteristics conducive to community defence, the social configuration of the built environment of the Kalinin neighbourhood enjoyed a number of advantages compared to the Oshskii raion. There is no large open space, similar to that in the Oshskii raion, to serve as a natural place for spatial co-presence and the violent mobilization of a large number of people. A lower density of housing, more homogenous population of the neighbourhood, and the absence of spillover effects from the grand bazaar made social control and community policing easier for local community leaders. Their power was reinforced by the physical self-isolation of the neighbourhood, which prevented the spatial mobility of local residents and any other actors who could threaten community policing and social order in the neighbourhood. The small- and medium-sized streets of Kalinin were convenient for constructing barricades to protect the neighbourhood from the potential attacks of combatant groups in neighbouring Cheremushki and other parts of the city. Thanks to the auto spares market, local residents were able to erect solid and dense roadblocks using cargo containers taken from the market. The absence of commercial objects made this neighbourhood less attractive for militants and looters.

Finally, the role of brokers such as Datka cannot be underestimated. Datka's mediating activities can be characterized as follows: "Brokers are people ... who can break down a variety of everyday spatial barriers and build new connections across space. They are able to do so because of their ability to physically and communicatively link unconnected social sites and connect them in a variety of ways" (Martin and Miller 2003, 152). With her connections to both ethnic communities and their leaders in the neighbourhood, and other actors such as police and criminal gang members, she managed to link the otherwise disconnected local residents of two ethnic communities for the collective and cooperative defence of a temporally self-contained territory. In other words, Datka and the other leaders connected the two previously uncommunicative, segregated groups of residents in their neighbourhood: the numerically dominant Uzbeks with minority Kyrgyz. This kind of brokerage was virtually invisible in the Oshskii raion. This is also in a striking contrast to the Uzbek and Kyrgyz leaders in Cheremushki, who did not manage to communicate and cooperate effectively between each other to protect their neighbourhood from violent groups. Dwellers in the Kyrgyz quarters and Uzbek mahallas in Cheremushki were mutually suspicious and fearful of each other. Some barricades were even built between Kyrgyz and Uzbek blocks within the neighbourhood.[7] Given that the social and built environment in two neighbourhoods are somewhat similar, the brokerage and community policing conducted by the Kalinin leaders underlines the great importance of spatial agency in community defence.

CONCLUSION

This chapter suggests new insights in the analysis of communal violence by connecting theoretical categories and concepts of space provided by scholars of political violence and applying them to the case of the 2010 ethnic conflict in the Osh city. As Leitner, Shepard, and Sziarto (2008) suggest, spatial categories are interdependent and co-implicated and should be considered in interaction rather than separately. My analysis of the communal violence in the city of Osh demonstrates how various spatial categories such as the built environment, spatial structures, mobility, and spatiality of power/socio-spatial positionality and brokerage are capable of explaining local dynamics and variation in violence across different neighbourhoods in one town. By analyzing dynamics of violence on the neighbourhood level, this research contributes to our understanding of the spatial dynamics of urban communal violence.

The comparison of two neighbourhood cases highlights several important points specified by the theoretical literature on space and contentious politics. First, this chapter shows that the built environment of public space, spatial differentiation and location of neighbourhoods, and spatial structures – especially road and communications infrastructures – play important role in violence dynamics. It demonstrates that a large and transit "unassigned" open public space in densely concentrated housing is especially vulnerable to violence and mobilization (see also Gieryn 2000). Oshskii raion, as a large and transit space with many streets converging onto its central square, was exposed to the incursion of combatant and looting groups of individuals from both ethnic groups. Thus, it enabled the spatial co-presence of hostile groups in one place. Violent confrontations between the members of these two ethnic communities took place in the neglected central square of the Oshskii raion. The significance of the physical co-presence of large numbers of individuals in a limited space for all forms of contentious politics was also emphasized by Sewell's (2001, 58) theoretical accounts. In addition, this chapter shows that, by isolating itself, the community of residents in the Kalinin neighbourhood managed to eliminate external spatial factors that contributed to the emergence of violence in the Oshskii raion.

Second, spatiality is not causally deterministic, and its impact should be accounted in interaction with human agency. The self-isolation enabled and empowered the local community leaders and constrained actors that might have undermined peace in the neighbourhood. Just as the physical isolation of the Beijing campuses increased the Chinese students' capacity to mobilize for protests in 1989 (Zhao 1998, 1518), in some Osh neighbourhoods, isolation allowed community leaders to enhance their capacity for community policing. The initially disconnected leaders of the two residentially segregated ethnic communities in the Oshskii raion and the Kalinin cases, remained passive in the former, while they managed to strengthen their position by building connections between the two segregated ethnic groups in the latter. By restricting and isolating the neighbourhood, the leaders of Kalinin gained greater social and mobility control over its residents. The change of public space strengthened the local leaders, who started playing an increasingly important role in in-group control thanks to the emergency regime imposed by them on the self-isolated space.

This observation goes along with Zhao's (2013) findings that emphasize the importance of the built environment for mobilization, which increases with a lower organizational capacity. However, while in the case of student protests in the Beijing universities, the built environment of university campuses was fixed and played a static role, the local activists in some Osh neighbourhoods transformed the built environment to protect them from violent mobs and to successfully police local communities. They did this by building artificial barriers and constraining the spatial mobility of the residents and other actors. Community leaders and local residents were able to create environmental conditions that would play in their favour. Thus, they became active agents interacting with spatial structures.

What Sewell (2001) calls the "spatiality of power" and Leitner, Shepard, and Sziarto (2008) call "socio-spatial positionality," play an important role in reconfiguring the built environment and making it effective for community defence. This is what happened in the Kalinin case. The spatiality of power or socio-spatial positionality is "one way to keep analysis open to the resilience of unequal power relations within networks, as well as the possible emergence of new power relations" (ibid., 163).

Third, the concept of "spatial brokerage" (Martin and Miller 2003; see also Auyero 2007; McAdam, Tarrow, and Tilly 2001) is crucial for understanding the relative fortune of the Kalinin and some other barricaded neighbourhoods. The Cheremushki experience showed that the spatial structures / built environment that was relatively similar with the Kalinin did not help the local Uzbek leaders in Cheremushki to protect their neighbourhoods from violent mobs. They failed to build effective cooperation and communication with the local Kyrgyz residents and leaders lacking such spatial brokers and intercommunal mediators as Datka. The absence of intercommunal brokerage in Cheremushki clearly was exacerbated by the problem of intercommunal civic engagement and a lack of bridging social capital between the Kyrgyz and Uzbeks in one neighbourhood. Further research to investigate the local dynamics of the communal violence in Osh should take the role of mediators and social capital into serious account.

Finally, I should mention some caveats. This chapter does not discuss the role of contingent factors in the local dynamics of violence. Not everything was under the control of the communal leaders, brokers, and mediators. I do not want to overstate the salience of spatial factors either. Some contingent events and factors, such as rumours and provocations as well as the (in)efficiency of the police forces in preventing violence, have a strong impact on the local dynamics and spatial distribution of violence. However, other factors being equal, the effects of spatial factors on violent dynamics are considerable.

The role of space and the built environment have rarely been applied to explain outcomes or the local dynamics of riots and ethnic conflicts and have never been evaluated in the analysis of the Osh conflict of 2010. As this chapter demonstrates, space considerably shaped the behaviour of the main actors in this conflict. In general, spatiality and its impact on the local dynamics of violence have been neglected in the literature on political violence and ethnic conflict. This chapter aims to bring attention to the role of spatiality and the built environment in the analysis of political violence.

Although this research has concentrated on the explanation of the relationship between ethnic violence and the social configuration of the built environment in one town, this case is far from being an idiosyncratic study. It has great relevance for many places beyond Kyrgyzstan. The built environment similar to the public space in Osh (the mix of modern multistorey building complexes and historical neighbourhoods with small curvy streets) can be found in cities and towns in many other riot-prone parts of the world; mahallas in Central Asia, Northern Africa, the Middle East, and India, favelas in Brazil, and ghettos in Belfast and Derry in Northern Ireland.[8] The spatial analysis presented in this chapter may shed light on similar processes in many other cities and towns in the world.

Intense ethnic violence in the Oshskii raion and other similar wards has revealed the real extent of crisis in urban public space. City authorities and international NGOs have made some efforts to change public space in neighbourhoods such as the Oshskii raion. Since 2010, public spaces in Osh have been renovated, streets illuminated, and the bazaar de-concentrated. The changing of the built environment does not eliminate the underlying causes of ethnic disorders. However, some of the conditions facilitating violent mobilization can be improved to mitigate the intensity of violence. This chapter will hopefully help to address relevant issues not only in the field of ethnic violence but also in various fields of policymaking: in urban planning and conflict resolution, for example.

6

Intragroup Balance of Power and Self-Policing in Osh Neighbourhoods

This chapter examines the effect of contingency and strategic interactions – both within and between groups – on violent dynamics across Osh's neighbourhoods along with the impact of environmental and spatial conditions. It shows how shifts in the intragroup balance of power between moderates and radicals influences the dynamics of intercommunal negotiations. This chapter underlines the critical role of communal brokers in connecting intergroup and intragroup preferences and thus, the main emphasis is on the intragroup interactions and their critical implications for the success of intergroup nonaggression pacts.

Environmental conditions and two-level interplay between the intra- and intergroup strategic interactions affect micro-spatial variation in violence. In other words, divergent outcomes result from the success or failure of local ethnic community leaders to conduct effective self-policing within the respective neighbourhood-based ethnic constituencies as well as from their ability to reach effective intercommunal nonaggression agreements with community leaders from rival groups. I make two paired comparisons of successful and failed pacts and self-policing between neighbourhood-level communal groups in Osh's southern and northern districts with complementary evidence from some other neighbourhoods. The selected paired comparisons explain the varying trajectories in escalation dynamics and divergent outcomes in dyadic interactions between neighbourhoods. The first paired comparison – between Toloikon and Uchar – provides comparative analysis of in-group policing and nonaggression pacts between communal groups that succeeded under different local environmental conditions. It shows how these two Kyrgyz-dominated neighbourhoods managed to implement nonaggression pacts with the neighbouring Uzbek communal groups despite initially having divergent intragroup conditions for achieving peace agreements. The second paired comparison – between Turan and Nariman – on the contrary, shows how the two Uzbek neighbourhoods with otherwise similar conditions reached diverse outcomes. All neighbourhoods represented in this chapter are cases of intercommunal pacts and in-group policing in ethnically segregated communities.

This chapter analyzes in-group policing and pact-making activities conducted by communal leaders and their interactions from perspectives of questions raised by scholars of IR (Moravcsik 1993, 24; Putnam 1988) regarding the logic of the two-level game model. Under what conditions can leaders act independently of constituent pressures? How do group configurations, institutions, and levels of uncertainty affect the strategies of leaders?

As the southern area was not the main flashpoint of ethnic violence, the level of information about what happened in the southern neighbourhoods of Osh is insufficient, both in official and international investigative reports and in the academic literature. Only some information about clashes between Uchar and Turan is provided and only in certain reports. I reconstruct the events and processes in the southern part of Osh from the scarce information that appears in the Memorial report but mainly from my interviews with local community leaders and residents.

Below, I make two nested paired comparisons of successful and failed pacts and self-policing in Osh's southern district of Turan and the northern district of Nariman – both Uzbek-dominated areas – with complementary evidence from some other neighbourhoods. The first comparison shows how the Kyrgyz leaders of Uchar and Toloikon conducted effective self-policing of the respective local Kyrgyz communities and made nonaggression pacts with Uzbek leaders of Turan that allowed local ethnic community leaders to contain initial violence and preserve peace. This provides comparative evidence for in-group policing and nonaggression pacts of two Kyrgyz neighbourhoods with an Uzbek community in Turan that took place under different local environmental conditions but with the consequent similar outcomes. In the second comparison, the case of failed self-policing in the northern Uzbek neighbourhood of Nariman is juxtaposed with the cases of successful self-policing and nonaggression pacts in Turan district. In Nariman, initially successful self-policing failed due to an influx of refugees. Failed self-policing caused the loss of control by Uzbek *aksakals* (elders) over their local constituency which resulted in the subsequent violence in this neighbourhood and led to the breakdown of a pact between the local Uzbek leaders and the state authorities. In the final section, I discuss factors which explain the difference in outcomes across these cases.

I explain the difference in outcomes in violence between Turan and Nariman by two-level power dynamics – intragroup and intergroup. Structural conditions, such as strength of social norms, homogenous composition of residents, social cohesion, and strong leaders, were favourable for effective in-group policing in both districts. Similar structural conditions highlight the effect of contingent factors. What made difference in these two districts is how local leaders negotiated at the in-group and intergroup levels. The important factor was how leaders dealt with in-group challenges such as the influx of outsiders into their respective ethnic communities. Local ethnic community leaders proceeded with a two-step negotiation process. First, at the domestic/in-group level, the key was to control the in-group constituency and neutralize and convince militant outsiders and local radicals not to fight against the other side. Second, if moderates dominated and radicals were marginalized at the in-group level, leaders managed to negotiate nonaggression pacts with signalling commitments to peace through effective self-policing to their counterparts from the other side.

Here I distinguish "outsiders" as a key intervening variable that affects intragroup balances of power in ethnic community neighbourhoods. Outsiders emerged in some neighbourhoods as mobilized radical groups of rural youths or vindictive male refugees. Where they emerged in sufficient numbers, they altered the local within-group balances by shifting power to radical forces in neighbourhood-based ethnic communities. This, in turn, affected local intercommunal negotiation environments. Outsiders, in alliance with local radical forces, put serious pressure on the community leaders against plans to negotiate nonaggression pacts with opponent groups.

In the southern neighbourhoods of Turan, Uchar, and Toloikon, leaders managed to contain initial violence, neutralize radicals and outsiders, and negotiate successful nonaggression pacts among themselves. On the contrary, in the northern neighbourhood of Nariman, local leaders initially conducted successful self-policing. However, after hundreds of mostly male refugees arrived in Nariman, they lost control of local constituency and in-group policing failed. Power shifted to vengeful radicals who broke a peaceful pact with the Kyrgyz side. The result was violence with brutal assassination of the chief of the district police and his driver, who was beheaded.

When analyzing these cases, we should adopt a two-level game approach from the IR analytical framework. As Kaplan argues (1998, 252), "[a] focus on either international systemic or domestic determinants alone cannot account for the differences" in outcomes. Adopting this IR perspective and juxtaposing international and domestic arenas with in-group and intergroup levels, I argue that neither intragroup nor intergroup factors alone can explain the variation in outcomes. An approach that approximates "the two-level negotiations game, allows for international and domestic factors to be taken into account simultaneously" (ibid., 252; see also Putnam 1988). The two-level game model underlines the critical role of leaders in connecting interstate and domestic policy preferences. Some assumptions of this model – namely, the importance of constellation of domestic forces for external negotiations and the linkage between domestic and international levels in mediation/negotiation processes – can be applied to the analysis of intercommunal pacts and "the two-level model should be tested in the context of ethnicity" (Kaplan 1998, 252).

The constellation of domestic/in-group forces generally divided across locals-versus-outsiders and moderates-versus-radicals categories. This situation was applicable both for Uzbek and Kyrgyz neighbourhoods. As this chapter shows, power dynamics at the two levels interacted and affected each other. Intragroup power shifts influenced the dynamics of intercommunal negotiations and perceptions of credible commitment problem in relation to an intergroup pact.

TURAN AND KYRGYZ NEIGHBOURHOODS: NONAGGRESSION PACTS

Intercommunal relations in Osh's southern neighbourhoods were characterized mainly by interactions between the large and predominantly Uzbek district of Turan and its surrounding Kyrgyz neighbours Uchar, Toloikon, and Abjalov. The southern neighbourhoods avoided large-scale destruction and mass ethnic violence. Although some violence took place on the border between Turan and Uchar, the violence was quickly contained.

All domestic and international investigative missions ignore this area in their reports. Memorial (2012) devotes no more than one and a half pages to this area, out of its overall 222-page document. This lack of attention is understandable since the southern neighbourhoods remained largely peaceful and so investigative reports and journalists therefore concentrated on covering violent events in other districts. I reconstruct and analyze events in this district drawing on my interviews with local residents and leaders. I selected leaders for interviews based on the evidence given to me by ordinary residents who indicated me the key figures who played important role in intergroup negotiations and intragroup community policing.

Turan is a large Uzbek-dominated neighbourhood – one of the ten official districts of Osh. Its population of around 25,000 to 28,000 is mainly Uzbek with a small Kyrgyz minority occupying a few of this district's multistorey buildings. Many residents of Osh call it *Yuzhnyi* – literally "the southern" – referring to its southern location in the city or sometimes *Bir Adyr* (One Hill) referring to its hilly landscape. This large district emerged in the 1960s to 1970s when the Soviet urban planners demolished the old Uzbek mahallas in the center of Osh and built in their place new four- and five-storey apartment buildings. The residents of the demolished mahallas were offered flats in these new apartment complexes but instead of moving into new flats, many of them preferred to build their new houses in the hills of southern suburbs which later became known as the Turan district (Liu 2012). Over time, Turan transformed into a prestigious district. It is encircled by three Kyrgyz neighbourhoods from the northern, western, and eastern directions. In the southern direction, there are mainly uninhabited hills. The district is spatially separated from the Kyrgyz neighbourhoods by a water channel. Three bridges connect Turan with its Kyrgyz neighbours. When ethnic clashes flared up in the city, the residents of Turan strategically used these bridges by building barricades on them to protect the neighbourhood from unexpected attacks. The Kyrgyz did the same on their ends of the bridges. In addition, the Uzbeks in Turan set up barricades blocking the entrances inside mahallas on the whole perimeter of Turan (see figure 6.1). Rumours and news about the ethnic violence in the city contributed to ethnic tensions, distrust, and uncertainty between local ethnic communities.

The relatively distant location of Osh's southern neighbourhoods from the city's major entrance roads in Osh partly explains the relative peace there. The main flow of groups from Kyrgyz rural areas entered the city from its eastern and western entrances in Furkat and Zapadnyi, respectively, where, at first, they clashed with local Uzbek self-defence and militant groups. The neighbourhoods that were located along the entrance roads and in the streets in close proximity to violent hotspots experienced spillover effects from these armed fights. As the violence spilled over to Uzbek mahallas located along these roads in the central and northern parts of the city, the relatively large distance between the main flashpoints and the southern neighbourhoods of Turan, Uchar, and Toloikon facilitated security

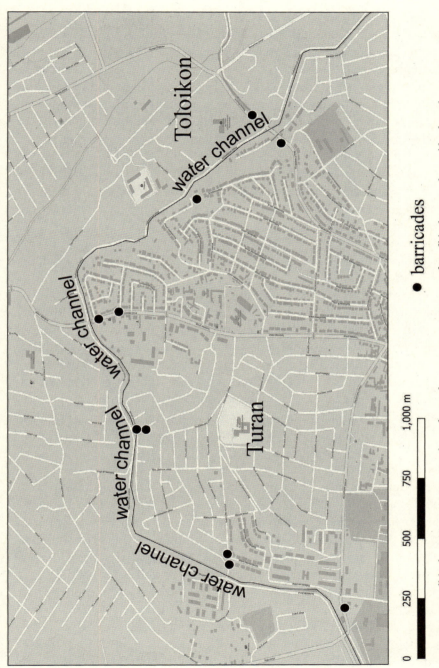

Figure 6.1 Roadblocks in Turan. *Note*: Circles indicate the main concentration of roadblocks near channel bridges that connect Turan with its Kyrgyz neighbours.

measures taken by the community leaders in these neighbourhoods. Nevertheless, the geographical distance does not fully explain why the southern neighbourhoods remained peaceful. The southern interregional road connecting Osh with the Nookat raion is situated in very close proximity to Turan and practically crosses Uchar. In fact, many Kyrgyz participants who gathered in the Zapadnyi neighbourhood and then participated in violence in Osh's western neighbourhoods of Cheremushki and Kyzyl-Kyshtak came to the city using exactly this road. Note that in the north-western direction from Turan (the upper left corner of figure 6.2), there is a roundabout that connects the regional road from the Nookat raion to various parts of the Osh city (indicated with a dark circle). From this roundabout, one can go to Zapadnyi, Dostuk, or Uchar village. Some rural Kyrgyz, mainly those who came from the Nookat raion, did reach Uchar through the same southern regional road. The newcomers became an important force which affected the intracommunal balance of power in Uchar and intercommunal relations between Uchar and Turan.

The balance of power in each neighbourhood explains why some communities managed or failed to reach an agreement with the other side. However, in each case, the distribution of power was not given and fixed. It shifted depending on various contingent factors including the dynamics of intercommunal relations. Therefore, in Uchar and in Toloikon and also in other places such as Uzgen, before negotiating a pact with out-group members, moderate leaders faced internal opposition, usually from young radicals. Before making a pact, leaders had to win a peaceful platform within their group. In some neighbourhoods and villages, leaders could not suppress the radicals, so during negotiations, the radicals tried to disrupt negotiations by pressure or threats.

The constellation of local forces and domestic constraints on leaders in the selected cases were different across communities. Domestic intracommunal constituencies in the city's southern districts, as in many other neighbourhoods, were generally represented by two sets of forces: moderates and radicals. Uchar was overwhelmed by a large number of rural outsiders who overpowered local moderates. Rural men who came to Uchar from outside areas coalesced with local radicals from the area called *dachas* (summer houses) – a migrant part of Uchar. In contrast, Toloikon did not receive an influx of outsiders; virtually all local inhabitants were long-term residents, so the power balance was leaning toward moderates. In Turan, the majority were local residents. Some radical outsiders infiltrated the local youth during the onset of

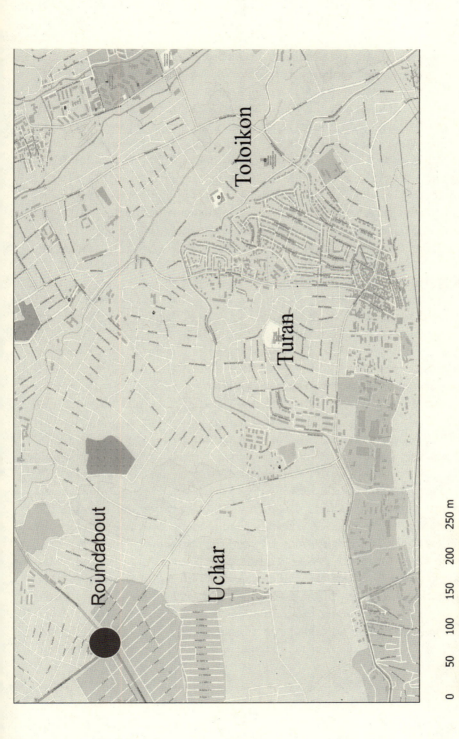

Figure 6.2 Location of Turan, Uchar, and Toloikon

violence in Osh, though the infiltration stopped when the southern neighbourhoods' entrances were choked by roadblocks. The division between moderates and radicals was acute in Uchar and less evident in Turan and Toloikon.

The information obtained from interviews with leaders allows us to follow internal debates and power struggles in Uchar regarding strategic move toward Turan; however, due to lack of evidence, I cannot provide the same-level observations about what was happening in Turan and their internal debates about security strategies toward Kyrgyz neighbours. In general, intercommunal communication between the leaders in the southern neighbourhoods can be characterized as follows. Toloikon chose the strategy of preventive diplomacy and pact-making. In Uchar, local leaders were initially unprepared for the influx of radical outsiders. Their first task was to regain control over the internal constituency, contain the violence that broke out between the radicals from Uchar and Turan, and then negotiate a pact. In Turan, the general policy was a peaceful defensive strategy that was followed by nonaggression pacts with Kyrgyz neighbours. In each neighbourhood, local leaders managed to conduct effective policing of the respective communities.[1]

The Uchar and the Toloikon pacts were negotiated with the same opponent but with different domestic conditions, constraints, and intercommunal negotiation environments. In Uchar, local leaders encountered strong pressures from radical outsiders who demanded to fight against Uzbeks in Turan. The negotiation environment, both in-group and intergroup, was exacerbated by violence that occurred between Uchar and Turan in the first days of the conflict, in which one or two people from each side were killed. In Toloikon, there was a more homogenous domestic constituency and less pressure on leaders from the radicals, allowing the former to carry out more active preventive diplomacy without frequently coordinating their positions with intragroup competing forces. In terms of spatial characteristics and the built environment, the two neighbourhoods were similar except for one important condition: Uchar was a more transitional location as it was linked to the southern regional road that connected Osh with the Nookat raion, while Toloikon was more protected from radical outsiders by its more isolated location. This condition had important implications for in-group control and self-policing activities in these two neighbourhoods. The variation on this factor caused the difference in intragroup balances of power in Toloikon and Uchar. While Toloikon was not linked to the (inter)regional roads and, therefore, did not experience an influx of outsiders from rural areas, Uchar and its local traditional leaders faced serious challenge from radical outsiders who came to this neighbourhood from the neighbouring Nookat raion and other more remote locations.

As for Turan, its spatial characteristics were ambiguous for effective self-policing and for defensive measures. On the one hand, this large Uzbek district was fully surrounded by Kyrgyz neighbourhoods. Being spatially isolated from other Uzbek neighbourhoods and encircled by the Kyrgyz territories, the Turan residents felt themselves under higher-level threat. They could neither flee to safe areas nor seek "military" help from other local Uzbek communities. On the other hand, the spatially strategic advantage of Turan was that it was located on a hill and encircled by a water channel on the whole perimeter from the western (Uchar), eastern (Toloikon), and northern (the Abjalov neighbourhood) sides, connected by three bridges to the adjacent Kyrgyz neighbourhoods. From the southern side, Turan was protected by uninhabited hills. This spatial advantage allowed the Turan leaders to concentrate their defensive efforts around three bridges where local Uzbek community had built barricades to prevent possible sudden incursions inside its territory. The neighbouring Kyrgyz communities chose the same strategy by setting up roadblocks on their side. According to Sewell (2001, 68), control over territory is synonymous with policing – the monitoring of local residents and the use of coercion and sanctions to maintain order. The spatial isolation of Turan as "an ethnic island" ensured its leaders' greater influence and control over the local constituency with ability to sanction violators. After Turan blocked the bridges, no disruptive outsiders such as instigators or vengeful refugees from other Uzbek neighbourhoods could arrive in Turan to pose an open challenge to local community leaders.

The most notable confrontation between Uzbeks and Kyrgyz in this area occurred on 12 June, on the border between Turan and the Kyrgyz-dominated suburban neighbourhood of Uchar. The Kyrgyz, a group of 300–500, who arrived in Uchar from the direction of Nookat region, attempted to enter Turan but were met by the 500–1,000 strong Uzbek group which stood behind barricades armed by two training APCs, one automatic weapon, several guns, around ten hunting rifles and numerous bottles of flammable oil (Memorial 2012, 177–8). In the gunfire that followed this encounter, several people were killed on both sides.[2] The full-scale clashes were prevented by riot police troops that arrived on the hotspot on an APC. This time they were more efficient compared to how they dealt with similar situations in other hotspots (interview with an Uchar resident; Memorial 2012, 175–9). After the police left the area, the two groups stood against each other separated by barricades. Local Kyrgyz leaders and mediators in Uchar and also in the

Abjalov neighbourhood, at Turan's northern end, intervened and held back groups of Kyrgyz youngsters in Uchar who wanted to enter Turan anyway.[3] After these interventions, the tensions calmed but the attempts by radical youngsters from rural areas to enter Turan did not stop. In the next sections, I discuss how the Kyrgyz and Uzbek leaders conducted in-group policing of respective communities and negotiated nonaggression pacts to prevent ethnic violence. Similar nonaggression pacts were negotiated between the Kyrgyz and the Uzbek neighbourhoods in some other southern parts of Osh as well. In some neighbourhoods, with more ethnically mixed population,[4] local Kyrgyz and Uzbeks together conducted coordinated defence against violent groups from both ethnic groups and established ethnically mixed patrols and self-defence groups (Memorial 2012, 176–8; interviews with a military officer and an Uzbek community leader).

There was also the exchange of hostages between Kyrgyz and Uzbek neighbourhoods. Some of local Kyrgyz who did not manage to leave Turan stayed in this neighbourhood, practically as hostages. There is at least one confirmed incident involving the exchange of hostages in Turan (interview with an Uzbek community leader in Turan, August 2012). Another incident was mentioned in the Memorial report when a Kyrgyz woman with her three children were caught in Turan. From her family, the kidnappers demanded an automatic weapon in exchange for their release. In the end, she was exchanged for three or four Uzbek women, residents of Turan (Memorial 2012, 179).

THE DYNAMICS OF NEGOTIATIONS BETWEEN TURAN AND UCHAR

This section provides original perspectives from the key figures who participated in intercommunal negotiations from both sides. Each side claims that they were the first to initiate a nonaggression pact. There is also some confusion about the dates and sequence of events. Although such details in the interviews of Kyrgyz and Uzbek leaders does not coincide, in general, they confirm the dynamics and the content of negotiations.

Turan's Nonaggression Pact with Uchar

One of my key respondents, Rahman, is one of the Uzbek leaders in Turan and also a well-known human rights activist in the city. The morning after communal violence broke out in the city, he was among those moderates who advanced the decision to start negotiations with the leaders of the adjacent Kyrgyz villages. I had a chance to interview him twice in July 2010 and in August 2012. His accounts over the two-year period between these two interviews remained consistent which gave me an additional reason to rely on his evidence. Below I provide extensive excerpts from my two interviews with Rahman as they well illustrate the environment of intercommunal negotiations. Here the first excerpt from the interview in 2010 (interview with Rahman, Osh, July 2010):

> Rahman: On the 10th there was this clash [in front of Alai Hotel, in the city center], on the 11th early in the morning I gathered about 20 Uzbek elders, aksakals [community leaders]. Then I came here [to the Kyrgyz-dominated neighbourhood of Uchar] to the aksakals, then went to Jindi Mahalla [literally crazy mahalla – an informal name for the Abjalov neighbourhood]. We went there and mentioned that someone had started the conflict in the city and addressed Kyrgyz and Uzbeks on the territory saying that we should protect each other ... Local Kyrgyz should protect us from the Kyrgyz militants and we will protect them if there are attacks from the Uzbek side. In the end, we all agreed and the aksakals blessed and prayed. Then we barricaded and closed the streets. We closed [the entrance to] Uchar, from that place to this it was barricaded. It was totally barricaded here.
> Joldon: Uchar was also barricaded?
> Rahman: Yes. It was a circular defence [*krugovaya oborona*, referring to the barricades across the water canal]. So, all the aksakals supported this idea. The other side of the circle was also barricaded separately. When the Nookat guys [rural Kyrgyz from surrounding villages of the Nookat raion] came, they came along that canal bank and entered the territory. Because it remained unclosed. On the way, they burnt a shop and shot a couple of people. Then they were confronted by other armed guys [Uzbeks] there, later after gunfire exchange and after a noisy grenade attack, they fled.
> Joldon: Who were the shooters?
> Rahman: First there were Kyrgyz who started the fire and shot dead a couple of people. Then when they entered deep inside the territory they confronted with Uzbeks, driving the car and

using their guns from the car windows. These Uzbeks also managed to kill one or two men. After this, the Kyrgyz fled and never came back again. That's why Yujnyi [Turan] was in peace.

In the 2012 interview (interview with Rahman, August 2012), Rahman basically repeated what he said in 2010 but also added new important details on what kind of arguments he used during the negotiations to "persuade" the Kyrgyz side:

> Rahman: On the 10th of June, I knew that was a high time [to act]. Then at around 3 a.m. I visited about ten old men [aksakals] in their houses, and gathered them. I explained to them the situation that there was unrest. I suggested to go to the Kyrgyz neighbourhoods and gather aksakals from there and decide on plans. We decided to defend each other from the opposite groups. If Uzbeks attacked the Uzbek aksakals would protect [the Kyrgyz], if Kyrgyz attacked then the Kyrgyz aksakals would protect [the Uzbeks]. When we went to Uchar, there were some aksakals already saying that "we are one people that we should protect each other." We promised this to each other. Then we went to Abjal, the Kyrgyz-dominated neighbourhood [on the northern side of Turan], where we also met Kyrgyz aksakals and we all gathered and continued strengthening our people's diplomacy. [During] 11–12 June [2010] we didn't encounter anybody from outside, and on the 13th there was an armed group in Yujnyi [Turan] district which started shooting and burning. Then Uchar people went to defend. The strength of people's diplomacy helped to save Yujnyi as well.
>
> Joldon: When you went to conduct reconciliation negotiations, what difficulties … did you have to overcome? Weren't you afraid of being attacked?
>
> Rahman: First, we weren't afraid because knowing we were acquainted with the people there for a long time – we used to greet, hug, have a tea together, used to meet in the weddings, funerals – so how could it be possible that they kill us if we go there? But yes, some young men behind the aksakals greeted us aggressively, then we said "Hey, you guys, please calm yourselves down, what will happen in the future only God knows, maybe tomorrow this will turn into interstate conflict between Uzbekistan and Kyrgyzstan.

This may turn into interstate war. Even in this case if the Uzbek [Uzbekistani?] people will come and attack the Kyrgyz, we will stand against them telling them not to attack our people, we will say this is our nation, this is our people. If necessary, we will confront them. And you should do this too, you should protect us if Kyrgyz attack; we will do so if the Uzbeks attack. No one knows what will happen in the future." We said all this without hiding anything.

The last excerpt reveals one changing condition in the dynamics of the intercommunal conflict. In the negotiation process, Rahman referred to the possibility of interstate war between Kyrgyzstan and Uzbekistan. As was discussed in the overview of violent events in chapter 4, on the night of 12–13 June, the rumour about the military intervention of Uzbekistan's 5,000 special forces troops spread in Osh and especially in its western neighbourhoods. This caused great panic in the city and many Kyrgyz residents in the western neighbourhoods left the city, abandoning their houses. This tide of panic caused many Kyrgyz who came to Osh to fight against Uzbeks to flee. The rumour about Uzbekistan's military intervention induced an important power shift in the city-level dynamics of the intercommunal violence. First, because after this rumour many Kyrgyz participants in combats fled the city. As the death-toll statistics show, the number of killings in Osh dropped significantly the next day after this rumour appeared. Second, those who remained in the city now considered the external factor of Uzbekistan. So, when during the negotiations, the Uzbek leaders faced pressure from Kyrgyz side, Rahman implicitly indicated to the Kyrgyz radicals about the shifting intergroup power balance related to the possibility of Uzbekistan's invasion. As we can see below, the changing intercommunal negotiation environment altered the power balance within the Kyrgyz community in Uchar and convinced the radicals to accept the nonaggression pact.

In the next interview excerpt (Osh, August 2012), Rahman highlights some conditions that facilitated the pact. One is connections among communal leaders. The fact that communal leaders from both sides had some knowledge about each other and that some had a history of past interaction helped them to build the trust necessary to initiate a nonaggression pact. This prior knowledge facilitated contacts between leaders under uncertainty, which proved to be an important factor in initiating intergroup pacts and reducing the level of uncertainty caused by the absence of the state and the security dilemma triggered by the onset of intercommunal violence in Osh. The main content of negotiations illustrated in quotations below was about self-policing by local respective communities and mutual guarantees of security and protection from outside forces.

> Joldon: You said that you knew those aksakals and had tea together. How were your relations before the events, did you have mutual plans?
> Rahman: Local people used to work there together, attending each other's weddings, funerals. There are three to four other people with whom I have close relations. When we worked at an NGO, we used to have intern students from the journalist department who were from Uchar. They came to us asking to get them an internship. We took some of them. Therefore, when we went there those guys accepted us well. And if, to my point, the Kyrgyz from Alay, Papan, Kara-Kulja, Nookat, those marginal guys, wouldn't come, the Osh Kyrgyz-Uzbek people would never fight because our ancestors were friends and had tea together.

The evidence about the peace negotiations between Turan and Uchar given by Rahman was confirmed by Umar, one of key figures at the Osh UNCC (Uzbek National Cultural Center).[5] Umar (interview, Osh, August 2012) also mentions pacts between the Uzbek district of Amir Timur and a Kyrgyz village of Ozgur:

> The same day, the events were on the 11th, the same day they [leaders in Turan district] had talks. On the 11th of June representatives of the Uzbek aksakals met with the reps of the Kyrgyz aksakals in the Uchar area. They made an agreement. The same took place in On Adyr [literally "ten hills," a large Uzbek neighbourhood. The official name is Amir Timur] and Ozgur [a Kyrgyz village]. That's why the Hills [*adyrlar*, Amir Timur neighbourhood] did not suffer. They made a peace agreement.

Umar went on explaining how these talks were organized:

> Joldon: So, what mechanisms did aksakals use, phone calls, visited each other, talked, weren't they afraid to be attacked in Uchar or Dostuk, for instance? How was it organized to stop the violence?

Umar: From 11 to 15 they went just by car, small cars. Our Uzbek people went to Uchar, although, at that time, they did not have time for pilaf lunch, they just shared some bread. They made a peace agreement on not to attack each other, not to make pressure and stop a possible threat if from the Uzbek side [comes], so the Uzbeks would stop it, if from the Kyrgyz side [some militants come] – then the Kyrgyz [would stop them].

Joldon: There were some rumours about possible attacks from Uzbekistan. Do you think the Kyrgyz were scared?

Umar: Everyone was scared about it, both the Uzbeks and the Kyrgyz. That was the case, yes.

Joldon: So, when they drove cars to Uchar, they weren't afraid of being attacked and shot?

Umar: No, they weren't. Because they negotiated in advance saying "we are four to five of us and we are coming," then they were met by another four to five people. There, they entered the houses, sharing bread, supportive of peace, negotiating, talking, finally agreeing that: "If you don't attack us, we don't attack you. If someone from our side comes, we will protect you, and if someone from your part attacks, you will protect us" was the point of the agreement. Aksakals knew each other before.

These interview excerpts display the negotiation environment in Turan that was generally favourable for negotiations. Uzbek moderate leaders dominated the process of decision-making and were open for negotiations. In contrast to Turan, in Uchar, the negotiation environment was very difficult as local leaders faced a strong challenge from radical opposition.

Peaceful Mediation under the Domination of Radicals in Uchar

Uchar with around 5,000 residents is located on the western side of Turan. The southern interregional road that connects Osh and the Nookat raion is situated in the western side of Uchar. On the southern side of Uchar, closer to the hills, there is another distinct settlement called *dachas*. Former summer houses now occupied by rural migrants, the dachas became an integral part of Uchar, although local residents until recently kept some degree of autonomy from the rest of the village. Many dacha residents preserved strong ties with their kinship in villages, mainly in the Nookat raion.

During the communal violence, they hosted people who came to Osh from Nookat's rural areas.

On 11 June, people from dachas started flocking around the southern road from the Nookat raion which was next to Uchar. Another group gathered on the bridge which connected Uchar and Turan. With no police or military seen at the time, the Kyrgyz crowd of 2,000 people who came to the bridge from dachas, Papan village, Nookat, and other regions had the intention of passing through Turan, which would trigger a fight with a local Uzbek self-defence group. By that moment, Kanybek – Uchar's most powerful leader – had already obstructed the movement of the crowd on the bridge toward Turan, literally telling them that they would proceed further only over his dead body. The crowd stopped also because some local Kyrgyz supported Kanybek. He and other leaders managed to hold back the crowd for the next two days. The crowd was angry with his peaceful attitude toward the Uzbek community in Turan. As an angry response, people in the crowd threatened to burn his house. They could not understand the reason why he was defending the local Uzbek community while, according to them, Uzbeks in the city were killing their Kyrgyz ethnic fellows.

To retain control over the crowd, community leaders appealed to the residents from dachas and Uchar, who, according to Kanybek, comprised about 200 individuals or 10 per cent of this crowd. Through his fellows, Uchar leaders tried to put pressure on the group. The appeal was effective because most of the outsiders coming to Uchar from nearby and remote villages and districts/raions found shelter among Uchar residents, and therefore, were dependent on them in terms of food and accommodation. This forced them to listen to the arguments of their hosts. Some of the outsiders were acquaintances or relatives of dacha and Uchar residents. Kanybek used his authority among his immediate constituency, and according to him, his words had "a command-like effect" on the residents of Uchar. Consequently, he decided to act directly through his local constituency that, in turn, was putting pressure on the outsiders.

In Turan, local Uzbeks erected barricades closing entrances to their mahalla. The Kyrgyz in Uchar organized a roadblock on the bridge connecting Uchar and Turan. By that moment, Kanybek and his followers had managed to stop the Kyrgyz outsider group. Appealing to the crowd, he also used religious rhetoric about irreversibility of punishment in the other world and the common religious identity with Uzbeks. He was in regular phone contact with Uzbek aksakals in Turan to monitor the ongoing situation. At one point, the Kyrgyz patrol at the bridge roadblock told him that young Uzbeks from Turan were constantly provoking them driving around in a car, showering abuse on the Kyrgyz at the bridge roadblock, and showing them fists and their middle fingers. The situation was so tense that one provocative spark could make it impossible to stop the Kyrgyz crowd from attacking the Turan neighbourhood.

Therefore, on 12 June, Kanybek went to Turan to have talks with Uzbek aksakals. Together, they held a short council where they assured one another of good intentions and prepared good ground for negotiating a peaceful pact. He asked to restrain those youngsters from provoking the Kyrgyz on the bridge roadblock. Otherwise, as he explained to them, he could not guarantee that he would manage to hold back the crowd from attacking the Uzbek mahalla. The Uzbeks accepted the fact that there were some violators and provocateurs and promised to punish them. In turn, Kanybek guaranteed to curb the aggression of the youngsters. "This was a first step to the peace," he said to me in an interview (Osh, September 2013).

After that meeting, the provocations stopped. The next day, communal brokers such as Rahman and Kanybek from both the communities created a joint commission which comprised local strongmen, aksakals, and imams both from Turan and Uchar – fifteen people with ten Kyrgyz and five Uzbeks. At the meeting, they decided to make a peaceful appeal to the youth of both ethnic communities and to pray together. They gathered and prayed together first among Uzbeks in Turan and then in Uchar near the bridge roadblock. They made speeches about interethnic friendship and the necessity of stopping bloodshed. However, at the end of the ceremony, the Kyrgyz youngsters who had come from outside of Uchar refused to finish the prayer with the utterance "Amen!" They tried to wreck the peaceful process by heaping abuse upon Uzbek aksakals. The radicals presented an ultimatum – the presumable purpose of which was to demonstrate their dominance over the peaceful process than to actually disrupt peaceful talks – which included the following conditions: Uzbek children must study in Kyrgyz schools, to make broadcasting of programs in Osh TV[6] only in Kyrgyz language, and demands like "you [Uzbeks] have to speak [only] in Kyrgyz." When Kanybek tried to calm the radicals down, the latter again threatened to burn his house. They were angry with his attempts to protect the Uzbeks. He was finally able to reach agreement with the non-Uchar fellows at the roadblock by slaughtering some cattle for them.

Another piece of evidence of Uchar's commitment to a pact was given by an Uzbek leader, a head of UNCC. According to him (interview, Osh, 2012), residents of Uchar stopped a crowd that was coming from Nookat and trying to enter Turan:

> Joldon: So, there is the road from Nookat. Were there attempted attacks [on Turan] by young men coming from that road?
> Leader: Yes, there were. They [rural Kyrgyz] were coming from that road. For example, if you are coming from the left side, on the right there is Uchar where Kyrgyz live, then through Uchar you can enter Turan. So, the [local] Kyrgyz managed stop those invading Kyrgyz. That's why they couldn't enter our street. Uchar people didn't allow them to go there.

Later Kanybek helped Uzbeks in Turan by sending a humanitarian aid. When violence broke in the city, Uzbek leaders in Turan evacuated people, mostly women and children, to a local school building. Uzbek activists contacted Kanybek in 3–4 days. They asked him to supply the mahalla with food and vegetables as the roads were blocked and people started experiencing food shortage. Kanybek asked his friends, local leaders in Aravan rural district to send two trucks loaded with twenty tons of potatoes, cabbages, onions, and other food products. The trucks got stuck in one of the Kyrgyz urban districts of Osh because the roads had still been blocked. Therefore, the food supply was delivered with the help of small porters (tiny trucks) to Turan, Dyikan Kyshtak, and to the area of the Kalinin Street.

At the end of our interview, surprisingly for me, Kanybek asked a question: "One question comes to my mind. Why did some areas in Osh city suffer violence while other districts in the same city remained peaceful?" That was basically the main question of my research that drove me to investigate the spatial variations in violence in Osh and other places. He immediately answered his question himself. According to him, it was the factor of local strong leaders that allowed them, including him, to conduct effective in-group policing and the key to that was strong ties between leaders and their constituencies that were possible only in Uchar, Turan, and other rural types of neighbourhoods in Osh. He argued further, "If I lived in Zapadnyi neighbourhood, [a modern Soviet-type neighbourhood with exclusively multi-storey apartment buildings like in Alymbek Datka (AD) and Manas-Ata (HBK)] I would barely be able to control the situation there. At a maximum, I could probably control the residents of the building where I would live but this is the maximum I could do." Kanybek's words accurately reflected the situation in multistorey apartment buildings neighbourhoods like Zapadnyi, where local leaders had little control over local developments.

The dynamics of negotiations between the Turan and Uchar leaders show that the environmental conditions for pact-making were different in these neighbourhoods. The intragroup balance of power was favourable for the moderate leaders of Turan while in Uchar, it shifted toward the radicals. However, the final outcome was a successful nonaggression pact. In Uchar, Kyrgyz leaders had strong internal pressures from the radicals when they negotiated a pact with the Uzbek leaders. The local radicals coalesced with outsiders. The majority of locals did not support aggression but on the other hand, they did not trust the Uzbeks and were uncertain about Turan's intentions. They feared that the city of Osh would be taken over by Uzbeks and Uchar could be attacked by Turan. Therefore, most locals stayed at home or were passive observers of the events except for the active group led by the Uchar leaders. In such circumstances, the arrival of outsiders from the Nookat region made a difference by shifting power balance toward the radicals. Radicals were a minority in Uchar as well as in many other neighbourhoods and they could not sufficiently press their agenda without external support. With the arrival of outsiders, the local in-group power balance shifted toward the radicals, who initiated attacks against Turan.

Uchar presents a question about how local leaders managed to hold radicals back under domination of the latter in this locality. Local leaders managed to hold the distribution of power in their favour strategically using their local constituency against outsiders. They and their counterparts from the adjacent Abjalov neighbourhood employed mixed strategy of putting pressure on outsiders through their constituency networks and on the other hand, using "carrots" (slaughtering cattle) to calm down radical outsiders.

TOLOIKON AND TURAN: SUCCESSFUL SELF-POLICING AND NONAGGRESSION PACT

Toloikon is a small Kyrgyz subrub on the southern border of the Osh city, squeezed between uninhabited hills in the south and the Turan neighbourhood in the north and the west. In the eastern side, the Ak-Buura river separates Toloikon from Osh's Kurmanjan Datka (Yugo-Vostok) district. Most of its residents are either farmers or have employment in the city. When ethnic violence erupted in the city, Toloikon hosted some Kyrgyz refugees from the city, mostly children and women. Toloikon and Turan are separated by a water canal and the connection between the two goes across a bridge. Local residents have practically no connections with the Uzbek residents of Turan except occasional and small-trade transactions, although some local community leaders have some connections among each other, but their encounters and interactions are random.

One of the leaders of Toloikon is Avasbek who formerly held high-ranking positions in the police. He played the key role in in-group policing within Kyrgyz community in Toloikon and in successful peaceful negotiations with Uzbek aksakals from Turan. According to him, he noticed ethnic mobilization one week before the onset of violence: locals started to gather in large numbers. There were multiple rumours about possible interethnic clashes. At that moment, Avasbek started communicating with the Uzbek community leaders in Turan.

Approximately at that time, some Uzbek youngsters beat two Kyrgyz cattlemen from Toloikon, an incident that had the potential to spark off violence between two local communities given that intercommunal tensions in the city had already been growing. After Avasbek and his associates complained to Uzbek aksakals about the incident, the latter quickly identified the culprits and brought them to Toloikon to be presented to him and the victims. In the presence of all involved parties, Avasbek urged both communities to refrain from anti-social behaviour that could lead to escalation of violence. The conflict was settled peacefully.

This incident demonstrates an example of efficient self-policing by Uzbek aksakals in Turan who identified the culprits and brought them for the punishment to the Kyrgyz side. By delivering the culprits to the victims' side, they clearly showed their credible commitment to intercommunal cooperation. The decision to hand them to the Kyrgyz side for punishment highlights the readiness of Uzbek aksakals to build trust and cooperate to avoid potential indiscriminate retaliation from the Kyrgyz side in Toloikon. The important thing here was that Uzbek aksakals identified the perpetrators and left the right of punishment to the victims' side, thus making sanctions against perpetrators visible and showing their capacity for effective self-policing within the local Uzbek community. According to Laitin and Fearon's (1996) interethnic cooperation model, the visibility of punishment is important for in-group policing equilibrium because it demonstrates that the sanctions for anti-social behaviour actually work. As a result, neither side had claims against each other in the end. On the other hand, the visibility of sanctions signalled the group leaders' credible commitments to a peaceful pact.

The Kyrgyz side was very active in contacts with the Uzbek leaders of Turan. Avasbek (interview, September 2013) says that the fact that it was the Kyrgyz side that first initiated a nonaggression pact refutes the general belief about the Kyrgyz being largely the aggressors in this ethnic conflict. In the process of communication between the leaders of Toloikon and Turan, the peaceful initiative actually came from Toloikon.

On the other hand, in the interviews with the Uzbek leaders of Turan, they stressed on the difficulties in their negotiations mainly with Uchar, while Toloikon and the Abjalov neighbourhood figure in their narratives as unproblematic cases. This is most likely because the Turan leaders correctly evaluated Uchar as the most dangerous zone in which they would experience violent encounters with the Kyrgyz side and the potential serious problems in the negotiation process. Already one week before the communal conflict broke out in Osh, the Kyrgyz leader of Toloikon had started actively meeting Uzbek aksakals and other leaders of Turan to prevent ethnic violence. During the meetings, they negotiated to implement strong in-group policing in the respective communities.

On the night of 10–11 June, people gathered in groups immediately when they heard news about first violence in central Osh. Avasbek urged local Kyrgyz not to join the riots. At the same time, Uzbeks also gathered in large groups in Turan. A large Uzbek group mobilized not far from the bridge that divided Turan and Toloikon. The Kyrgyz patrol took the position on their end of the bridge. The two groups looked at each other with distrust. Both sides barricaded the entrances to their neighbourhoods. Among the Turan Uzbeks, some instigators emerged who began to incite the local Uzbeks. The rumours about ethnic slaughter spread in both ethnic communities. As instigators emerged in both communities, Avasbek policed his own community and suppressed the local radicals' attempts to foment violence against the Uzbeks. His high social status, connections with the police, and reputation within his community helped him to gain support from the local moderate Kyrgyz. The Kyrgyz patrols, each consisting of approximately twenty men, protected and monitored the village. Sixty men in total were mobilized to protect the security of the village. These patrols and self-defence groups were the main tool used by Toloikon's moderate leaders to enforce self-policing within the local Kyrgyz community. In Turan, young Uzbeks also were disgruntled by the "passive" stance of the local aksakals. They strove to go to the downtown – where main clashes between the Uzbeks and the Kyrgyz had been taking place – to help their ethnic fellows. In order to prevent violence with Turan, Avasbek decided to speak directly to the local Uzbek population.

On 11 June, the first day of violence, Avasbek – with the support of, and accompanied by, the Uzbek leaders – decided to speak in front of residents of Turan, who gathered in large numbers in six or seven locations of this district, upon hearing news about the ethnic riots in the downtown. Always escorted by at least two local Uzbek leaders, he attended mass gatherings where he called for interethnic peace and urged local residents not to succumb to instigation. However, during one of these meetings, Uzbek leaders suddenly asked Avasbek to leave Turan immediately as they noticed the increasing presence of unfamiliar faces among the locals in the crowd. The outsiders were mostly young Uzbek lads. Aksakals forced him to leave the meeting, warning that they could no longer guarantee his security and assuring him that they would continue community policing and calls for peace in the same vein.

This incident demonstrates some important points. One is that the presence of a sufficient number of outsiders seriously threatens the community-policing capacity of local leaders. Uzbek leaders interrupted the speech of the Kyrgyz leader after they realized the hazard of potential attacks against their Kyrgyz guest. The fact that they could not identify many youngsters in the crowd made them wary and fearful. They could not control or deter aggressive behaviour of individuals who did not belong to their constituency and who would not recognize their traditional authority. The Uzbek aksakals got anxious because they realized that they could not exert community control over the outsiders, especially amid the intercommunal tensions and emerging violence. Neither could they guarantee the security of the Kyrgyz mediator. This highlights the limits of traditional authority which the Uzbek aksakals realized themselves. Another implication of this incident demonstrates Uzbek leaders' alertness of the possible attack against the Kyrgyz leader from the unknown young radicals. Even worse, his assassination would bring undesired consequences for intergroup relations. Trust between the communities would be completely eliminated and violent intercommunal confrontations would be inevitable. Any assassination would change the intragroup balance and shift power toward radicals not only in Toloikon but also in other neighbouring Kyrgyz communities – in Uchar and in the Abjalov neighbourhood. With this favourable advantage, local radicals in each Kyrgyz neighbourhood would instigate vindictive and non-discriminative violence against the Uzbeks in Turan. By asking the Toloikon leader to leave the scene, the Turan aksakals recognized both the limits of their authority and responsibility for the intercommunal peace.

The leaders of Turan and Toloikon agreed on some conditions of the nonaggression pact. In the atmosphere of growing tensions and escalation of violence in the city, the leaders in both neighbourhoods put a lot of effort into counteracting instigators. They also agreed that the violence is not in interests of both communities and in case the riots would break out on their territory they would not yield to the general tide of violence.

Several facts that observed Turan and Toloikon exhibit examples of effective self-policing and local leaders' credible commitments to the conditions of nonaggression pact. In Turan, there are several multistorey apartment buildings, mainly occupied by Kyrgyz people who became trapped in this neighbourhood during the conflict. Local Uzbek radicals threatened them with vengeful violence. Some of the Kyrgyz called their relatives in Toloikon informing them about these threats. The Kyrgyz leaders in Toloikon identified the exact addresses of the trapped Kyrgyz in Turan and handed the list with the addresses to the Uzbek community leaders. The latter managed to evacuate twenty-three Kyrgyz households from Turan. On the other hand, the Uzbek aksakals guaranteed the safety of their property and arranged guards to keep Kyrgyz houses and flats safe from looters. In turn, the Kyrgyz in Toloikon handed in several migrant workers and artisans from Uzbekistan (all ethnic Uzbeks) who worked in Toloikon and then got trapped there when the violence broke out in the city and Turan blocked the bridges. The Kyrgyz let several Uzbek women pass through the village to get to the maternity hospital in Toloikon and provided security for the hospital and its patients. Six or seven Uzbek women delivered babies in those days.

Here is another example of cooperation. When the interethnic tensions grew on the eve of the conflict, one Uzbek crowd attacked passing by cars with Kyrgyz passengers in Turan. They beat some Kyrgyz civilians and a couple of Kyrgyz policemen, and broke the windshield of one of the cars. Fortunately, the local elders became aware of this incident and rushed to rescue the victims. They apologized and even paid compensation for the broken windshield.

In Avasbek's view, effective communication, and eventually successful self-policing, was facilitated by the fact that both ethnic communities – although living in ethnic and resident segregation – still had experience of cohabitation and knew about each other. Avasbek (interview, Osh, 2013) said that although he got acquainted with the majority of the Uzbek leaders for the first time during those days (he had known only two of them before), they knew about each other indirectly. According to Avasbek, that he was well known in his community helped him to build trust with the Uzbek leaders. This confirms the main assumptions of the literature on pacts, which claims that a legitimate leader is a necessary condition for effective pact-making (Collins 2006; O'Donnell 1986; O'Donnell and Schmitter 1986).

Avasbek was satisfied with the level of cooperation and the way the Uzbek leaders in Turan complied with all his requests during mediating activities. They made sure to bring all those groups of authoritative figures to meetings with Avasbek at his request. He kept contact with the Uzbek aksakals on daily basis. The main contingent of aksakals who held communication with the Kyrgyz leaders consisted of authoritative figures such as the chair of the territorial council of Turan, kvartkoms, a deputy of the city council, and a well-known Uzbek human rights activist. Avasbek asked them to organize appointments with other types of leaders in Turan, including sportsmen, imams, and other influential people. He conducted peaceful talks with each of these segments. In addition, he was in touch with the Kyrgyz leaders in Uchar. They updated each other about the situation and inquired about the developments. He also kept contacts with the head of the Osh police.

Another important factor that helped to build trust was the history of past interactions between these two communities. For Kyrgyz neighbourhoods near Turan, the important precedent was that in 1990, residents of Turan had not participated in ethnic violence against Kyrgyz. This memory helped to rebuild trustful relations between these neighbourhoods. Furthermore, the fact that Turan had neither common boundaries with other Uzbek mahallas in the city nor direct access route to Uzbekistan's border was also critical. The absence of exit options for the Uzbeks in Turan pushed its communal leaders to carry out more efficient and careful in-group policing and incentives to effectively communicate with the Kyrgyz neighbouring communities. Minor number of residents in the Kyrgyz neighbourhoods surrounding Turan may have created similar incentives for the Kyrgyz side, particularly among Kyrgyz community leaders.

Avasbek shared how his concerns – along with humanitarian beliefs – drove him to actively promote peace and restrain those who wanted to fight with the Uzbeks. Uncertainty and fear created the security dilemma situation among the Kyrgyz and Uzbeks and pushed some of them to think that aggressive attacks against neighbouring communities would provide security and deterrence. However, Avasbek's rational calculations and pragmatic measurement of the intergroup balance of power made him think that the aggression would have created grave consequences for the Kyrgyz community in Toloikon. He feels a situation of tense, fearful, and distrustful relations between two communities would have morphed into one in which immediate or deferred retaliation against the Kyrgyz in Toloikon was likely. Avasbek (interview, September 2013) argued, "If Kyrgyz attacked Turan, the consequences for the Kyrgyz in Toloikon would be grave. There are thirty thousand residents in Turan and in Toloikon there are only ten." According to him, as a hunted and cornered animal, the Uzbeks from Turan would assault the Kyrgyz in Toloikon in a retaliatory attack or out of fear and panic. If the Kyrgyz attacked the Turan Uzbeks from Uchar or from the northern direction to the city (e.g., the Abjalov neighbourhood), Uzbeks would most probably flee toward Toloikon and no one could predict what would happen further. During the meetings with the Uzbeks in Turan, Avasbek also called for peace saying that an open conflict would bring grave outcomes for the Uzbeks too.

The main in-group policing in Toloikon was conducted by three or four authoritative figures under Avasbek's leadership. To enforce self-policing decisions, the leaders relied on a group of about fifteen men, all approximately 40–60 years old and known to the residents of the village as respected and constructively minded persons. This group would pressurize individuals who openly challenged the decisions of the leaders and threaten instigators with harsh sanctions. During his mediating and explanatory activities, Avasbek paid special attention to newcomers and outsiders. He (ibid.) explained the difference in attitudes between locals and outsiders toward Uzbeks: "Those who come from the regions have a particular mood. They are more aggressive [toward Uzbeks]. But in Toloikon, [we] local residents live here. They have their houses here and therefore, they are more cautious and prudent. The most important is to explain things to people competently and then they will listen."

Initially, his peaceful attitudes toward the neighbouring Uzbek community in Turan faced some opposition. When residents first gathered after hearing news from the city, Avasbek and his moderate counterparts made speech about the necessity to keep peace with Turan but some radicals opposed this, calling him a coward and an accomplice of the Uzbeks. However, he managed to quickly suppress the few challengers by threatening them with force. In the end, clear-headed moderates dominated the meeting and the peaceful platform won. To prevent further possible escalation, he prohibited the sale of alcohol in the neighbourhood. Avasbek (ibid.) said, "In every conflict, there are their own leaders emerge among outcasts. They should be immediately suppressed by stronger and sensible leaders." Young men in Toloikon were willing to join "the fight" against Uzbeks out of ethno-nationalist sentiments but Avasbek and his colleagues held them back relying on their traditional authority. In addition to his high social authority, what helped him to maintain authority in the neighbourhood was some welfare activities in everyday life.

Despite sharing many similar structural characteristics such as same location, ethnicity, population size, socioeconomic conditions, and initial structural balance of power, Uchar and Toloikon underwent divergent trajectories to peace. Uchar initially experienced violence but then managed to contain the violence while Toloikon's trajectory was nonviolent without serious challenges to the peace. The divergent trajectories were produced by several factors. Table 6.1 presents the list of structural, spatial, and contingent factors that affected the efficiency of local in-group policing and intergroup non-aggression pacts. These factors are not independent variables but rather a combination of sequential contingent events and independent spatial and structural conditions. If the structural conditions were equal for both Kyrgyz communities, the spatial conditions diverged. More precisely, one but very important spatial condition was different in these two communities – the proximity to interregional roads. As discussed earlier, this factor is crucial for explaining the divergent trajectories in Uchar and Toloikon.

The proximity to interregional roads in Uchar brought into effect another important factor – outsiders. Arrival of outsiders produced several important subsequent changes in the community. It changed the intragroup balance of power and the intergroup negotiation environment by increasing domestic constraints on moderate leaders in Uchar. The leaders were challenged by radical outsiders. This threatened in-group policing and the negotiation process with Turan leaders. However, spatial proximity of interregional roads is not a determinant of violence. As we have seen, Uchar leaders managed to change a violent trajectory toward a peaceful settlement. That what leaders in Nariman failed to do, which we explore in the next section.

FAILED SELF-POLICING AND BROKEN PACT IN NARIMAN

Turan and Nariman are two large Uzbek districts in Osh. This section reconstructs the violent dynamics and juxtaposes structural, spatial-environmental, and contingent factors in Nariman to the same set of conditions in Turan.

Table 6.1
Variation in structural, spatial, and contingent factors and their impact on peaceful/violent trajectories in Toloikon and Uchar

Factors	Toloikon	Uchar
STRUCTURAL		
Ethnodemographic	Segregated, stable community	Segregated, mostly stable community
Initial structural balance of power (constellation of local forces)	Moderates	Moderates
SPATIAL		
Spatial proximity to interregional roads	No	Yes
CONTINGENT (INTERACTIONAL)		
Arrival of outsiders	No	Yes (coalition with local radicals)
Intragroup power shifts	No	Yes (towards radicals)
Negotiation environment	Favourable	Tense (after violent clashes)
Domestic constraints	Small pressure from local radicals	Pressure on moderate leaders from radicals and outsider alliances
In-group policing	Successful	Partially successful
Nonaggression pact	Successful (preventive diplomacy)	Successful
OUTCOME	Peace	Initial violence and then peace

Source: Based on the author's own research.

This structural comparison demonstrates how different types of intragroup and intergroup interactions in these districts caused the variation in outcomes between these two neighbourhoods. Table 6.2 presents the variation in structural, spatial-environmental, and contingent (interactional) factors and their causal impact on the dynamics of violence in Turan and Nariman. It shows that structurally these two districts were similar. Prior to the onset of violence, both districts were segregated with strong social norms and community leadership. These similarities allow us to control for structural conditions. However, spatial-environmental and contingent factors were different. Spatial differentiation has important effect on the security dynamics in these two neighbourhoods.

Nariman presents a case of initially well-conducted in-group policing that later broke down. The interference of external actors, mainly refugees from other locations (such as Furkat) and additional instigators, undermined local policing efforts by Nariman's community leaders.

Table 6.2
Variation in structural, spatial, and contingent factors and their impact on peaceful/violent trajectories in Turan and Nariman

Factors	Turan	Nariman
STRUCTURAL		
Ethnodemographic conditions	Segregated, Uzbek	Segregated, Uzbek
Social norms and community control	Strong	Strong
Initial structural balance of power (constellation of local forces)	Moderates	Moderates
SPATIAL-ENVIRONMENTAL		
Location within the city and surrounding neighbourhoods	Insecure, encircled by Kyrgyz neighbourhoods ("ethnic island")	Secure, mostly surrounded by Uzbek neighbourhoods
Spatial proximity to interregional roads	Yes	Yes
Spatial proximity to Uzbekistan	No	Yes
Environmental conditions for defense (built and natural)	Favourable	Favourable
CONTINGENT (INTERACTIONAL)		
Intragroup power shifts	No	Yes (towards radicals)
Arrival of outsiders	No	Yes (embittered Uzbek refugees)
Negotiation environment	Tense (after violent clashes)	Initial negotiations terminated
Domestic constraints	Small pressure from local radicals (infiltrated by outsiders)	Failed authority of moderate leaders under domination of radical outsiders
In-group policing	Successful	Initially successful but then failed
Nonaggression pact	Successful (pacts with surrounding Kyrgyz neighbourhoods)	Broken agreement with state authorities
TRAJECTORY	Initial violence and then peace	Initial peace and then violence

Source: Based on the author's own research.

More than ten suburban neighbourhoods – practically all located in the northern outskirts of Osh and along the Kyrgyzstan-Uzbekistan border – constitute the Nariman district. Technically a part of the Karasuu raion, the district's mahallas are distinct suburban and predominantly Uzbek neighbourhoods with the total population of around 45,000 residents. Four of this district's mahallas – Nurdar, Nariman, Jim, and Jiydalik – figure in the investigative reports in relation to the ethnic violence. However, in this section,

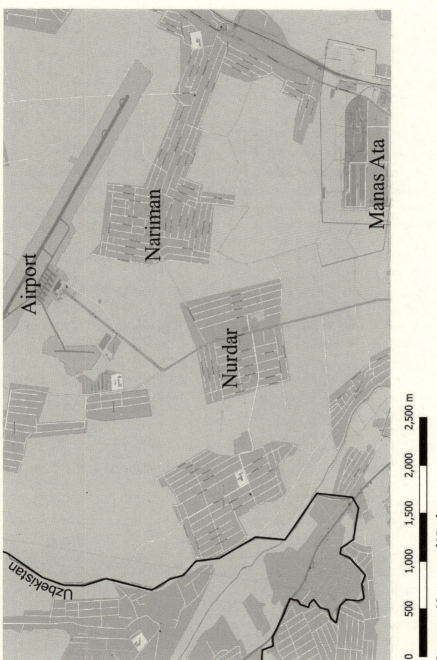

Figure 6.3 Nariman and Nurdar

I discuss the events that took place in one neighbourhood – Nariman – the administrative center of the respective district.

Nariman is a suburban mahalla on the northern outskirts of the Osh city, with around 10,000 people, most of them (82 per cent) being Uzbeks (the Kyrgyz comprise 6 per cent). Like the southern neighbourhoods of Uchar and Toloikon, Nariman and the district's other Uzbek mahallas are extensions of the Osh city in the northern direction. Its geographical position makes it an important and strategic location. The neighbourhood connects Osh with the Osh airport and the Karasuu raion which is the largest raion in Kyrgyzstan, with about 400,000 residents. In the town of Karasuu, there is the famous Karasuu bazaar, the largest commodity bazaar in southern Kyrgyzstan. It emerged in the late 1990s as the main market selling products to entrepreneurs from Uzbekistan. Nariman also hosts a petroleum storage depot – the largest in southern Kyrgyzstan, with a capacity of 7,000 tons.

In international and domestic reports on the communal violence in Osh, Nariman is usually mentioned in relation to the assassination of the head of the Karasuu raion police and his driver by a rioting crowd in Nariman neighbourhood and a subsequent ambiguous sweep operation conducted by the Kyrgyz law-enforcement professionals. However, the reports do not discuss the local violence dynamics in Nariman that led to these assassinations in the first place, and the retaliatory operation by the Kyrgyz police. I argue that the assassinations emerged as a result of failed self-policing in the neighbourhood.

When violence erupted in the city of Osh, the scared local police immediately left Nariman. On 11 June, the first day of violence in Osh, local residents gathered in the neighbourhood and started blocking the main highway connecting Nariman with Osh and the airport. In the initial stages, local community leaders, following instructions from the Osh city administration, managed to convince people to unblock the road. According to Memorial (2012, 179), on the same day, an Uzbek group captured a petroleum storage depot on the outskirts of Nariman, wounding one guard and taking another hostage. However, shortly after, the depot was taken into protection by a local self-defence group.

According to international investigative reports (KIC 2011, 35; Matveeva, Savin, and Faizullaev 2012, 23; Memorial 2012, 179), the depot was instrumental in preventing possible attacks on the neighbourhood by Kyrgyz militant groups. According to the local residents, there were several attempts to enter the neighbourhood by some Kyrgyz groups. A self-defence group that took control over the petroleum storage depot used it as deterrence tool to prevent possible attacks on Nariman, by issuing a threat of exploding the fuel tanks (KIC

2011, 33, 35; Matveeva, Savin, and Faizullaev 2012, 23; Memorial 2012, 179, 181). Local authorities that needed fuel for humanitarian and police operations negotiated a pact with the Nariman residents about access to the fuel tanks. Apparently, the self-defence group in the depot operated independently of the events unfolding in Nariman. When embittered Uzbek refugees tried to take over the depot, a local guard from the self-defence group forestalled their entry by threatening to explode one of the fuel tanks with his rifle (interview with communal leader Nariman, September 2013). While the petroleum tanks helped local residents to prevent possible attacks on Nariman from outside, they did not help them to prevent disorders inside the neighbourhood.

After some groups of Kyrgyz militants attacked various Uzbek mahallas in the Osh city, thousands of Uzbeks fled to the borders shared with Uzbekistan, and Nariman became one of the corridors for refugee flows in that direction. However, as Uzbekistan admitted only women and children to the refugee camps set up in its territory, rejecting all adult men – many of male refugees came back to Nariman which was only a few kilometres away from the border. With the arrival of many displaced Uzbeks in Nariman the situation in the mahalla changed. Local leaders lost control over their constituency. As many of refugees who arrived in the neighbourhood were from the damaged areas exposed to ethnic violence, they began to put pressure on local male residents to "fight" against the Kyrgyz. The situation in the neighbourhood became tense and aggressive. Later, on the evening of 11 June, a 200-strong Uzbek crowd attacked and burned the local police station. According to the head of the local district, the attackers were mostly refugees from other districts (Memorial 2012, 180). The refugees from Furkat, Shark, and other damaged areas played prominent role in creating disorders and calling for retaliating actions. Some Uzbeks in several cars running through the streets of the neighbourhood called for "jihad" against Kyrgyz through loudspeakers (ibid., 180–1).

The excerpt below from an interview with a community leader (Osh, 2013) demonstrates local leaders' initial attempts to conduct in-group policing by efforts to isolate the local constituency from external influences. Under conditions of uncertainty and rumours, when thousands of refugees were passing through Nariman, the primary goal of the local aksakals was to impede a merging of the local population with radical outsiders who could pose a challenge to the traditional authority of Nariman's leaders. The main signal to the local constituency was not to host outsiders in their houses. By attempting to isolate the local constituency from outsiders, local leaders tried to keep the distribution of power in their favour.

When rumours about Kyrgyz wrongdoing emerged on the first day, our aksakals and the imam of the mosque deterred people [from joining the radicals] by saying: "Stop listening to instigations. There is the state. It has the army and police. The state has power. Don't believe such rumours. Those are the [false] words of instigators." I also spoke in front of people on the first day and people dispersed to their mahallas. At that moment, the city [of Osh] was burning. Above the city there was smoke. It was a horrible picture. We told people that the city would be responsible for itself, and we would be for ourselves: "We won't accept anyone [in Nariman], we won't let anyone go out and we won't let anyone enter our neighbourhood. Don't host refugees in your houses. Let them go and pass elsewhere, wherever they want to go. And don't join and don't let your kids join these people. These disorders will stop in a day or two and then you will get what you deserve [according to your actions]. Don't join these people." So, with the aksakals we shouted and told them these words.

The next excerpt shows how the situation changed in Nariman after the onset of ethnic violence in Osh.

When violence broke out on 10 June, we managed to effectively police our community for the first and second days of disorders [in Osh]. We didn't let people go beyond neighbourhood. Some people had already started blocking the main highway. Due to strategic importance of this road, we received the following order [from state authorities]: "You don't have any right to block the road. Everyone should block only [secondary] entrance roads to mahallas. Don't let any [outsider] cars or individuals in and stay inside [mahallas] and restrain your kids [from violence]. Only in this case, will we remain in peace."

And then, starting from the second day, those refugees who had tried to flee to Uzbekistan began to arrive. Our neighbourhood became a corridor to the border with Uzbekistan for those wounded and burned in the disorder. They crossed the neighbourhood toward the border [with Uzbekistan] on Porters [small trucks]. After they [Uzbekistani border guards] had allowed crying women and children to cross the border and rejected males, those young guys moved again toward our neighbourhood. But even then, we still managed to keep order. Later, when new arrivals from other towns [from Osh and surroundings] arrived they ignored and stopped listening either to us or to the neighbourhood council. There, a crowd emerged in the main road and newcomers infiltrated local residents. So, you don't know what their goal is. They don't have any plan and no leaders. It was just a crowd that was not willing to listen to anyone. (interview with local community leader).

The growing number of refugees turned the situation in Nariman increasingly tense and confrontational. A few Kyrgyz residents living in the neighbourhood had to hide in their houses on the advice of the local Uzbek aksakals. In their turn, the Uzbek aksakals tried their best to provide maximum security to the local Kyrgyz residents by organizing a duty roster for guards for, at least, some Kyrgyz houses (interview with local resident September, 2013). The following excerpt from my interview with a leader of the Kyrgyz minority (Osh, 2013) in Nariman shows how security deteriorated and self-policing in Nariman failed.

I was a Kyrgyz living in an Uzbek mahalla. And on the second day, there were a growing number of outsiders in our neighbourhood. In order to avoid their aggression toward me, the aksakals convinced me to go and hide at home. They instructed me not to go out from my house. They told me "Please go home, we will control and protect your house, taking turns (one after another). We will call you back only if there will be a necessity for this and when we have managed people. Otherwise, we won't be able to protect you." So, they made me hide at my house when the number of strangers and outsiders increased in the streets. Then disorder broke out in that place [Nariman]. Unknown people came and burned the police station. They killed the police head of the Karasuu district and his driver. However, I didn't see it because I was at home and couldn't go out. For five days, I remained in my house because every day we had unknown outsiders in our streets. Every day there was disorder, every day there were crowds. Youngsters with their calls to disorder and petrol bombs in their hands didn't want to listen to anybody. They all were outsiders, those who came from down areas [Osh]. They were not our local fellows. They mixed with [infiltrated] our people. They had sticks and metal bars in their hands. Those armed guys increased in numbers in our neighbourhood and infiltrated local people.

The entrance to Nariman was blocked again. On 12 June, a military officer convoying a humanitarian shipment was killed in Nariman by a shot in the head (Memorial 2012, 181). This was a first incident signifying the breakdown of the pact between state authorities and local residents.

Similar events were unfolding in Nurdar, the neighbouring Uzbek mahalla. On 12 June, about 1,500 to 2,000 young Uzbeks, armed with sticks and some with hunting rifles, gathered in the central highway of Nurdar that connected Osh with the Osh airport. The youngsters asked elders not to interfere in the situation. They set up barricades and prepared petrol bombs. The firefight with the military who arrived at the barricades resulted in three deaths among local self-defence groups. Later, officials negotiated with Nurdar to unblock the road connecting the city with the Osh airport for the transit of humanitarian aid (ibid., 181).

On 13 June, while the ethnic violence de-escalated in Osh, it escalated in Nariman. By that time, the outsider militant groups of male refugees from damaged areas enjoyed total domination in the neighbourhood. The involvement of outsiders was a key factor that explains the broken self-policing in this neighbourhood. The radicals who came to Nariman from other locations put pressure on and forced local young males. These groups that witnessed ethnic violence in their own mahallas in Osh, now desired retaliation against the Kyrgyz. They forced local youth to join them and together they stopped passing cars with Uzbek refugees, disembarking the Uzbek males, and demanding that they stay for the defence of Nariman. The following passage from the interview with the communal leader (Osh 2013) shows how outsiders in Nariman tried to pressurize locals into joining fight against Kyrgyz.

> Joldon: However, the outsiders came in anyway?
> Leader: It's a crowd anyway. At that moment, I understood that there were such guys. Then I felt the presence of third and fourth parties. They shouted: "Are you a man? Are you an Uzbek? Why are you not together with people? The Kyrgyz kill all [Uzbeks] one by one. Look, the state now sent the army, airplanes, and tanks [against Uzbeks]. Why should we just sit and wait? Uzbekistan will help us, that's what you will see." There were such calls among people. Then I could see instigation attempts. There was a guy with a covered head – a ninja style, who spoke these words. Then the head of the district came and with the words "what kind of things are you talking about?," and he tore masks off from two of them. There were four guys in masks. All four had knives in their hands.

When the police chief of Karasuu district, together with his driver, both unarmed, arrived in Nariman to negotiate peace, the agitated and uncontrolled crowd of 300 Uzbeks – mostly refugees – attacked the car and brutally killed them both. The police chief came to Nariman together with a deputy head of the Karasuu raion – an ethnic Uzbek – presumably to mediate the situation and to have talks with local residents. The crowd pulled the two policemen out of their car, beat them with sticks and stones and then killed them. The police chief was burned inside his car while his driver was beheaded and pulled down to a river (KIC 2011, 38; Matveeva, Savin, and Faizullaev 2012, 25; Memorial 2012, 183–4). According to the local residents, many of the attackers were Uzbeks from Furkat – one of the most damaged neighbourhoods in the Osh city (Memorial 2012, 184). KIC's version describes the situation as follows: "There was an Uzbek crowd of about 150. Three masked men emerged from the crowd and murdered the police chief and his driver" (KIC 2011, 38). The fact that the deputy head of Karasuu raion did not suffer in this attack highlights the ethnically framed retaliatory character of these killings.

This infamous incident clearly shows that at that moment, local aksakals had completely lost control over the situation and the disorder had been initiated and led by the newly arrived young Uzbek refugees from other districts and neighbourhoods in Osh. The fact that the district police chief arrived without reinforcements and without any arms implies that there was a tentative agreement between him and local leaders about the possibility to unblock the road. However, local elders had already lost control and were not in a position to police their local constituency. As a result, they did not manage to protect the police mediator. The situation remained tense till 19 June (Memorial 2012, 183) when local authorities convinced local residents to unblock the entrance and the main road.

During the conflict, Nariman did not conduct intercommunal nonaggression pacts with neighbouring Kyrgyz blocks as some other Uzbek neighbourhoods in the outskirts of Osh had. One of the main reasons was the above-detailed failed self-policing after local elders lost control over the situation with arrival of hundreds of vindictive young male refugees in the neighbourhood, who undermined the traditional power of the local aksakals and took over domination of the local residents. When a delegation of activists from the Kyrgyz Manas-Ata (HBK) neighbourhood attempted to negotiate reconciliation pact with Nariman they were not able to approach the neighbourhood due to gunfire from Nariman's barricades. Nevertheless, Nariman negotiated an agreement with state authorities that allowed the latter to access the petroleum depot and to use the highway that connected Osh with Nariman. A similar pact was conducted between state authorities and the Uzbek neighbourhood of Nurdar.

The violence in Nariman did not take the shape of open clashes between Kyrgyz and Uzbek combatants and with neighbouring blocks, as happened in some other neighbourhoods in Osh. Generally, Nariman is surrounded by Uzbek neighbourhoods and the only Kyrgyz neighbour – Manas-Ata (НВК) – is one kilometre away from Nariman. However, the disorder in Nariman and the assassination of policemen signified the breakdown of both self-policing and the nonaggression pact.

CONCLUSION

The initial outbreak of violence in Osh triggered fears, distrust, and uncertainty about intentions between ethnic neighbourhoods. For many neighbourhoods striving for survival, the response strategy was to ensure credible peace through negotiating a nonaggression pact with the neighbours.

All cases selected for the comparisons in this chapter were from ethnically segregated neighbourhoods. Therefore, they represent the comparable dynamics of violence and disorder that took place in many other similarly segregated neighbourhoods of Osh. In each selected neighbourhood, there were strong and legitimate local leaders who, under conditions of uncertainty, attempted to conduct in-group policing and negotiate nonaggression pacts to secure their communities. Yet, variation in the outcomes across compared neighbourhoods is evident. While in the southern neighbourhoods, local ethnic communities managed to stop disorder by conducting effective in-group policing and negotiating intercommunal nonaggression pacts, in Nariman, local leaders failed to conduct both in-group policing and a nonaggression pact. The difference in the outcomes between the southern and northern neighbourhoods highlights the importance of the dynamics of intra- and intergroup relations. More specifically, intergroup and, to higher extent, in-group power shifts affected the capacity of leaders to control local communities and to negotiate nonaggression pacts with their counterparts. The local intragroup balance of power within the neighbourhoods was especially important for shaping violent or peaceful outcomes in the localities.

As the paired comparisons selected for this chapter were segregated neighbourhoods, structural conditions were similar in many but not all respects. In particular, spatial factors played an important role in setting local intra- and intergroup power balances. The location of these neighbourhoods within the city as well as the built and natural environments and characteristics of the local road infrastructure had effect on local power distributions and alliance configurations.

One line of comparison in this chapter has been between two Kyrgyz neighbourhoods, Uchar and Toloikon, that managed to keep peace. They negotiated pacts with the same Uzbek partner – Turan. However, each had different domestic constituency configurations and intercommunal negotiation environments. The constellation of domestic forces was different in each neighbourhood, and this affected the dynamics of intercommunal negotiations. The environment of negotiations between Turan and Uchar was difficult due to the strong internal challenge from radical forces that the Uchar leaders faced in their neighbourhood. This variation in domestic constituency configurations resulted from the influx of outsiders in Uchar but not in Toloikon. The proximity of Uchar to Osh's southern regional road made it a destination for outsiders coming from Nookat region. Community leaders experienced strong pressure from outsiders and managed to negotiate with Turan even after violent clashes erupted between these two neighbourhoods. The outcome was contained violence and a nonaggression pact with Turan. On the other hand, Toloikon's remote location from interregional roads prevented arrival of outsiders and ensured more homogenous domestic constituency, lesser internal pressure from radicals, and a successful preventive diplomacy. In Toloikon, the Kyrgyz initiated the pact with Turan, although at the aggregate picture, they were a part of the winning group in Osh. So, both sides were equal in determining the pact despite Toloikon being much smaller than Turan. Nevertheless, Avasbek, the Kyrgyz leader, was interested in negotiating peace as radicals from his neighbourhood could have instigated violence between these two neighbourhoods and then the outcome of possible intercommunal violence could have been grave for Toloikon (interview with Avasbek, September 2013).

The above discussion of negotiation environments in Toloikon and Uchar demonstrates that Uzbek moderate leaders practically remained unchallenged in Turan regarding the question of negotiations with Uchar and other Kyrgyz neighbourhoods. They managed to establish control over the local constituency, forcing out the few radicals from the decision-making process. They maintained communication with the Kyrgyz leaders and were open to negotiation. Effective in-group policing and sanctions against the violators demonstrated that these leaders were credibly committed to the peaceful settlement of intercommunal tensions.

Another condition that helped to reach a local agreement was a perception of rising costs of conflict for both parties. In Osh, rumours of Uzbekistani intervention contributed to such perceptions, especially among the Kyrgyz. The threat of intervention by Uzbekistan and other rumours altered the balance of power in Osh and, according to developments, increased the bargaining leverage of the Uzbek leaders while decreasing the leverage of the Kyrgyz radicals. The dynamics of intergroup power shifts helped to moderate the radicals. In Uchar, the radical coalition was aware of the developments on the Kyrgyzstan-Uzbekistan border and this contributed to the moderation of their demands. On the other hand, the arrival of several Kyrgyz groups in Osh and the attacks on the Uzbek mahallas created incentives for many Uzbek leaders to initiate pacts with the Kyrgyz.

Another line of comparison is between the northern district of Nariman and the southern district of Turan with its Kyrgyz neighbours. Turan/Uchar and Nariman are two cases with contrasting dynamics of disorders. The situation between Turan and Uchar started with an armed clash, but then they managed to contain the violence and restrain the radicals, while in Nariman, local leaders started with effective self-policing, then lost control over situation after the influx of refugees from affected districts in Furkat, Mady, and Shark. Violence broke out in Nariman that resulted in the assassination of the head of district/raion police and his driver.

In this light, the comparison between Nariman and Uchar is instructive. Both experienced intervention by outsiders but the outcomes diverged. In Nariman, initial good policing broke down and violence ensued, and in Uchar, initial violence was contained and an intergroup pact was negotiated. Environmental conditions, including spatial factors, were important as Nariman and Uchar were spatially more disadvantaged in terms of their location. Being located on the main highway leading to the Uzbekistan border exposed Nariman to many aggravated and vindictive male refugees. The influx of outsiders changed the local balance of power. This led to the breakdown of both self-policing and external pact with state authorities. The Kyrgyz leadership in Uchar was also challenged by outsiders from rural areas. The difference in outcomes can be explained by how local leaders dealt with outsiders and how they used the local constituency to keep the in-group balance of power in their favour. Different types of constituency networks and styles of policing affected the final outcomes.

7

Security Dilemma and the Variation in Neighbourhood Responses to Uncertainty in Jalalabat

This chapter explains the puzzle of why neighbourhood-level ethnic communities react differently to ethnic fears by depicting the dynamics of violence in Jalalabat. News and rumours about the violence in Osh produced ethnic fears, intercommunal distrust, and uncertainty. Growing mobilization of ethnic communities produced a security dilemma and triggered preemptive attacks in some neighbourhoods, while prompted intercommunal nonaggression pacts in segregated areas and interethnic alliances based on territorial solidarity in ethnically mixed neighbourhoods. The chapter outlines this notable variation in the neighbourhood responses by comparing the cases of four neighbourhoods. Each neighbourhood displays a distinct response and diverges in conditions that shaped that response toward the emerging uncertainty. The concluding section of this chapter compares the outcomes in these four neighbourhoods. It also accounts for the general patterns and differences in dynamics of violence across towns of Jalalabat, Osh, and Uzgen.

The city of Jalalabat is the second largest city in southern Kyrgyzstan and an administrative center of the Jalalabat oblast. In 2010, it was the second most violent locality after Osh. The town's official population is more than 100,000, but this does not include about 20,000–30,000 unregistered internal economic migrants living in the city and around 30,000–50,000 people, who, according to an official in the provincial administration, come and go from the rural districts to Jalalabat on an everyday basis for business, shopping, employment, and administration and bureaucracy-related issues.

The urban landscape visibly divides the city into three distinct parts: (1) the center, dominated by individual unit house type of neighbourhoods with few apartment buildings of two to five storeys dispersed across those neighbourhoods; (2) the Sputnik district, with its high concentration of apartment buildings of four to six storeys; and (3) suburban neighbourhoods and residential areas that are officially not a part of the city but socially and economically integrated in the city's urban life. Jalalabat is surrounded by the Kyrgyz and Uzbek villages of the Suzak raion. Few villages in the suburban districts are ethnically mixed; most are thus either predominantly Uzbek or Kyrgyz by ethnic composition. The Kyrgyz villages are chiefly located in the mountainous and hilly landscape, with a few in the valley. The Uzbek villages are in the valley, mainly along the Uzbekistan borders.

The violence diffused to Jalalabat on the second day of communal warfare in Osh. The scenario of events was similar to Osh and proceeded in two stages: the first stage was violent mobilization of Uzbeks in Jalalabat and Suzak and attacks on Kyrgyz. This was followed by a second stage characterized by countermobilization of rural Kyrgyz from the mountainous villages and Jalalabat's surroundings, followed by clustered mass arson of Uzbek houses in the town.

The following section presents the chronology of violence in Jalalabat. It shows that just as in Osh, neighbourhoods in Jalalabat produced divergent responses to the similar threat. The second section outlines this notable variation in neighbourhood responses by presenting the cases of four neighbourhoods. Furthermore, it discusses the impact of spatial factors on the dynamics and distribution of violence in Jalalabat. The concluding section summarizes the findings of this chapter and compares outcomes in four neighbourhoods.

CHRONOLOGY OF VIOLENCE IN JALALABAT

One of the main problems in reconstructing violent events in Jalalabat is that clashes in this town did not receive close attention from investigative commissions who were mainly focused on investigating violence in Osh. Therefore, this short reconstruction of events is based on my witness interviews, brief mentions in investigative reports and mass media, and my informal conversations with local residents.

11 June

It was calm on the morning of 11 June, but in the afternoon the streets suddenly became deserted upon arrival of news and rumours about the violence in Osh. Some Uzbeks began to leave their houses and to flee Jalalabat and refugees from Osh started arriving in the town. Various rumours spread among both ethnic communities. A group of 100–300 Kyrgyz gathered at the roundabout between Jalalabat and Suzak, while Uzbeks gathered at another roundabout located on the Bishkek-Osh road. Around 500 Uzbeks gathered in Suzak to discuss the situation in Osh. They decided to organize the barricading of streets at the entrances to Suzak, Jalalabat's suburban area, and to organize self-defence groups. Some wanted to go to Osh to help their ethnic fellows. Uzbek communities in Jalalabat initiated evacuation of women and children toward Uzbekistan's border (Joint Working Group 2012). This caused rumours among the Kyrgyz that by evacuating women, the Uzbeks were preparing for war and attacks against the Kyrgyz. An atmosphere of fear and panic emerged in Jalalabat, fuelled by rumours and horrible news from Osh. The streets of Jalalabat became deserted.

At 2 p.m., a Kyrgyz journalist tried to evacuate his family from the suburban Suzak, which was ethnically dominated by Uzbeks. He could not get into the village as shuttles, taxi, and regular cars had already stopped their trips to Suzak fearing attacks or possible provocations. His family had managed to escape Suzak and flee to Sputnik, a Kyrgyz neighbourhood in Jalalabat, when local Uzbeks started constructing barricades at the entrance streets. The journalist also managed to hail a passing car at the Suzak roundabout. When the car was passing near the University of Peoples' Friendship (hereafter UDN)[1] toward the town at very high speed, there was already a large Uzbek crowd armed with metal bars and sticks. The crowd had already crashed down several cars. At the same time, some Kyrgyz people from the nearby mountainous villages came down to the town's hippodrome. According to a police officer, around 500 Kyrgyz gathered on the central square after hearing news that Uzbeks were shooting and killing Kyrgyz motorists and passengers on the Bishkek-Osh highway near the Sanpa cotton factory located close to Suzak and to the west of Jalalabat. However, the mobilization was still weak and by the evening the Kyrgyz crowd in the square dispersed (interview with a police officer, October 2013).

12 June

The next morning, a group of about 500–600 Kyrgyz people moved from central Jalalabat toward Suzak. On their way to Suzak, the Kyrgyz came upon a large Uzbek crowd of 3,000–5,000, who had gathered around UDN, which is located along the street connecting Jalalabat and Suzak. Violence near the Sanpa cotton factory continued. A group of Uzbeks from Suzak set a trap for passing cars along the Bishkek-Osh highway. They poured oil on the hill slope, so that cars going uphill would slow down. Uzbeks at the Sanpa factory then shot and killed Kyrgyz drivers and passengers. Dozens were severely beaten and some taken hostage. Attackers released the non-Kyrgyz passengers. "An uncontrolled crowd of 2,000 Uzbeks" from Suzak participated in these mass violent disorders at Sanpa (interview with an Uzbek community leader, Suzak, October 2013). The killings at Sanpa had a negative escalating effect on dynamics of violence in Jalalabat. They fuelled violent attitudes and mobilization among the Kyrgyz rural population, especially those who gathered at the hippodrome.

At approximately the same time, a large group of armed Uzbeks attacked the central provincial police headquarters from the side of the VLKSM Park in the central part of the city. A deputy head of the provincial police (interview, Jalalabat 2013) was sitting in his office on the ground floor when he observed several armed Uzbek men through his window running near his office. He jumped out of his chair and rushed to his lock box where he kept his automatic rifle. He called the police officers to arms. The police left the building and moved toward the park to face attackers but fell into a trap. Surrounded by Uzbek combatants who were hiding in the park and on the roofs of some houses in the adjacent Uzbek mahalla, the police officers came under heavy fire. In this gunfire exchange, the police lost two officers and a further sixteen were wounded. After this, the police ran back into the building of the police headquarters. At that moment, special police troops (SOBR) arrived to aid the trapped police. Some of the Uzbek attackers fled toward Uzbek Kojo mahalla in Tash Bulak, the northeastern part of the town. Other attackers continued to keep their positions in the Uzbek mahalla adjacent to the park and the central mosque firing at the police from rifles and small-bore guns. According to the same police officer, the police managed to detain two of the attackers in possession of firearms, which had allegedly been distributed at the UDN.

During the next days, the Central Provincial Police Headquarters underwent further attacks, but this time from Kyrgyz combatants. The first Kyrgyz crowd captured Tashiev, a prominent politician from the ousted president Bakiev's inner circle, demanding firearms. Being a local strongman in Jalalabat he was unsuccessfully trying to mediate the crowd. Later the same group brought him on an APC toward Suzak where he managed to convince the Kyrgyz not to attack the suburb. Of the other Kyrgyz groups that attacked the Central Provincial Police Headquarters, one was headed by Bakiev's brother Ahmat and another was led by a criminal gang. Both groups demanded weapons but were refused (interview with a high-ranking police officer, Jalalabat, October 2013). According to another police officer (interview Jalalabat, 2013), he heard the trapped police officers' calls for help through police radio transmitter but was unable to help because his squad was also in difficult situation on the Lenin Street.

On that day, Kyrgyz men assembled at the hippodrome and waited until afternoon. They did not see any representatives of the authorities or police. Then Kamchybek Tashiev, an opposition politician at the time, addressed those gathered, stating that he had negotiated peace with the Uzbeks and the men should go home. The crowd did not want to listen, as bodies of dead Kyrgyz killed by the Uzbeks were carried past them for burials. Women shouted at them to "go and save Jalalabat." The men grew agitated, and finally attacked the Uzbek mahallas along the Pushkin Street in the afternoon. (Matveeva, Savin, and Faizullaev 2012, 32).

Another group of Kyrgyz people from the villages of upper Suzak raion also gathered at the town's hippodrome. A governor of Jalalabat province attempted to address the crowd but was beaten by people in the crowd. Tashiev, mentioned in the previous episode, tried to disperse the mob but news about killings of Kyrgyz at Sanpa and attacks on Kyrgyz near the UDN aggravated people in the crowd. They stopped listening to the politician and moved toward the city. The report prepared by some former members of the KIC mission (ibid., 32–3) describes the movement of the Kyrgyz crowd from the hippodrome toward the city center:

> As they advanced, they were shot at from locations at the mosque, lyceum and the city hospital. Uzbeks fired hunting rifles, hiding behind KAMAZ lorries used to block the roads. Some Kyrgyz were wounded and taken to the hospital in Oktyabrskoe [village]. The Kyrgyz armed with sticks, retreated, but returned with firearms and shot back at the Uzbeks. The Kyrgyz crowd grew, although it lost several wounded and dead, and the Uzbeks started to retreat. Uzbek-owned shops were burned because of anger that the Uzbeks shot, and the Kyrgyz could not respond, but now they at least could destroy their properties. Kyrgyz explained that if the Uzbeks did not shoot at them first, violence would not happen in Jalalabad.

As this report shows, the Kyrgyz group was attacked from Kojo mahalla in Tash Bulak district where the city hospital and Khazret-Ayub Mosque are in close proximity. As some of my Kyrgyz respondents indicated, the Kyrgyz crowd was making its way along Pushkin Street toward the UDN when they

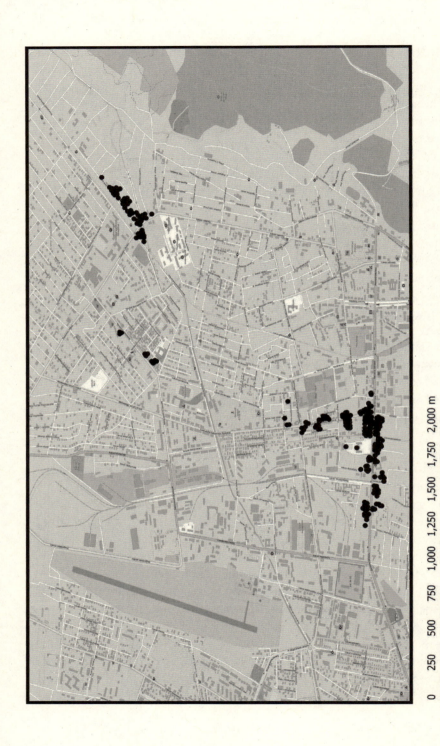

Figure 7.1 Overview of the property damage in Jalalabat

were attacked by Uzbeks from Tash Bulak. This gunfire attack made Tash Bulak a flashpoint of violence. Being unarmed, the Kyrgyz retreated, coming to the conclusion that they could not resist the Uzbeks without first acquiring firearms. The Kyrgyz attacked a military garrison in Kokart, in the western outskirts of the city, and later the abovementioned provincial police building. They apprehended an APC and three Kalashnikov automatic rifles (Joint Working Group 2012). With this weapon, they returned to Tash Bulak and attacked the mahalla. The Kyrgyz burnt several dozen already deserted empty houses in the peripheral area of the mahalla but could not penetrate deep inside because of intensive gunfire exchange.

Another Kyrgyz group of 500–600 people, started moving toward Suzak, Jalalabat's suburban area. Near the UDN, they came across a large Uzbek group of several thousand people. The Uzbek group – all men – burned several buildings, including Jalalabat TV, a customs outpost, and traffic police building, along with six Kyrgyz-owned cafes located along Suzak-Jalalabat road. The two crowds stoned each other. A direct clash was prevented by forty police troops who formed a thin line between two groups. Sometime later, twenty special police troops were re-routed to the Sanpa factory. After some of the police left, a group of Uzbeks went out from the UDN building and adjacent mahallas and shot at the Kyrgyz, killing one or two of them. The Kyrgyz were forced out. The police also were attempting to persuade the Kyrgyz, in their own interests, to retreat. The remaining twenty police officers were forced out as well to the Krasin Street. Youngsters of Uzbek nationality were aggressively springing from the narrow mahalla streets behind the police line. The police slowly retreated. The crowd was aiming to go to the city center but at that time an APC arrived and Uzbeks dispersed. It was already late evening (around 8–10 p.m.). The police also sought refuge in the building of the town police as there were many aggressive groups roaming the city streets. On a radio transmitter, they heard calls for aid from the provincial police department, which was taking gunfire from Uzbek attackers, but were unable to help. Throughout the night, there were intensive gunfire exchanges between unidentified groups (interview with a police officer, Jalalabat, 2013).

13 June

The next day, the Kyrgyz crowd continued their attacks against the mahallas in Tash Bulak and near UDN. The advantage was now on the Kyrgyz side. The day before, the Kyrgyz had captured some weapons by storming military garrisons in the Chatkal, Toktogul, and Mailuu-Suu raions, all located in Jalalabat province. However, the Uzbeks took active actions in different parts of the city. A Kyrgyz crowd tried to enter some ethnically mixed blocks in the Dostuk and Kurmanbek districts in the central part of the city but were rebuffed at barricades by local residents. The crowd then turned toward Tash Bulak. Another group of more than 1,000–2,000 people attacked UDN and the adjacent mahallas, burning empty Uzbek houses along the Krasin and Lenin streets; the highest concentration being at the intersection of these two streets where UDN was located. This area became the largest cluster of property destruction in Jalalabat. This was a final blow to the Uzbek militant groups as the territory within and around UDN served as the basis for Uzbek mobilization. The destruction of UDN and the surrounding area completed the defeat against Uzbek armed groups. Although some Uzbek combatant groups still operated in the city, the general intergroup balance of power conclusively shifted toward the Kyrgyz groups. The report by Matveeva and her collaborators (Matveeva, Savin, and Faizullaev 2012, 33) describes the dynamics of violence on 13 June:

> On 13 June, the Uzbeks could no longer contain the Kyrgyz advance. Crowds moved in from two directions. The one equipped with an APC, moving along Pushkin Street, attacked Uzbek neighbourhood of Tash Bulak/Hodja [Kojo] mahalla. Uzbek armed groups operated throughout the city, clashing with the Kyrgyz. A crowd of rural Kyrgyz men besieged the police headquarters and the administration, demanding weapons and threatening to overpower the authorities. A tense standoff ensued, but the shots fired by the troops over the rioters' heads created a sobering impact. This opened the way for negotiations between informal leaders and the authorities, after which the Kyrgyz men agreed to disperse. Some did indeed go away, while others engaged in wanton destruction and looting. Sporadic fighting between Kyrgyz and Uzbek groups continued at several city locations on 14 June.

The same day, police reinforcements arrived from Bishkek and the police took greater control over the city.

14 June

The police managed to establish roadblocks at some streets, on the previous day, and to send police troops to Sanpa on 14 June, to stop violence. Young Kyrgyz looted Uzbek houses but when police fired in the air they fled. Furthermore, a large Kyrgyz crowd of 7,000–8,000 mostly young people moved to attack Suzak where they thought many radical Uzbek leaders were hiding. At the entrance to Suzak, Tashiev and other community leaders convinced Kyrgyz not to attack this suburb.

Assessment of the Situation

During 12–15 June, the city streets were closed by barricades. One police officer that I spoke with (Jalalabat, October 2013) wanted to go to the district of Sputnik but could not reach it till 14 June due to heavy firefights in the city and the roadblocks built in many neighbourhoods that substantially impaired transport communication and movement in the city. The troops came under fire in Uzbek mahallas. The officer's family lived in an Uzbek mahalla near Sputnik. When violence broke out, they hid in a house of an Uzbek traffic police officer. When he and his troops managed to reach Sputnik in the early morning of 14 June, his squad came under fire from a Kyrgyz group led by an APC and a black car that sought to attack the Uzbek mahalla.

In Suzak, local residents blocked the entrances to the neighbourhood. Militant groups of Uzbeks dug trenches around a local police station (Matveeva, Savin, and Faizullaev 2012, 34). They besieged and attacked the police station which had before sent half of its contingent to Jalalabat. Attackers demanded firearms and release of Uzbek prisoners from jail. Local Kyrgyz families living in this area were in difficult and ambiguous situation. They could not leave the neighbourhood and found themselves practically being hostages.

How was it possible that a large crowd of several thousand stopped and agreed to disperse just in front of the entrance to Suzak? First, among many there were perceptions that the Uzbeks were heavily armed and well prepared to rebuff Kyrgyz attacks with firearms. These perceptions were founded on rumours, stereotypes, and also some concrete evidence. Rumours about Uzbeks arming themselves had been circulating among Kyrgyz in Osh, Jalalabat, Uzgen, and other locations long before the 2010 communal violence. As the various investigative reports indicate, many Kyrgyz believed that Uzbeks had started arming themselves after the 1990 communal violence. In May and the beginning of June 2010, circulation of these rumours sharply increased along with increasing intercommunal tensions. Perceptions about strong Uzbek communalism made the Kyrgyz believe that the arms distribution was taking place at communal level. When violence broke out in Jalalabat, the advantage was on the side of the Uzbeks as they used some firearms against the unarmed Kyrgyz during first intercommunal clashes in the city. This fact convinced the Kyrgyz even more that the Uzbeks had been preparing for insurgency. Sometimes, police officers exploited this rumour in an attempt to demobilize the Kyrgyz groups. According to a police officer (interview, Jalalabat 2013), during the intercommunal clashes near UDN on 12 June, the police was persuading the Kyrgyz crowd not to attack the Uzbek mahalla behind UDN by claiming that the Uzbeks were heavily armed. This tactic probably had some preventive effect. The Kyrgyz participants did not risk advancing in internal parts of the densely populated Uzbek mahallas out of fear being trapped and killed by the armed Uzbek groups.

Second, the Kyrgyz were aware that some Kyrgyz families remained in Uzbek mahallas and particularly, in Suzak. Kyrgyz mediators emphasized this reason to stop youngsters from attacking Suzak. The following excerpt from an interview with a Kyrgyz nationalist journalist (Jalalabat, 2013) and reveal perceptions and concerns among the Kyrgyz in the crowd.

> Journalist: On 14 June, I observed movements of the [Kyrgyz] crowd. They wanted to go to Suzak and attempted to enter the village. But thanks to Tashiev – and I also participated – we managed to stop the crowd telling them that there was no need to enter Suzak. Why? Because, according to our information in Suzak they [local Uzbeks] were heavily armed and prepared. Then they would massacre our unarmed crowd. And after that, in turn, Kyrgyz [from villages] would rise with vengeful intentions and then the real massacre [of Uzbeks] would start. Thanks to Tashiev, we managed to stop it. At that point, disorders in Jalalabat had stopped. It is not the authorities who stopped [violence] but wise Kyrgyz citizens. They stopped this slaughterhouse. I am a witness; I was among these people. But, of course, I did not participate in those disorders. On 12 June, I didn't go to the streets. On 13 June, I went to the streets, but I was fearful with my other fellows to join the crowds. We were on our own.
> This was a very dangerous moment. It was not so tough here as in Osh thanks to prudent Kyrgyz. Because Kyrgyz stopped each other. We told youngsters: "There is no need [to continue]. Uzbeks got what they deserved. Let's stop this. What's done is done." I myself was among numerous youths. I admonished them: "My family is taken

Figure 7.2 The largest cluster of property damage in Jalalabat

hostage there [in Suzak]. If you go there, they [Uzbeks] will kill them." I repeated this in different ways and we managed to stop them.
Joldon: Did not your family manage to get out from there?
Journalist: They did. Nevertheless, there were other families remaining as hostages. They gathered in one large house. If something happened, they [Uzbeks] would finish them off. They stayed there as hostages. First, we stopped [the Kyrgyz crowd] in order to save them [Kyrgyz hostages]. Second, we spared the lives of these young boys [in the Kyrgyz crowd]. We had the following information, real or false: they [Uzbeks in Suzak] were armed. They received weapons from Uzbekistan. They had made accurately all reconnaissance in advance. They were waiting for us correctly selecting all firing standpoints. If our boys approached, they [Uzbeks] would massacre them. And when we received such information, we tried to stop them to avoid big, big bloodshed. That day our boys would get massacred and this would not stop like this. All Kyrgyz would mobilize, gather, and enter Suzak and then severe massacre would start. That would bring serious consequences. Our state would disappear. Therefore, at this point we had to think with cold blood.

As soon as violence broke in the town, many neighbourhoods erected barricades fearing attacks from the other side. This was especially characteristic of the neighbourhoods with densely clustered individual housing units. Almost the whole central zone of the town was barricaded, making free movement across the neighbourhoods extremely difficult. Barricades and roadblocks not only paralyzed the mobility of police, firefighters, and ambulances, but they also constrained the movement of raging crowds and combatants. In such situation, barricading the main streets became counterproductive for those local self-defence groups who wanted to secure themselves by blocking central streets and avenues. Those barricades especially triggered the outrage of the Kyrgyz mobs as they considered them as an act of Uzbek hostility toward the Kyrgyz (interview with a local leader, Jalalabat 2013). After demolishing barricades, furious crowds would attack neighbouring houses. This particularly happened on Krasin Street (Kyrgyz Respublikasy/Kyrgyz Republic Street), which became a part of the largest cluster of mass arson in the town.

DIVERGENT RESPONSES OF THE JALALABAT NEIGHBOURHOODS TO UNCERTAINTY

The sections below assess the divergent responses of four neighbourhoods selected from each of Jalalabat's four districts. Each neighbourhood displays a distinct response and conditions that shaped its response to the emerging ethnic violence and uncertainty.

Quarter 1 (Aitmatov District, Southeastern Neighbourhoods): Nonaggression Pact with Kyrgyz Neighbourhoods

Some neighbourhoods in Jalalabat relied on informal pacts with the adjacent Kyrgyz or Uzbek neighbourhoods and villages. Among those few were Uzbek-dominated neighbourhoods in the southeastern part of the town, in the Aitmatov district. They negotiated intercommunal cooperation with Kyrgyz neighbourhoods and villages of the Barpy suburban district. Below is an example of one interethnic cooperation pact initiated by the Kyrgyz leaders from Barpy which had positive implications for preserving peace and order in the mostly Uzbek neighbourhood despite being negotiated among a very small number of community leaders. This pact shows that in some instances negotiations among few leaders could produce peaceful outcomes on the condition that the leaders were in relatively full control of their constituency and able to successfully police their neighbourhood communities. This and some other nonaggression pacts in the Osh city brokered by the Kyrgyz side show that despite being in a less vulnerable position during this ethnic conflict – relatively to many Uzbek neighbourhoods that were under great threat, some Kyrgyz leaders took the initiative to preserve peace and rebuild trust between two ethnic communities. This goes against the widely portrayed image of the Kyrgyz as being the aggressors in this conflict.

On 12 June, when violent mass disorders broke out in the streets of Jalalabat, neighbourhoods in the Aitmatov district experienced different outcomes in terms of violence. A railway divides this district into two distinct parts. Those neighbourhoods located along Lenin Street near UDN were a stronghold zone of Batyrov – a leader of the Jalalabat's Uzbek community. They became active hotspots in violent Uzbek mobilization and were later attacked by Kyrgyz rural groups. Some youngsters from these neighbourhoods participated in anti-Kyrgyz mobilization and violence, joining a crowd of several thousand Uzbeks that belonged to the clientelist networks of Batyrov. Armed groups from these networks attacked the central police headquarters killing two and wounding nineteen police officers. Later they attacked a Kyrgyz group near UDN, killing one or two Kyrgyz. When a large Kyrgyz crowd came to take a revenge, it attacked neighbourhoods located near UDN, including those in the western part of Aitmatov district. According to a senior secretary of this district (interview with a local official, Jalalabat, October 2013), in the territory of Aitmatov district, forty-three houses were burned along the Lenin Street and ten along the Nizami Street.

The eastern part of the district, comprising both ethnically mixed and homogenous Uzbek neighbourhoods, remained silent and peaceful. On the first day of communal violence, leaders of neighbourhood called "Quarter 1" set up headquarters to monitor the situation. Two Kyrgyz men came to the headquarters from the neighbouring Kyrgyz district of Barpy. They inquired about who was the head of the headquarters. Makam, a local Uzbek community leader, responded identifying himself as the head.[2] When he introduced himself the two Kyrgyz men recognized him by his name. They asked Makam not to block the old Jalalabat-Osh road which connected the Kyrgyz communities in Barpy with central Jalalabat. They gave Makam assurances of the security of his community. They explained that Barpy needed access to the town. The Kyrgyz warned that if the road was blocked, they could not ensure the security of Quarter 1 and the neighbourhoods of the eastern part of Aitmatov district in general. Blocking the road would trigger an accumulation of young people in front of barricades and, in that case, the Kyrgyz from Barpy could not guarantee that they would be able to deter those youngsters from attacking Makam's neighbourhood. Makam and his Kyrgyz guests exchanged phone numbers. It turned out that the Kyrgyz men were heads of similar headquarters in Barpy. At the end, they suggested Makam to call them if youngsters from Barpy created problems in his neighbourhood.

Problems emerged very soon. One young Uzbek resident of Quarter 1 was beaten by some unknown Kyrgyz. They hijacked his small porter truck. Makam called the headquarters in Barpy, informing them about the fact of this opportunistic behaviour from the Kyrgyz side. In two hours, the Kyrgyz headquarters in Barpy called him back notifying that the hijacked truck was found. The Kyrgyz returned the truck with apologies. On the next occasion, still during the conflict, the Kyrgyz from Barpy made a phone call to Makam seeking his assistance. Among the Kyrgyz in Barpy, some rumours emerged about young Kyrgyz women being taken hostage by Uzbeks and held captive and possibly sexually abused in the basement of the medical college in the neighbouring Kurmanbek district. The leaders of Barpy suggested Makam accompany them to the medical college to check the plausibility of the rumours. In case they were stopped by Uzbeks, Makam had to talk to Uzbek self-defence groups and negotiate their passage through the Uzbek-dominated areas. Makam agreed to accompany the Kyrgyz, but under one condition: the Kyrgyz had to guarantee his personal safety. Both parties agreed on terms of security and went toward the medical college. When they were approaching the areas affected by violence near the medical college, Makam and his Kyrgyz counterparts heard an intense gunfire exchange. The Kyrgyz decided that they could not guarantee Makam's safety and brought him back home. The above example clearly shows that Kyrgyz leaders from Barpy committed to their responsibility to keep Makam safe also because it was essential for keeping trust between two communities.

One important aspect in keeping peace between Uzbek-dominated quarters in the city and Kyrgyz suburban communities in Barpy was that residential community in Quarter 1 decided – as they were advised – not to block the main street that connected Barpy with the city of Jalalabat. In the beginning, a natural reaction to the emerging uncertainty among the Uzbek residents in the Aitmatov district, and in Quarter 1 particularly, was to block the road with their Kyrgyz neighbours. This initiative was raised by the younger Uzbek residents of this neighbourhood shortly after the violence broke out in the city. The blocking of the road was prevented by local community leaders, especially after the representatives of the Kyrgyz community in Barpy requested them not to do so. In their dispute about the construction a barricade along the old Jalalabat-Osh road, Makam argued that any barricade could be demolished by machinery, yet this would trigger accumulation of Kyrgyz people in front of barricades and eventual attacks on the neighbourhood and mass arson of houses. The elder managed to convince against blocking the road and his platform won the dispute.

In general, the local community decided to refrain from building barricades as it felt itself at a sufficiently secure distance from major flashpoints of violence in the city. Only in some neighbourhoods did they establish ethnically mixed patrols that inquired from strangers entering the neighbourhood about the purpose of their visits. This strategy proved effective as the Kyrgyz youths from Barpy who wanted to participate in clashes in flashpoint areas in

Jalalabat peacefully passed through Makam's and other neighbourhoods of the eastern part of Aitmatov district. No one attacked the local Uzbeks there throughout the period of communal violence.

Quarter 8 (Dostuk District):
Self-Policing and Interethnic Cooperation

The Dostuk district is located in the central part of the city. Officially it has a population of around 27,000 residents with nearly equal distribution of Kyrgyz and Uzbek populations – 9,500 and 7,600 registered voters respectively (interview with a local official, October 2013, Jalalabat). Dwellers live in seventy-six multistorey apartment buildings, many of them between two and four storeys high, and 3,800 individual housing units. Uzbeks mainly dominate in older historical quarters while Kyrgyz live in the multistorey apartment buildings. However, Dostuk is the most ethnically mixed urban district in Jalalabat where in many of its neighbourhoods the Uzbeks and the Kyrgyz live side by side. The VLKSM Park, the Central Provincial Police Headquarters, the Imam-Bukhari Central Mosque, and the Krasin Street – locations that figured earlier in the earlier description of violence – are all located in this district. In contrast to Osh, the bazaar in Jalalabat is decentralized into several specialized markets: food, furniture, construction materials, and household goods. The majority of them, except the food market, are located in Dostuk.

The zone with the most property damage during communal violence was along the Krasin Street, especially in the location where it intersects with the Lenin Street, near UDN. Houses on the Krasin Street were burned by the Kyrgyz crowds which moved from the hippodrome toward UDN. According to local witnesses, those houses were torched after their movement was hindered by massive roadblocks. It is unclear if the Kyrgyz moving toward UDN through the Krasin Street were provoked by gunfire from the local Uzbek armed groups as happened on the Pushkin Street, in the area of the Khazret-Ayub Mosque and the town hospital, near the Kojo mahalla/Tash Bulak mahalla. However, the roadblocks enraged the crowd which after demolishing them started torching nearby houses. Fortunately, the large destruction of property in this area did not cause a high death rate among civilians as many local Uzbek residents had abandoned their houses beforehand and evacuated their valuable property. However, the highest concentration of property damage and probably of highest mortality was at the intersection of the Krasin and Lenin streets, in the close vicinity of UDN, where the most militant participants of mass disorders from both sides clashed.

As we have seen in the cases of Quarter 1 in Jalalabat and Furkat and Cheremushki in Osh, the decision about building barricades on principal streets is a controversial issue could be a counterproductive strategy. Before the violence escalated, local neighbourhood communities in Dostuk had held some meetings where the neighbourhood leaders discussed their strategic responses toward the escalating violence. Despite some local Kyrgyz leaders' warnings to Uzbeks against building barricades on principal roads such as the Krasin Street, the latter decided to erect the roadblocks expecting attacks by the Kyrgyz horse riders from the nearby mountainous villages (interview with a local official, October 2013).

Nevertheless, most neighbourhoods in Dostuk district did not experience attacks from violent groups despite the fact that local dwellers had constructed barricades. But these were typical neighbourhoods of small streets with individual unit houses. Those neighbourhoods selected a self-isolation strategy by encircling themselves by a set of barricades on small and secondary streets. Residents set up ethnically mixed patrols that did not let strangers enter their neighbourhoods. When militant groups approached roadblocks, local residents of the same ethnicity would deny the passage through a neighbourhood and protect their neighbours of the other ethnicity. For instance, when groups of rural Kyrgyz from the hippodrome came to Dostuk neighbourhoods, they were calmly but decisively rebuffed and redirected by the local Kyrgyz residents.

One example of such a self-isolation strategy is a neighbourhood called Quarter 8 in the Dostuk district. Being one of the typical neighbourhoods which one can find in the central part of the town, Quarter 8 comprises 24 small streets and 530 individual housing units. The quarter's 2,750 residents are distributed equally along ethnic lines: 1,390 Uzbeks and 1,300 Kyrgyz living together, house by house. This makes Quarter 8 one of the most mixed neighbourhoods in Jalalabat.

When armed fights erupted in the town, the residents of Quarter 8 closed their internal streets with roadblocks. On 12 June, a local domkom, a Kyrgyz aksakal named Konokbek, collected 100 soms (2 US dollars) from each household to slaughter a cow. The neighbourhood's residents prayed together to consolidate their communal unity. Both Kyrgyz and Uzbek residents came forward together in defence of their neighbourhood. According to Konokbek (interview, Jalalabat 2013), those neighbourhoods in Dostuk with strong

Kyrgyz-Uzbek cooperation did not let in fighters of any ethnicity and managed to redirect them to other places. His neighbourhood dealt mainly with a Kyrgyz group that came from the hippodrome. Consequently, the Kyrgyz men from the hippodrome turned their route toward the Kojo mahalla without attempting to assail any Uzbek houses in Quarter 8. Later, another Kyrgyz group that came from the direction of the Krasin Street was also rebuffed by local dwellers. In the end, there were no killings and no active clashes in this neighbourhood despite being closely located, approximately one kilometre, to a hotspot of violence near the provincial hospital. Quarter 8 did not suffer property damage either, except one burnt house located in the periphery of the neighbourhood along the principal street that leads to Tash Bulak. This is in sharp contrast with a neighbouring community located on the other side of the road on the border with Quarter 8. That neighbourhood had thirteen houses destroyed and three damaged as result of attacks that spilled over from fierce fights between the Kyrgyz and the Uzbeks on the Pushkin Street, near the Kojo mahalla/Tash Bulak.

The fortunes of Quarter 8 in avoiding violence can be explained by combination of strong self-policing and interethnic cooperation stemming from intercommunal trust and lack of fear and based on relatively strong quotidian civic engagement among the residents of the neighbourhood. Community-based activities such as festivities, feast, funerals, celebrations, and weddings take place with participation of both ethnic groups. Each resident, irrespective of ethnicity, contributes a small amount of money every month for community needs. These common funds are usually used for community works aimed at improving local infrastructure or to help to needy families to organize funerals. Each event of this kind is discussed with elected neighbourhood aksakals where they decide on reasonable expenses. The community assigns responsible young men to enforce rules and to monitor and control the situation during festivities and prevent possible violations and brawls.

Community leaders conduct strong social control over the neighbourhood's residents. There is a relatively low number of internal migrants and all of them are registered by the quarter's head who closely monitors them. The low number of outsiders makes this neighbourhood socially homogenous and cohesive and relatively easy for communal leaders to monitor and manage the domain. Konokbek, a head of the quarter, conducts interviews with each new arrival and interrogates them about the purpose of their stay in the neighbourhood. He monitors them to make sure that they pay utility costs in time and do not violate local social norms and order. In his personal journal, he registers each migrant (*kvartirant*) and their passport data. This, he does to monitor them within his neighbourhood. Elected aksakals help him in managing and organizing the neighbourhood. The example of Quarter 8 shows the mechanisms of self-policing and represents the situation that that is similar to some other ethnically mixed neighbourhoods in Jalalabat.

Kojo mahalla/Tash Bulak (Kurmanbek District): Preemptive Aggression

The Kurmanbek district is located in the eastern part of the town. It officially has around 25,000 inhabitants, both Kyrgyz and Uzbeks. The majority of the district's residents live in old mahallas, comprising more than 4,000 individual housing units. Newer neighbourhoods in the district are ethnically mixed, while the mahallas in the older historical blocks are inhabited mainly by Uzbeks. The most segregated neighbourhood with the largest Uzbek cluster in this area is called the Kojo (Hoja) mahalla. The district once was a historical core of the town. The Kojo mahalla is squeezed between Pushkin Street and a range of hills that are a natural boundary of the town from its eastern part. It became one of major flashpoints of violence and intergroup clashes in the city – the zone with the second highest level of property damage after the UDN area. This large neighbourhood includes three official urban quarters and, in addition, the Tash Bulak suburban community, which is also an integral part of this informal neighbourhood but formally located outside the town's boundaries. Together, the Kojo mahalla and the Tash Bulak neighbourhoods have a population of around 12,000–15,000, which makes the combined neighbourhood one of the largest and densely concentrated Uzbek ethnic clusters in the Jalalabat city area.

According to my respondents, the Kojo mahalla was an active supporter of Batyrov, once the most influential Uzbek leader in Jalalabat, and many residents of this neighbourhood allegedly participated in ethnic rallies organized by him. Residents of the Kojo mahalla constituted Batyrov's strong mobilizational force during the demonstrations of May 2010. According to some local officials and residents, they created "jamaat," a collective-action community that supported Batyrov politically and contributed financially to organized events.

This neighbourhood includes several blocks both from the town and the Tash Bulak area densely located between Pushkin Street and the hills on which Jalalabat's resort place, famous for its curative mineral water, is located. Local residents believe that they are descendants of the prophet Muhammad as "kojo" ("hoja") literally means "a descendant of the prophet." They have local strong identity and pride for being a part of this neighbourhood. Inside the Kojo mahalla, there are also blocks named the "Tajik mahalla" and the "Kurt (Kurd) mahalla." The names of these internal blocks within the Kojo mahalla presumably refer to the ethnic affiliation of its residents. The traditional authority of their leaders is high. For instance, when the head of the Kurt mahalla is sick, the local residents never celebrate any events. "The words of the head of Kurt mahalla have law-like effect for its residents," said a local low-ranking official (interview, Jalalabat 2013) in Kurmanbek district. Nevertheless, as was indicated above the residents of this neighbourhood are ethnic Uzbeks. Kojo mahalla represents itself as a strong community with strong inward-looking social capital.[3] To enforce strong policing over the community, aksakals also use "tough guys" to force someone to comply with local rules or to punish anti-social behaviour but this is done on very rare occasions. As one respondent noted (interview with a communal leader, Jalalabat 2013), "if the mosque's imam is strong then the social organization of the mahalla is also."

However, this neighbourhood was one of the flashpoints of violence. If self-policing was strong in the Kojo mahalla then why did local leaders fail to restrain some residents from fighting against groups of rural Kyrgyz? One presumable explanation is that ethnic fears, the lack of intercommunal trust, and uncertainty about group survival caused panic and confrontational attitudes among some Uzbek leaders in the Kojo mahalla, who then conceded to the arguments of the radical groups to strike Kyrgyz preemptively in order to secure their neighbourhood.

The preventive aggression of the residents of the Kojo mahalla illustrates the mechanism of the security dilemma at work. When local residents heard news from Osh about the escalating interethnic violence and, especially, when they heard that rural Kyrgyz were gathered in the town hippodrome, they blocked streets leading to the mahalla. Fearful of Kyrgyz attacks, they formed self-defence groups. It is not clear, how a dispute between the radicals and the moderates decided upon the defensive strategy. However, the dynamics of violence in the town affected the local intragroup balance of power. One trigger for the intragroup power shift toward the radicals was Kyrgyz mobilization in the town's hippodrome and, especially, its movement toward the city center. When communal violence broke out in the town, the balance of power in this neighbourhood was favourable toward the radicals, as many radical leaders – supporters of Batyrov – were based in the Kojo mahalla. The radical party in this neighbourhood might have taken initiative in defensive decision-making.

When the Kyrgyz group from the hippodrome started moving along the Pushkin Street toward the city center, some members of Uzbek self-defence groups started shooting toward the moving group of rural Kyrgyz. As the report by Matveeva, Savin, and Faizullaev (2012, 22–3) suggests, the Kyrgyz were unarmed and retreated under the gunfire coming from the Kojo mahalla. Presumably, a Kyrgyz mobilization was interpreted as a direct aggression and threat toward the Kojo mahalla that produced security dilemma for its residents. This miscalculated strategy backfired. The Kyrgyz retreated then, but later returned with firearms that they had obtained after attacking military depots and garrisons around Jalalabat. The firearms obtained by the Kyrgyz changed the intergroup balance of power. Local Uzbek self-defence groups were no longer able to deter the rural Kyrgyz. As shown in the section on violent events in Jalalabat, the Kyrgyz attacked the Kojo mahalla, burning Uzbek houses at the forefront of this neighbourhood that were adjacent to the Pushkin Street (which were deserted as local residents and self-defence groups had already evacuated from this area). The Kyrgyz attackers did not risk to advance deeper into the inner parts of mahalla fearing attacks from an ambush. As Dhattiwala (2016) convincingly shows from her research on Ahmedabad, attackers in dense urban neighbourhoods often act with regard to self-protection in selecting the location to attack.

Another possible reason of the preemptive violence from the Uzbek was the desire to protect their ethnic fellows near UDN, as the self-defence groups in the Kojo mahalla realized that the Kyrgyz group moving toward city center would sooner or later encounter the Uzbeks near UDN.

This security dilemma mechanism evident in the case of Kojo mahalla/Tash Bulak at the level of interpretation of and response to the real or perceived threat is well-explained in the relevant literature regarding interstate relations: "Because of unavoidable uncertainty about intentions ... powerful states, feeling insecure, will act offensively in order to ensure their survival [and] the way to cope with existential uncertainty at the level of interpretation is to impose operational certainty at the level of response" (Booth and Wheeler 2008, 37). So, if we extend this logic of macro-level interstate uncertainty to the meso-level behaviour between two groups, then it becomes clear that the Uzbek self-defence groups in the Kojo mahalla attacked the Kyrgyz moving along the Pushkin Street based on a worst-case-scenario thinking. The latter resulted from two main factors: "the difficulty of distinguishing from between offensive and defensive forces, and the history of past interactions" (ibid., 74; also Posen 1993). As Booth and Wheeler (2008, 74) argue, "In the situation of emerging anarchy ... even if particular ethnic groups were arming for defensive reasons, they nonetheless had capabilities to conduct offensive operations, and this generated fear about future intentions on the part of those groups that might consider themselves as potential targets – especially those constituting ... ethnic islands." (See also Posen 1993, 32–3.) The Kyrgyz people walking along the Pushkin Street were unarmed, but the large size of the crowd and their marching near the Kojo mahalla was interpreted by the Uzbek residents as an intention to attack their neighbourhood. The residents of the Kojo mahalla, squeezed between hills and the Pushkin Street, felt even more vulnerable because this neighbourhood became "an ethnic island" being cut off from other large Uzbek mahallas and the Uzbekistan border.

On the other hand, for the residents of the Kojo mahalla, an experience of past interactions with the Kyrgyz from the villages was absent or limited to random contacts. Among many Uzbeks, there is a widespread perception of the rural Kyrgyz as being unruly, aggressive, and savage.[4] Furthermore, although Jalalabat was not a flashpoint of violence during the Kyrgyz-Uzbek communal violence in 1990, the Jalalabat Uzbeks were very well aware of the Kyrgyz rural mobilization in Osh and Uzgen at that time. The recent experience of Kyrgyz rural mobilization during political upheavals in Jalalabat in May 2010 certainly did not contribute to mutually trustful intercommunal relations either. The relations between two groups can be better characterized as mutual ignorance. However, the most important shortcoming was the absence of contacts between the leaders of the Kojo mahalla and the rural Kyrgyz aksakals. Communication and negotiations between them could have reduced uncertainty and lessened fears.

Therefore, the inability to distinguish between real and perceived intentions as well as, to a lesser extent, the negative past interactions with the rural Kyrgyz generated fears and worst-case thinking among the Uzbeks in the Kojo mahalla, who decided to strike first against the Kyrgyz. To use Booth and Wheeler's (2008) vocabulary, the preemptive aggression was committed in order to reduce existential uncertainty at the level of interpretation and to impose operational certainty at the level of response. As described above, Uzbeks attacked Kyrgyz from locations at Hazret-Ayub Mosque, the provinicial hospital, and the lyceum (Matveeva, Savin, and Faizullaev 2012, 32–3).

Sputnik District:
No Pact and Neutrality

In Sputnik, there were no clashes. It is a district inhabited mainly by Kyrgyz residents living in densely concentrated block apartments buildings, usually of four to five storeys. Out of the 178 multistorey housings in Jalalabat, 84 are located in Sputnik (interview with a local kvartkom, October 2013). On the margins of this district, there are few quarters with individual housing units. Generally, these individual house neighbourhoods have an Uzbek majority. Most internal migrants, normally Kyrgyz from rural areas, tend to settle in the flats in Sputnik. It has a large share of the town's economic migrants. Officially the number of residents is around 28,500, but, in reality, there around 35,000 residents living in this district. The difference between the official and the de facto number is unregistered tenants.

Communal self-policing was practically absent but there were attempts to control the neighbourhood territorially in order not to let outsiders enter the neighbourhood. In general, the Kyrgyz that gathered in the hippodrome made very few attempts go to this district and therefore did not create any trouble for local residents. Some local influential residents made sure that militants did not enter the few Uzbek neighbourhoods in this district. These local leaders – including several Uzbeks – tried to influence and control the situation in Sputnik. When there were attempts to enter the district, they redirected rural Kyrgyz toward the downtown. However, the leaders lost sight of two Uzbek houses being torched by the unknown people despite this policing of the territory. The owners of these two houses were prominent supporters of Batyrov, one was his lawyer and another was a businessman (interview with a local kvartkom in Sputnik, Jalalabat 2013). The houses had been deserted, however, like many other Uzbek houses in this district.

Despite the fact that the Kyrgyz neighbourhoods in Sputnik share a border with the large Uzbek mahallas, there were no pacts negotiated between them. These conditions, in general, are applicable to all neighbourhoods with densely concentrated multistorey apartment building complexes. The main reasons for the absence of pacts were: (1) absence of communication between the Kyrgyz Sputnik and the Uzbek neighbourhoods even at community leaders' level, and (2) lack of credible commitment – the Kyrgyz leaders had limited power to control and police the local residents in the neighbourhoods due to weak authority of the local leaders and lack of social norms conducive for social control. The majority of residents did not know the local kvartkoms or recognize their authority. This is in contrast to individual unit house neighbourhoods, where kvartkoms have more authority. Many Uzbeks had fled to Suzak and other Uzbek-dominated areas. Sputnik was mainly left aside from the main events unfolding in the central parts of the town, chiefly, due to its location and spatial separation from the city.

SPATIAL FACTORS

Spatial factors were important to explain the geographical distribution of violence in Jalalabat. Sputnik is separated from the rest of the town by an airport and the hippodrome that divides the city into two parts: the western and the eastern. All clashes took place on the eastern side. The hippodrome – a focal point for the Kyrgyz mobilization – is located in the northern outskirts of the town not far from the districts of Sputnik, Dostuk, and Kurmanbek. The hippodrome is a large open space and a convenient point for gathering and meetings, especially because of the road leading to Jalalabat from the mountainous areas and the Kyrgyz villages of Kokart valley, which eventually crosses a roundabout near the hippodrome at the northern entrance to the town with roads leading further from this roundabout to the eastern part of the town. The hippodrome had once been a meeting point for Kyrgyz rural mobilization against the interim government and later against Batyrov during the disorder of May 2010 when the Kyrgyz clashed with the Uzbeks in front of UDN. In June, the hippodrome once again became a focal point for hundreds of Kyrgyz mobilizing from rural areas. When first news and rumours about Uzbek attacks against Kyrgyz in Jalalabat spread to the rural areas of the Kokart valley and the mountainous areas, hundreds of rural Kyrgyz rushed to Jalalabat and gathered in the hippodrome. When they gathered at the hippodrome in large numbers, several high-profile leaders unsuccessfully tried to pacify and restrain the crowd. The provincial governor was beaten as Kyrgyz people considered him a traitor for allowing and being present at Batyrov's Uzbek rallies in front of UDN. Another figure, Tashiev – a prominent politician from Bakiev's close circle – was respected by the Kyrgyz crowd for his nationalist stance. However, people did not listen to him either. When news about killings of Kyrgyz people at Sanpa and near UDN arrived, people in the crowd got furious.

From the roundabout near the hippodrome, the roads lead to two directions. One direction leads along the Pushkin Street toward the administrative and business center passing between the Dostuk and Kurmanbek districts, the provincial hospital, and the Kojo mahalla (with Tash Bulak). The second direction leads toward the airport, the VLKSM Park, and along several streets, including the Krasin Street, toward UDN. The mob flooded into these two directions. These road communication structures as well as the location of barricades explain how Kyrgyz groups proceeded through the town and how they moved to certain streets rather than others. Barricades considerably constrained movement of the militant groups, police, and residents. The substantial part of the town, especially neighbourhoods in its central zone including almost the entire districts of Kurmanbek and Dostuk from a foot of eastern hills (the Kojo mahalla) to the airport area were fully barricaded. As one high-ranking police officer confessed to me in an interview (Jalalabat, October 2013), his troops could not freely move throughout the city to react on emerging flashpoints of violence as many streets were blocked. The police troops operated under high risk of getting under heavy gunfire in certain neighbourhoods. Basically, his troops operated in a small zone, still free of barricades, around the central police headquarters. Furthermore, those days, because of a high concentration of barricades or of militant groups on the roads, he could not reach his house to help his own family to evacuate from a dangerous area to a safer one. Only on 14 June, when reinforcements from the capital city of Bishkek arrived in Jalalabat, unblocking some streets, did he manage to reach his family that was hiding in the basement of his Uzbek traffic policeman colleague's house (ibid.).

In such circumstances, large groups chose to move on broad principal streets which were more difficult to block. However, one of them, Krasin Street, got blocked by the Uzbek groups in the area closer to UDN. A Kyrgyz group, that was moving toward UDN through the Krasin Street, encountered this barricade. What exactly happened between two groups on different sides of the barricade is not very well known. The standoff ensued in a violent clash in which the Kyrgyz group overpowered Uzbeks at the barricade. As the Kyrgyz group broke through the barricade, it moved toward UDN burning houses alongside the Krasin Street, already deserted by local residents and evacuated to Suzak and to the Uzbekistan's border. At the intersection with the Lenin Street, this Kyrgyz group merged with the group coming from Pushkin Street. Together they attacked and torched the UDN, executing a final blow to the Uzbek armed groups in Jalalabat. The Kyrgyz moved further to attack a large Suzak village, where they were stopped by Kyrgyz elders as described in the previous sections.

The clash at the barricade on the Krasin Street shows that the location of the barricades was important for determining the spatial distribution of violence. Like in Osh and other towns, setting up barricades in the secondary streets and entrances to neighbourhoods generally increased security of local communities. This did not allow potential sudden incursions inside these neighbourhoods. Wandering militant groups often ignored them preferring to move along principal streets. However, erecting barricades on main principal streets was a counterproductive measure because it would block the street and, thus, communication in the city. It would eventually lead to accumulation of people and combatants at the barricade and then to a violent standoff.

A final observation on the importance of spatiality relates to the built environment of the town. Among factors that account for the relatively lighter intensity of violence in Jalalabat is the variation in levels of concentration of multistorey buildings and bazaar areas in Osh and Jalalabat. In the latter, multistorey buildings as well as bazaars are deconcentrated. In Osh, the grand bazaar occupies very large territory in the central part of the city adjoining neighbourhoods, with densely concentrated multistorey buildings. As already discussed in chapter 5, communal policing is especially difficult in such areas due to chaotic residential mobility and spillover effects coming from the bazaar. In Jalalabat, there are only two neighbourhoods with high concentration of multistorey buildings – Sputnik and Kokart – and they are far from the town bazaar, which, in fact, is deconcentrated into several smaller bazaars. The borderside location of Sputnik does not contribute to overcrowding of the bazaar areas (as in the Oshskii raion). This is in contrast to Osh where several specialized bazaars and multistorey building microdistricts are concentrated in one area, making it one huge area that is very difficult to control. These relative advantages made communal policing easier in Jalalabat and partially explain why the area around the town's bazaar remained undamaged.

CONCLUSION

This chapter demonstrated that the neighbourhoods in Jalalabat chose different strategies to deal with uncertainty and fear depending on such structural conditions as their location in the city, ethnic composition and the degree of residential segregation in the neighbourhoods, the level of quotidian intercommunal contacts among leaders and ordinary residents of Uzbek

Table 7.1
Divergent defense strategies and responses to emerging anarchy

Neighbourhood	Ethnic composition	Defensive strategy	Response to emerging violence
1st quarter	Homogenous Uzbek	Intercommunal pact and self-policing	Interethnic cooperation at leaders' level (between segregated neighbourhoods)
8th quarter	mixed	No pact; self-isolation	Interethnic cooperation within neighbourhood
Kojo mahalla	Homogenous Uzbek	No pact; self-isolation	Confrontation and failed self-policing
Sputnik	Homogenous Kyrgyz	No pact	Neutral (no centralized response)

Source: Based on the author's own research.

and Kyrgyz local communities, and the strength of local self-policing. These structural conditions provided the context, constrained, and affected contingency in the in-group and intergroup interactions within and between the Uzbek and the Kyrgyz groups. The choice of the type of response and defensive strategy in each neighbourhood was an outcome of the interplay between the contingent interactions and structural conditions.

Neighbourhoods adopted strategies/responses that were of confrontational, cooperative, and self-isolationist character (see table 7.1) and the type of strategy/response to uncertainty that they chose affected the spatial dynamics of violence and (non)violent outcomes in neighbourhoods. The action–reaction dynamic was important for determining peaceful and violent outcomes. How neighbourhood communities reacted to uncertainty and the decisions taken by leaders influenced the dynamics of violence. Rumours played a less-important role in the violence dynamics and mobilization if we compared Jalalabat with Osh but still they should not be ignored when analyzing the dynamics of violence.

Several communities chose preemptive aggression. Some because of failed self-policing and weak leaders, others with strong leaders but under strong influence of ethnic entrepreneurs who used their traditional authority to play an ethnic card to gain political benefits. For example, the Uzbek neighbourhoods in the Krasin Street, the UDN area, and the Kojo mahalla/Tash Bulak were, to a great extent, exposed to fears which triggered preventive attacks against the rural Kyrgyz by the Uzbek self-defence groups. They discarded the possibility to negotiate nonaggression pacts with Kyrgyz groups. The comparison between the following Uzbek neighbourhoods is illustrative.

Quarter 1 is a contrasting case to those mahallas such as the Kojo mahalla/Tash Bulak that resorted to preemptive violence. In the latter cases, local residents were fearful of rural Kyrgyz coming to the city. They built barricades (Krasin Street) but also attacked rural Kyrgyz (Kojo mahalla, Sanpa, and the UDN area) provoking them to acts of vengeance. The implication is the following: Quarter 1 and other Uzbek neighbourhoods of the Aitmatov district established relatively trustful relations with the Barpy rural district. These communities had common experience of coexistence and intercommunal relations were maintained through their leaders' participation in each other's communal events such as feasts, celebrations, and funerals. On the other hand, residents of the Kojo mahalla and their leaders never knew Kyrgyz people coming from the villages of Kokart and mountainous areas. The absence of communication between these two groups and their leaders prevented negotiations and facilitated the emergence of the security dilemma. Out of fear, local Uzbek residents made preemptive strikes on the Kyrgyz who otherwise would not have attacked their mahalla. Leaders on both sides did not know each other and there were no points of communication and little space for peaceful brokerage. In the Krasin Street, which was one of principal streets connecting the northern outskirts of the town with its central areas, the local Uzbek residents constructed barricades on the road. As discussed in this and previous chapters, erecting barricades on the principal streets was another counterproductive defense measure. The barricades triggered outrage and perception of threat among rural Kyrgyz who considered access to the town as their natural right to "Kyrgyz town." The fact that the Uzbeks were obstructing the access to the city drove them furious as for the Kyrgyz, it was a clear sign that the Uzbeks "had been preparing for war in advance" (interview with a local official). The combination of violent provocations, instigation, rumours, and the mix of false and real information about attacks against the Kyrgyz allowed the Kyrgyz groups to justify their aggression against some Uzbek mahallas.

Pacts played a less-important role in Jalalabat if compared with Osh and Uzgen. To the best of my knowledge, the only neighbourhoods in Jalalabat that conducted nonaggression pacts were in the southeastern part of the Aitmatov district. The lack of pacts can be explained by the smaller degree of ethnic segregation in Jalalabat. Nevertheless, in those segregated neighbourhoods, where pacts were implemented and backed with strong in-group policing, there were higher chances for peaceful outcomes. In general, pacts between separate segregated neighbourhoods or territorial units were normally negotiated between suburban communities and adjacent peripheral neighbourhoods, as in case of Quarter 1 and some other neighbourhoods in Osh. In the city center, there were no pacts but mainly interethnic cooperation within ethnically mixed neighbourhoods as it was in case of Quarter 8. Segregated neighbourhoods in the city center generally did not produce pacts, probably because there were no credible partners from the other side, especially in the chaotic, multistorey-building Kyrgyz neighbourhoods in Osh and to a certain extent in Jalalabat, who could credibly conduct self-policing of local constituencies and, therefore, to credibly commit to the conditions of pacts. In the busy city center's multistorey building neighbourhoods, people did not know each other and the informal authority of local leaders eroded. Therefore, successful pacts were usually negotiated between Uzbek mahallas and the adjacent Kyrgyz communities as the conditions for self-policing in the Kyrgyz suburban areas were relatively similar to those in the Uzbek mahallas.

In fact, neighbourhoods in the city center tried to secure themselves by physical self-isolation whereas neighbourhoods in the city periphery additionally resorted to diplomacy with the neighbouring suburban communities. This was clearly showed in description of the cases of Quarter 1 and Quarter 8. However, Jalalabat is less ethnically segregated then Osh and Uzgen. Its central neighbourhoods are mostly ethnically mixed, but many peripheral Uzbek mahallas do not have common borders with the Kyrgyz villages, and many Kyrgyz urban neighbourhoods do not share a border with the Uzbek villages. This spatial feature can partly explain the relative lack of intercommunal pacts in Jalalabat. In such mixed neighbourhoods, residents establish interethnic alliances on the grounds of neighbourhood solidarity. For example, the Kyrgyz protected "Uzbek co-villagers from outsider Kyrgyz, because they were members of the same community" (Matveeva, Savin, and Faizullaev 2012, 35).

Finally, the passive and neutral response of the Sputnik neighbourhood can be partly explained by its remote and isolated location in the city. As discussed in the section on the spatial factors, this neighbourhood was isolated from the main flashpoint locations of the town. The few attempts by outsiders to enter this Kyrgyz neighbourhood were repulsed by local leaders who policed the territory but not the local population. Those who wanted to participate in ethnic clashes could easily do it by joining the Kyrgyz group in the hippodrome and other flashpoints in the city. The neighbourhood leaders did not negotiate pacts with the Uzbek leaders from adjacent neighbourhoods.

The divergent strategic responses by the Uzbek, the Kyrgyz, and the ethnically mixed communities toward the emerging anarchy at local level, demonstrate that the analysis of ethnic conflict should take different spatial scales and levels of aggregation into consideration.

8

Conclusions

This book's main goal has been to analyze the spatial variations in violence and mechanisms in urban neighbourhoods' responses to uncertainty by explaining the following important puzzling questions: why did ethnic violence break out in some urban neighbourhoods but not in many others? Why did neighbourhoods with similar ethnic composition and social and economic contexts exhibit a variation in, and different levels of, ethnic violence?

This research employed a unique approach in the analysis of urban communal violence with the application of the neorealist approaches from the IR field at the neighbourhood scale.

The book's findings advance our knowledge of violent urban conflicts and might apply to similar instances of urban communal wars and conflicts in fragile states and divided societies such as sectarian violence in Iraq, Lebanon, and Northern Ireland; religious violence in Nigeria, India, and Indonesia; armed conflicts in Syria and Liberia; clan-based and ethnic conflicts in Somalia and The Democratic Republic of the Congo; and even gang violence in Brazil, Haiti, and Mexico. The study outcomes demonstrate that violent outbreaks, similar to one in June 2010 in southern Kyrgyzstan, produce a unique environmental change: a temporal breakdown of state institutions that may trigger divergent responses in the urban neighbourhoods toward the emerging violence, such as the "decision to fight, to negotiate, or to remain at peace" (Walter 1999, 2). The divergent responses to the similar threat and ethnic fears are contingent on the intergroup and intragroup interactions among neighbourhood-level ethnic subgroups. This demonstrates that many assumptions of neorealist IR literature, can be scaled down to the neighbourhood level. However, due to the large number of deaths and the fact that the majority of deaths resulted from gunshots, the armed conflict in southern Kyrgyzstan had features of both warfare and ethnic riots.

The first outbreaks of violence in the city of Osh, in June 2010, produced uncertainty and fears in the relations between the Uzbek and Kyrgyz communities, especially in ethnically segregated neighbourhoods in the many towns and villages of southern Kyrgyzstan. This became especially evident as soon as local-level ethnic communities realized that the state was incapable of intervening to stop the emergent violence in a credible manner. Basically, the weak central state withdrew itself from solving interethnic tensions and this created a sense of "the emerging anarchy" and a power vacuum. Uncertainty and fears caused by this power vacuum triggered different responses across towns, villages, and neighbourhoods. Local ethnic communities responded to escalating violence, emerging anarchy, and uncertainty mainly in three essential ways; namely, by: (1) initiating preemptive attacks against the opponent ethnic group members; (2) barricading and closing streets across borders of their neighbourhoods and cutting out contacts with other neighbourhoods and external groups; and (3) negotiating nonaggression pacts with the neighbouring "opponent" communities.

The importance of this study is highlighted by the fact that it explains the causes of violence and peace at a micro scale by identifying the local-level factors and conditions that affected the security dynamics in each locality. The aggregate picture and the level of violence in towns resulted from micro-outcomes in urban neighbourhoods. The outcome in each locality was determined by the combination of structural and contingent factors. In this book, my approach is beyond the agency-versus-structure framework (see Jones Luong 2002). I have argued that contingent factors – namely, intra- and intergroup interactions – directly affected the dynamics of violence and security outcomes at the local level. However, structural conditions provided the context, shaped, and constrained the contingent interactions.

Another contribution of this book is linking the arguments of structure- and contingency-oriented studies on ethnic conflict. Macro-level research highlights the importance of mostly socioeconomic structural conditions. It seeks to explain generalizable patterns of determinants and, frequently, at the expense of underestimating the short-term dynamics and local actors' behaviour. Micro-level studies accentuate the importance of the strategic behaviour and the dynamics of interactions (Przeworski 1991, 47). However, excessive attention on strategic interactions underemphasizes the influence of long-term factors and structural conditions. In this book, I showed that both short-term strategic interactions and long-term structural conditions interacted and influenced violent and nonviolent outcomes. This contrasts with studies that usually focus just on either of these dimensions. Yet, another distinction of this book is that in explaining the dynamics of violence and its cross-spatial outcomes, it adopted a micro-comparative research design. It considered town-level structural conditions and neighbourhood effects with local-level interactions as opposed to studies on ethnic conflict that generally aim their attention toward the national and regional-level socioeconomic conditions and intergroup relations. Importantly, I gave special attention to spatial factors such as urban neighbourhoods' built environment, the natural landscape, and strategic location. These variables rarely figure in the literature on civil wars and ethnic conflicts, mainly remaining in the domain of political geography.

Two different mechanisms explain peace in mixed and segregated neighbourhoods. In mixed neighbourhoods, interethnic cooperation was fostered by relatively strong civic links between ordinary residents. This type of cooperation was demonstrated by the case of Quarter 8 in Jalalabat where the Uzbek and the Kyrgyz residents of that quarter cooperated on the grounds of neighbourhood solidarity. This mechanism was emphasized by Varshney (2002), who argues that everyday intercommunal engagement between members of different communities increases the likelihood of peace. The case of Quarter 8 illustrates the security dynamic that was prevalent in other ethnically mixed neighbourhoods in Osh and Jalalabat. Communicating on a daily basis, Kyrgyz and Uzbek residents in the ethnically mixed neighbourhoods did not generally fear one another. When violence broke out, many mixed neighbourhoods barricaded the access streets and organized mixed patrols and self-defence groups. They did not take sides in the conflict and did not let outsiders enter or pass through their neighbourhoods, thereby conducting a strong territorial and community policing.

Ethnically segregated neighbourhoods constitute the majority in Osh, Uzgen,[1] and Jalalabat, but they exhibited striking variations in violence. Violence spread mainly across segregated neighbourhoods. Yet, many segregated neighbourhoods escaped trouble. Nonaggression pacts and in-group policing were the mechanisms that helped them to avoid violence. On the scale of ethnic segregation, there were varying degrees of segregation, with Uzgen being a completely segregated town, Osh being a highly segregated, and Jalalabat being largely segregated (to a lesser degree when compared to

Osh). However, as the evidence shows, the degree of segregation does not directly correspond with the level of violence each town experienced.

This is especially evident when comparing Osh and Uzgen. The latter is an entirely Uzbek town with only two Kyrgyz neighbourhoods and is completely surrounded by Kyrgyz rural districts. Having such a disadvantageous strategic location, Uzgen could be an obvious target for retaliatory attacks from the surrounding Kyrgyz villages as it already happened in 1990. However, despite being the most segregated town and an ethnic "island," Uzgen's communal leaders managed to protect both the Kyrgyz minority within the town and the Uzbek communities from the possible external threat. With Uzgen being geographically located between Osh and Jalalabat, which were both raged by violence, its leaders maintained order through effective in-group policing and security negotiations with the Kyrgyz leaders. The result was remarkable: the town remained peaceful. Local Uzbek radicals were neutralized and Kyrgyz radicals from surrounding areas preferred to go to Osh.

This evidence contradicts the widespread perceptions among international experts and journalists about the fully opportunist behaviour of the participants in this conflict. To be more precise, a high degree of opportunistic behaviour was apparent in many observed cases of attacks and looting, however, this should not allow simplistic accounts to prevail. If Kyrgyz radicals around Uzgen area were motivated solely by opportunist incentives, why would they go to Osh instead of attacking a closer and more convenient target – i.e., Uzgen? Many Kyrgyz participants in violence were driven by fear because information and rumours coming from Osh about killings of Kyrgyz people convinced them that their immediate enemies were the Uzbeks in Osh, not Uzgen. On the other side, some Uzbek militant groups in Osh and Jalalabat initiated the violence – a preemptive move based on a fear of potential Kyrgyz aggression.

The evidence from Uzgen and some other segregated places also complements Varshney's (2002) argument. His model does not explain what happens when there is a low level – or complete absence – of intercommunal associational and everyday engagement. Segregated groups in multiethnic societies are a widespread phenomenon in many countries. However, what we observe is that most communities and towns with complete absence of intercommunal associational quotidian engagement and civic ties remained peaceful despite the ethnic tensions (Fearon and Laitin 1996, 715–17). In other words, ethnic communities can remain peaceful even in the absence of cross-cutting bonds. As Varshney (2002) himself admits that the gaps in his argument about peace between segregated communities can be addressed by another mechanism of peace – namely, in-group policing, as advanced by Fearon and Laitin (1996). He suggested that this mechanism may be applicable to segregated environments and proposed that the model should be examined empirically. If exerted by elders and ethnic organizations, "intraethnic policing may lead to the same result that interethnic engagement does in India" (Varshney 2002, 300). This research sheds light on the identified gap and, as proposed by Varshney, empirically tested Fearon and Laitin's model of interethnic cooperation by applying it to the case of the June 2010 ethnic violence between Uzbeks and Kyrgyz.

In-group policing often implicitly requires mutual understanding or explicit agreements. In practice, geographically concentrated or residentially segregated groups that are engaged in in-group policing often make an informal pact which serves their interests. As Fearon and Laitin (1996, 722) suggest, groups, by adopting a policy of in-group sanctions against violators, "they take advantage of the fact that each group has better information about the behaviour of its own members than about the other group and so can target individuals rather than whole groups". Fearon and Laitin's (ibid., 715) model of interethnic cooperation suggests that in-group policing – an informal institutional mechanism – emerges when the state authority is weak or breaks down, to reduce the problem of opportunism in intergroup relations. It thus helps to preserve interethnic peace. In-group policing is a key mechanism that explains micro-outcomes in many segregated neighbourhoods not only during the June 2010 ethnic violence in southern Kyrgyzstan but also in the context of many other communal conflicts.

However, if peace breaks down, in-group policing can be complemented by nonaggression agreements not to let a violent conflict to spiral further between local ethnic communities still unaffected by the ethnic violence. When violence breaks out, it can undermine trust between ethnic communities and therefore, group leaders may engage in open negotiations to mediate tensions, reassure each other in peaceful intentions, and recover trust. Therefore, in such situations, explicit agreements about mutual nonaggressive intentions can foster restoration of trustful relations between ethnic communities.

This research highlights the critical role of communal brokers and mediators in connecting intergroup and intragroup interests. It identifies several structural and contingent factors requisite for the occurrence, efficiency, and stability of intragroup policing and nonaggression pacts. An essential condition is the ability of group leaders to publicly punish in-group members for opportunist behaviour and violation of intergroup peace. If leaders fail to "publicly sanction one's co-ethnics [in-group members] for violations against the out-group [it] will lead the out-group to begin a spiral or feuds [and] the in-group equilibrium will break down ... when sanctioning is costly" (ibid., 723). The ability to publicly sanction violators without high costs requires leaders to exercise strong social control over their constituency. The leaders' legitimacy and power must be accepted by the majority members of local community and backed by strong communal social norms.

A strategic response to communal violence is partially contingent on informal leaders' ideology. Leaders can influence the balance of power between radicals and moderates within their communities, which can shape the community's overall response to uncertainty and promote trust and reduce uncertainty in intercommunal relations, as demonstrated by actions of the moderate leaders in Uchar, Toloiokon, Turan, and Uzgen. If they are passive or suspicious of the neighbouring community, uncertainty may lead to fears and radicalization within groups and to escalation between communities that can spiral into a violent conflict.

Leaders' legitimacy and the strength of social control over their respective constituencies develops under long-term influence of local structural factors. However, once the violence breaks out and the emerging anarchy dominates the scene, short-term contingent factors come into play in an increasingly significant way, affecting the capacity of local leaders to conduct self-policing and to commit to the conditions of nonaggression pacts. Particularly, strong local social norms provide the basis for effective in-group policing in the long-term based on the structural-historical context, while the constellation of domestic forces and, to a lesser extent, intergroup balance of power, at the moment of conflict, affect the efficiency of in-group policing and the probability of pact occurrence in the "immediate strategic context" (Jones Luong 2002). If community social norms developed historically under influence of structural and institutional factors help communal leaders to exert social control, the dynamics of ethnic violence and contingent events alter power relations and trigger power shifts. Thus, local intragroup and intergroup power balances form under the effect of both structural and contingent factors. Leaders and local communities face a difficult choice to develop a strategic response to emerging anarchy and uncertainty. The strategic response of local communities is often determined in intragroup and intergroup interactions where actors contribute to the strategic action based on evaluation of their relative power. As Jones Luong (2002, 14) argues that individuals "utilize both the previous institutional setting (or the structural-historical context) and present dynamic circumstances (or the immediate strategic context) in order to assess the degree and direction in which their relative power is changing, and then to develop strategies over the *outcome* to be vis-à-vis other actors." (emphasis as in original). Similarly, neighbourhood responses to uncertainty are contingent on the degree of the strength of in-group policing which, in turn, depend on the strength of local social norms and power balances.

As discussed in chapter 5, in Osh and other towns, strong community norms developed in neighbourhoods with mostly long-term residents living in individual housing units. On the other hand, districts with a high concentration of multistorey apartment complexes and high and unstable residential mobility suffered from the problem of social disorder and opportunistic behaviour. In-group policing is effective in strong and homogenous communities with established rules and good knowledge about members of the group. Examples among others include Turan district and Toloikon in Osh, Quarters 1 and 8 in Jalalabat, and local communities in Uzgen. Spiral violence is more pertinent to larger communities with a large share of outsiders who do not have incentives to comply with intragroup rules due to weak ties with local communities. They are not long-term residents in those communities, so residential rotation is high, ties with the community are weak, as are the incentives to long-term community commitments. Leaders in such neighbourhoods are weak; community norms are unstable, fragile, and not widely shared within the neighbourhood; and sanctions against anti-social behaviour are costly. I discussed the problems in such neighbourhoods in chapter 5, exemplified by the case of the Oshskii raion and other similar neighbourhoods located around the grand bazaar. This difference in the neighbourhoods' socioeconomic and ethnodemographic characteristics derive from the previous urban and social policies of town administrations.

Nevertheless, contingent events and strategic interactions can mitigate or even remove structural constraints (Beissinger 2002, 2007). Even though structural factors provide a strong basis for the strength or weakness of local communities and norms that facilitate or hinder local leaders in exerting strong social control over respective communities, in-group policing failed in some strong communities. Still other strong communities were involved in violence even if intragroup policing did not fail. These failures resulted from spillover effects and contingent intra- and intergroup interactions. In the first case, the main cause of the failure of in-group policing results from spillover effects related to intragroup interactions. This happens when a strong and peaceful community is infiltrated by thugs and radicals or exposed to an influx of outsiders such as embittered refugees or militant co-ethnics from other areas. In both cases, they change local intragroup balance of power. Influx of aggressive outsiders shifts the power toward radicals. Outsiders subvert policing activities of moderate leaders by instigating retaliatory attacks or preemptive violence. They sabotage any attempts by moderates to initiate a nonaggression pact with the out-group members. Sometimes extremist outsiders replace moderate leaders and force local young males to join violence against the out-group.

This pattern took place in Nariman, where radical leaders of embittered refugees took over local power and instigated violence. The same script was precluded in Uchar where local moderates managed to resist the aggressive outsiders. This shows that having structural advantages moderate leaders can revert spillover effects. In weak communities, even a small band of opportunists can cause disorder. Infiltration of instigators and thugs assumes some elements of pre-planning. In interviews with me, several community leaders reported about the infiltration of unknown outsider instigators in their communities at the onset of the communal violence. Similar accounts appear in international investigative reports regarding the trigger event at the Alai Hotel. In Turan, the local leaders informed me about their concern with the infiltration of a growing number of unknown aggressive young males in their neighbourhood at the onset of violence, which was disrupted by the closure of the neighbourhood borders. This book does not have sufficient evidence on the infiltration activities, which requires more research.

Outsiders are an important variable that allows us to understand the micro-scale security dynamics in local communities. Some communal leaders wanted to keep outsiders away and not to involve them in the neighbourhood affairs even for the sake of security. They realized that appealing to outsiders involves high risks of losing control over their constituencies. On the other hand, some other neighbourhoods, distrustful and suspicious of out-groups' intentions, were probably willing to seek support of co-ethnic outsiders to secure their own physical safety. This example is illustrated by the Zapadnyi neighbourhood, where the local population supported outsiders out of fear of possible Uzbek attacks. Outsiders gained the upper hand especially in areas with weak community policing, and where leaders of ethnic communities had distrust and ethnic fears toward their out-group neighbours.

Yet another scenario refers to the cases where violence erupted in strong neighbourhoods even without involvement of outsiders. Unlike the previous scenario where violence was a result of intragroup interactions, in this case, violence was affected by the dynamics of intergroup interactions. Obviously, some strong neighbourhoods were attacked due to a spillover of violence coming from the neighbouring areas. However, here I refer to strong communities exposed to non-spillover violence. Radicals dominated in such neighbourhoods which became a hotbed for violent ethnic mobilization. Leaders in such neighbourhoods were exposed to interethnic fears and/or radical views against the out-group members. Violence broke out in such neighbourhoods following the action–reaction dynamics of the security dilemma. One example discussed in this book is the Kojo mahalla/Tash Bulak neighbourhood in Jalalabat (analyzed in chapter 8) and another is Furkat in Osh (described in chapter 4). These Uzbek neighbourhoods attacked large Kyrgyz groups out of fear. Preemptive attacks backfired. Violence spiralled. Kyrgyz first retreated but then returned with weapons. Retaliatory attacks were horrible, especially in the case of Furkat. Preemptive attacks were counterproductive, as they shifted the balance of power among the Kyrgyz toward the radicals.

Analyzing the dynamics of the two-level strategic interactions is important for understanding variation in communal responses to violence in segregated neighbourhoods. Although self-policing is mainly an intragroup mechanism, this institutional arrangement was developed precisely to solve problems of tension and lack of trust in intercommunal relations. As Fearon and Laitin (1996, 727) suggest, "interactions between individuals from different ethnic groups are marked by a distinct tension and lack of trust, which we explain as a strategic consequence of problems of asymmetric information due to the lower density of social networks across groups and to the differential ability to distinguish types inside versus outside the group." Low density of intercommunal social ties was identified by Varshney (2002) to be the main mechanism leading to intercommunal violence. In ethnically mixed neighbourhoods, problems of asymmetric information and lack of trust is mitigated by the higher density of interethnic social networks. Therefore, residents in mixed neighbourhoods develop mechanisms of cooperation similar to what Varshney (ibid.) argues in his work. According to him, higher density of intercommunal ties leads to lower probability of ethnic violence. In segregated neighbourhoods, interethnic social networks are at a very low level which leads to asymmetric information that produces tensions and creates problems of opportunism in interethnic interactions and a mechanism of in-group policing is designed to manage them (Fearon and Laitin 1996, 727). In this sense, intergroup agreements complement intragroup policing well. They help to deal with lack of trust and uncertainty in intercommunal relations.

Intergroup networks and a constellation of domestic actors are important to explain the success and failure of nonaggression pacts and in-group policing. Intercommunal networks between moderate leaders were crucial to initiate negotiations, but, without credible commitment, a pact is not viable. Strong in-group policing and visible in-group sanctions against opportunists signals toward credibility of commitments.

In pacted neighbourhoods, there should be legitimate leaders and strong intracommunal ties and social norms. To make a pact, leaders of both sides should exercise strong social control over their respective constituencies, if one of the negotiating parties cannot control its constituency then such pacts become meaningless as one side cannot guarantee nonaggression of its members. Therefore, a necessary condition for the success of pacts is strong in-group policing on both sides. Other requisite conditions for pact-making include social ties between local leaders and absence of outsiders in the community. Social control is more effective if pact-making communities are located in non-transit territory to avoid disruptive influence from outsider radical groups and spillover effects.

In this book, I do not want to overestimate the causal power and influence of in-group policing and nonaggression pacts on peaceful outcomes. These mechanisms played a key role in preventing local-level violence; however, some limitations must be mentioned. The very fact of pact-making is that it does not automatically lead to peaceful relations. In-group policing cannot fully explain what causes violence between communal groups. Similarly, the absence of pacts does not imply the presence of violence. Pacts cannot guarantee peace, if, especially under the influence of external factors, environmental conditions change, triggering unpredictable dynamics of contingent events and "noise" in intragroup and intergroup interactions. However, pacts signify attempts to normalize relations, reestablish trust, reassure peaceful intentions across groups, and reduce chances of violent outbreaks among the pacted neighbourhoods.

Pacts contribute to peaceful outcomes. However, even when pacts ensure short-term peace, they do not guarantee strong and long-term cooperative relations between two communities in the future. Agreements have short-term stabilization effect on relations between two neighbourhoods during or in the aftermath of ethnic violence, but, by itself alone, a pact is unlikely to sustain long-term ethnic cooperation. If intercommunal nonaggression continues and even transforms into cooperation between leaders, then it is more likely that the cooperation develops because of these favourable structural conditions that brought leaders together and made it possible for them to negotiate the pact. Agreements also create opportunities and space for future cooperation by bringing the leaders together. During these short interactions leaders have opportunity to build common ground for determining the future course of relationships. Some peaceful agreements indeed led to progress in social relations between communal leaders. During my fieldwork, I observed post-conflict progress in interethnic cooperation between communal leaders in several neighbourhoods. For example, one outcome was a deliberate post-conflict arrangement by a fraction of Kyrgyz and Uzbek leaders from the Uzgen raion to meet frequently and mitigate ethnic divisions.

However, reaching full-scale sustainable peace and long-term consolidated cooperation requires intercommunal civic engagement at the grassroots level, which is possible with the development of intercommunal associational civic engagement and civil society (as emphasized by Varshney 2002) and the changes in local structural and social conditions. In-group policing and intercommunal agreements at leaders' level do positively influence intercommunal cooperation in the short-term. However, in the long-term such delegative cooperation and diplomacy may lead to the retention of high levels of ethnic segregation and interethnic and intergroup interactions and dependence on ethnic leaders. Intercommunal relations that are delegated exclusively to local ethnic leaders who enjoy the power to make decisions regarding ethnic diplomacy can create incentives to conserve such relations and to abuse intergroup relations for personal interests. In other words, ethnic peace based only on interactions between leaders, pacts, and self-policing is vulnerable to external factors and politically oriented ethnic manipulation and is susceptible to ideological views of the local leaders. In-group policing is based and depends on intracommunal mechanisms. It can be effective when social capital and intercommunal civic links within a community are weak or absent. However, these mechanisms of peace are fragile and provide an inferior alternative to a strong civil society.

Consequently, the conclusions delineated in this chapter are designed to help policymakers, organizations, and practitioners in taking appropriate decisions when dealing with intense violent conflicts in segregated urban areas.

Notes

PREFACE AND ACKNOWLEDGMENTS

1 I would like to thank Andreas Hasenclever for helping me to clarify these points.

CHAPTER ONE

1 More detailed overviews of the ethnic violence in Osh and Jalalabat are provided in empirical chapters.
2 The fourth type of response was neutrality without pro-active in-group policing and without direct aggression acts against out-groups. This type of response was characteristic to communal groups located in ethnic strongholds. Being surrounded by co-ethnic groups such communities did not have common borders with out-group communities and therefore, they were not immediately exposed to security dilemmas. However, members of such groups could participate in violence and defense activities by going to neighbourhoods located in the frontier zones.
3 See Little (2007) on the interaction between local and general levels of balance of power.
4 Due to space constraints, I had to drop from the book a chapter on Uzgen – the third largest town in southern Kyrgyzstan. Uzgen – an Uzbek-dominated town completely surrounded by Kyrgyz rural districts – entirely avoided violence thanks to unprecedented level of ethnic diplomacy and peace-keeping activities that local Uzbek leaders conducted with their Kyrgyz counterparts from surrounding rural areas. A detailed analysis on Uzgen can be found in Kutmanaliev (2017).

5 Throughout the book, I place the original terms, as narrated by my respondents in local languages, in square brackets.
6 According to Varshney (2001, 372), the death toll in Aligarch (1950–95) was 160.

CHAPTER TWO

1 In this study, I use the terms "leaders," "brokers," and "mediators" interchangeably. Although these terms have different connotations, in the context of social life in southern Kyrgyzstan, same community leaders who conducted in-group control and policing were often acting as communal brokers and mediators in intercommunal negotiations.
2 My theoretical propositions are strongly influenced by O'Donnell's (1986, 12–13) analysis of transitional pacts and party politics in Latin America in the 1970s to the 1980s.

CHAPTER THREE

1 The modern city of Kokand is located in Uzbekistan's part of the Fergana valley.
2 On genealogical imagination among tribal nomads in Central Asia see Edgar (2004).
3 In his analysis of nationalist mobilization in the late Soviet Union, Beissinger (2002) argues that late risers were distinguished by more violent repertoires.
4 At that time, the profession of taxi driver was considered relatively prestigious and well-paid among blue-collar workers. For instance, in Bishkek, taxi drivers were, for the most part, ethnic Russians.
5 Note that there is the Osh city and the Osh province, with the former being an administrative center of the latter. The same refers to the city and the province of Jalalabat.
6 Mandatory residential registration.
7 For the detailed analysis of peacekeeping activities and intercommunal pacts in Uzgen see Kutmanaliev (2017).
8 The most notorious political assassination during Bakiev's rule was conducted by security services on the president's brother's direct order, and with his direct participation.
9 Allegedly, during the attack, the Uzbeks burned and trampled on the national

flag and the traditional Kyrgyz *yurt* (a mobile nomadic tent house), which is one of the most important Kyrgyz ethnic symbols.

10 The Uzbek National Cultural Centers (UNCCs) are organizations usually established by rich Uzbek businessmen operating at different levels. For example, Kadyrjan Batyrov, Jalalitdin Salakhutdinov, and Inomjon Abdurasulov were leading members of a national level UNCC. In contrast, the Osh UNCC operated at town level in Osh.

11 *Aksakal* literally means "white beard." The meaning of this term nowadays is twofold: (1) respectable elder, and (2) influential, respectable, and authoritative person. In this context, the term often refers to community leaders.

CHAPTER FOUR

1 See a comprehensive account of the violent events in Osh in Kutmanaliev (2017) and Memorial (2012).

2 This chapter presents only a general overview of the violence dynamics. Those who are interested in the more detailed review of communal warfare in Osh with the district-level breakdown of local violence can find the full-length analysis in my dissertation (Kutmanaliev 2017).

3 "Zapadnyi" translates from Russian as "western." Zapadnyi is an informal name of Kulatov micro-district.

4 The street starts as Pamirskaia from Furkat and continues as Monueva within the official boundaries of the city.

5 This death toll does not account for killings that took place after 15 June 2010 when open armed clashes stopped. After 15 June, violence continued in the form of hostage-taking and clandestine attacks.

6 Some researchers treat interviews as complementary to participant observation – see Bray (2008).

7 The snowball sampling method is a technique where interview participants refer to future interview respondents through their social networks. The territorially representative sampling is a technique where interview respondents' sample correctly represents location- and territory-specific characteristics of a larger population.

8 *Domkom/kvartkom* is a position on volunteer basis because it is not paid. The amount of a symbolic honorarium that a domkom/kvartkom receives is so small, so that it cannot be treated as public office salary. Even unemployed people would hardly bother to pursue this position as amount of work and

activities is simply overwhelming. This ensures that only local neighbourhood activists and informal leaders would pursue this position.
9   Unfortunately, I could not get access to these materials, as the mission did not respond to my email requests.
10 See the Memorial's critique of the KIC mission's report in the introductory part of its report.
11 For the discussion of weaknesses of partisan, political, normative biases in the study of conflicts see Kalyvas (2006, ch. 2).
12 In my view, the most detailed and objective accounts have been given by Memorial (2012) and by Matveeva et al. (2012).

CHAPTER FIVE

The content of this chapter has been published earlier in Kutmanaliev (2015).
1   For the few exceptions see Kutmanaliev (2015) and Megoran (2013).
2   This information was corroborated in conversations with an employee of international organization, a Kyrgyz resident of this neighbourhood (August 2012 and September 2013). Another my respondent, a former high-level Uzbek politician well known in Osh, was kidnapped by a Kyrgyz group in the same area but later managed to escape (interview August 2012).
3   Osh is the name for both the city and the province. In this chapter, unless I specify the province, by "Osh," I normally refer to the city.
4   In the citation, the Kalinin neighbourhood is indicated as Amir Timur Street which is now an official name of the street but I use instead its previous Soviet time related and now its informal name – Kalinin. I do it to avoid some confusion because there is also a large district in the eastern part of the Osh city, also called Amir Timur.
5   The Sulaiman-Too is a single mountain/hill located right in the city center and considered a holy place at regional level.
6   Uzbeks in Kyrgyzstan are considered to be more religious than the Kyrgyz. The mosque was located in an Uzbek-dominated area.
7   To be fair, if compared to Kalinin, Cheremushki neighbourhood was more disadvantaged in terms of its location as it received first strikes from rural mobs coming to the city through its western entrance.
8   I would like to thank Lorenzo Bosi for indicating me this point.

CHAPTER SIX

1 My evaluation of the security strategies in each neighbourhood is based on interviews with local leaders and aksakals and residents. I contacted key participants in pacted negotiations after my local respondents mentioned their names in interviews and conversations highlighting their contribution to peaceful mediation.
2 According to Memorial (2012, 178), four Uzbeks were killed, but Rahman, one of local Uzbek community leaders, told me that two persons were killed from each side.
3 The Memorial report (2012, 177–78) mentions the names of these Kyrgyz mediators and leaders which was also corroborated in interviews with the Uzbek aksakals in Turan.
4 For example, in Dostuk, the area of the bricks factory, the south-western part. Memorial also reports about other successful cases of intercommunal nonaggression pacts. Negotiations in Dostuk district along the southern regional road, where the then vice-mayor of Osh negotiated to avoid clashes in Turan and Mamyrova Street. In the night of 12–13 June, rumours spread about a Kyrgyz crowd from Ak-Tilek going to Dostuk. On the morning of 13 June, peaceful negotiations took place between Dostuk and Ak-Tilek with agreement on mutual aid in case of attacks from outsider rioters. On 14 June, negotiations took place between Kyrgyz and Uzbek community leaders near Kirpichnyi brick factory to form interethnic patrols to keep order (Memorial 2012, 178).
5 UNCC is an ethnic cultural organization which play an important role in organizing the life of ethnic Uzbeks. As noted in the previous chapter, the radical leaders of Uzbek communities in Osh and Jalalabat used UNCCs for ethnic mobilization for political reasons. A Kyrgyz journalist based in Osh suggested that each Uzbek who gets rich and influential tries to establish his own UNCC.
6 A TV channel broadcasting in the Uzbek language and at that time owned by an Uzbek entrepreneur.

CHAPTER SEVEN

1 UDN (in Russian – *Universitet Druzhby Narodov*) was a primarily Uzbek university founded by Kadyrjan Batyrov, an informal leader of the Jalalabat Uzbek community. He used the territory of the university as a focal point for ethnic mobilization.

2 Makam is the head of Quarter 1 neighbourhood committee with around 1,500 residents under his responsibility. All live in individual housing units. He became the head of the neighbourhood committee on account of his fair and honest attitudes toward people in his neighbourhood. They elected him to be a kvartkom in an open meeting. He is also a member of the court of elders in the Aitmatov district.
3 See the introductory chapter in Halpern (2005) for the discussion of the conceptualization and sub-types of the social capital concept.
4 On ethnic stereotypes see Horowitz (1985).

CHAPTER EIGHT

1 Although the case of Uzgen is not included in this book, I use it here as a reference point to make a cross-city comparison.

References

Agnew, John, and Ulrich Oslender. 2013. "Overlapping Territorialities, Sovereignty in Dispute: Empirical Lessons from Latin America." In *Spaces of Contention: Spatialities and Social Movements*, edited by Walter Nicholls, Justin Beaumont, and Byron Miller, 121–40. Farnham, Surrey: Ashgate.

Ataeva, Nadezhda, Dmitrii Belomestnov, and Janyl Jusupjan. 2011. "Kyrgyzstan: sexual violence during ethnic conflict." Association Droits de l'Homme en Asie Centrale. Le Mans.

Auyero, Javier. 2006. "Spaces and Places as Sites and Objects of Politics." In *The Oxford Handbook of Contextual Political Analysis*, edited by Robert E. Goodin and Charles Tilly, 564–78. Oxford Handbooks of Political Science. Oxford: Oxford University Press.

– 2007. *Routine Politics and Violence in Argentina: The Gray Zone of State Power*. Cambridge Studies in Contentious Politics. Cambridge: Cambridge University Press.

Beissinger, Mark R. 2002. *Nationalist Mobilization and the Collapse of the Soviet State*. Cambridge: Cambridge University Press. http://hdl.handle.net/2027/heb.05462.

– 2007. "Structure and Example in Modular Political Phenomena: The Diffusion of Bulldozer/Rose/Orange/Tulip Revolutions." *Perspectives on Politics* 5, no. 2. https://doi.org/10.1017/S1537592707070776.

Berenschot, Ward. 2011. "The Spatial Distribution of Riots: Patronage and the Instigation of Communal Violence in Gujarat, India." *World Development* 39, no. 2: 221–30. https://doi.org/10.1016/j.worlddev.2009.11.029.

– 2020. "Patterned Pogroms: Patronage Networks as Infrastructure for Electoral Violence in India and Indonesia." *Journal of Peace Research* 57, no. 1: 171–84. https://doi.org/10.1177/0022343319889678.

Bhavnani, Ravi, Michael G. Findley, and James H. Kuklinski. 2009. "Rumor Dynamics in Ethnic Violence." *The Journal of Politics* 71, no. 3: 876–92. https://doi.org/10.1017/S002238160909077X.

Boone, Catherine. 2014. *Property and Political Order in Africa: Land Rights and the Structure of Politics*. Cambridge Studies in Comparative Politics. New York: Cambridge University Press.

Booth, Ken, and Nicholas J. Wheeler. 2008. *The Security Dilemma: Fear, Cooperation and Trust in World Politics*. Basingstoke: Palgrave Macmillan.

Brass, Paul R. 1997. *Theft of an Idol: Text and Context in the Representation of Collective Violence*. Princeton Studies in Culture/Power/History. Princeton: Princeton University Press.

– 2003. *The Production of Hindu-Muslim Violence in Contemporary India*. Seattle: University of Washington Press. http://site.ebrary.com/id/10468612.

Bray, Zoe. 2008. "Ethnographic Approaches." In *Approaches and Methodologies in the Social Sciences: A Pluralist Perspective*, edited by Donatella Della Porta and Michael Keating, 296–315. Cambridge: Cambridge University Press.

Brosché, Johan. 2022. "Conflict over the Commons: Government Bias and Communal Conflicts in Darfur and Eastern Sudan." *Ethnopolitics*, January, 1–23. https://doi.org/10.1080/17449057.2021.2018221.

Brosché, Johan, and Emma Elfversson. 2012. "Communal Conflict, Civil War, and the State: Complexities, Connections, and the Case of Sudan." *African Journal on Conflict Resolution* 12, no. 1: 9–32.

Brubaker, R., and D. Laitin. 1998. "Ethnic and Nationalist Violence." *Annual Review of Sociology* 24: 423–52.

Bunte, Jonas B., and Laura Thaut Vinson. 2016. "Local Power-Sharing Institutions and Interreligious Violence in Nigeria." *Journal of Peace Research* 53, no. 1: 49–65. https://doi.org/10.1177/0022343315614999.

Christia, Fotini. 2012. *Alliance Formation in Civil Wars*. Cambridge: Cambridge University Press.

Collins, Kathleen. 2002. "Clans, Pacts, and Politics in Central Asia." *Journal of Democracy* 13, no. 3: 137–52. https://doi.org/10.1353/jod.2002.0041.

– 2006. *Clan Politics and Regime Transition in Central Asia*. Paperback reissue, transferred to digital printing. Cambridge: Cambridge University Press.

Coppedge, Michael. 1999. "Thickening Thin Concepts and Theories: Combining Large N and Small in Comparative Politics." *Comparative Politics* 31, no. 4: 465. https://doi.org/10.2307/422240.

Dhattiwala, Raheel. 2016. "The Ecology of Ethnic Violence: Attacks on Muslims

of Ahmedabad in 2002." *Qualitative Sociology* 39, no. 1: 71–95. https://doi.org/10.1007/s11133-015-9320-5.
— 2019. *Keeping the Peace: Spatial Differences in Hindu-Muslim Violence in Gujarat in 2002*. Cambridge: Cambridge University Press.
Doyle, Michael W., and Nicholas Sambanis. 2000. "International Peacebuilding: A Theoretical and Quantitative Analysis." *American Political Science Review* 94, no. 4: 779–801. https://doi.org/10.2307/2586208.
Driscoll, Jesse. 2015. *Warlords and Coalition Politics in Post-Soviet States*. Cambridge Studies in Comparative Politics. New York: Cambridge University Press.
Edgar, Adrienne Lynn. 2004. *Tribal Nation: The Making of Soviet Turkmenistan*. Princeton: Princeton University Press.
Elfversson, Emma. 2019. "The Political Conditions for Local Peacemaking: A Comparative Study of Communal Conflict Resolution in Kenya." *Comparative Political Studies* 52, no. 13–14: 2061–96. https://doi.org/10.1177/0010414019830734.
Elfversson, Emma, Ivan Gusic, and Kristine Höglund. 2019. "The Spatiality of Violence in Post-War Cities." *Third World Thematics: A TWQ Journal* 4, no. 2–3: 81–93. https://doi.org/10.1080/23802014.2019.1675533.
Elfversson, Emma, and Kristine Höglund. 2021. "Are Armed Conflicts Becoming More Urban?" *Cities* 119 (December): 103356. https://doi.org/10.1016/j.cities.2021.103356.
Epkenhans, Tim. 2018. *The Origins of the Civil War in Tajikistan: Nationalism, Islamism, and Violent Conflict in Post-Soviet Space*. Lexington Books. http://www.vlebooks.com/vleweb/product/openreader?id=none&isbn=9781498532792.
Evans, Peter B., Harold Karan Jacobson, and Robert D. Putnam, eds. 1993. *Double-Edged Diplomacy: International Bargaining and Domestic Politics*. Studies in International Political Economy 25. Berkeley: University of California Press.
Fearon, James D. 1998. "Commitment Problems and the Spread of Ethnic Conflict." In *The International Spread of Ethnic Conflict: Fear, Diffusion, and Escalation*, edited by David A. Lake and Donald S. Rothchild, 107–26. Princeton: Princeton University Press.
Fearon, James D., and David D. Laitin. 1996. "Explaining Interethnic Cooperation." *American Political Science Review*, 715–35.
— 2003. "Ethnicity, Insurgency, and Civil War." *American Political Science Review* 97, no. 1: 75–90. https://doi.org/10.1017/S0003055403000534.

—— 2011. "Sons of the Soil, Migrants, and Civil War." *World Development* 39, no. 2: 199–211. https://doi.org/10.1016/j.worlddev.2009.11.031.

Fergana News. 2010a. "Кыргызстан: Чёрные Списки Июня." (Kyrgyzstan: June Blacklists). Ferghana - International News Agency. 2010. https://fergananews.com/article.php?id=6841&print=1.

—— 2010b. "Кыргызстан: В Оше Бесчинствуют Организованные Банды, Целенаправленно Уничтожающие Мирных Жителей." (Kyrgyzstan: Organized Gangs Rampage in Osh Destroying Civilians). Ferghana - International News Agency. 12 June 2010. http://www.fergananews.com/news.php?id=14945.

Fergana.ru. 2010. "Ошская Резня 1990 Года. Хронология Трагедии" (The Osh Massacre of 1990. The Chronology of Tragedy).- Ferghana - International News Agency. 2010. http://www.fergananews.com/articles/6601.

Fierman, William. 1991. *Language Planning and National Development: The Uzbek Experience*. Berlin: De Gruyter.

Figueiredo, Rui de, and Barry R. Weingast. 1999. "The Rationality of Fear: Political Opportunism and Ethnic Conflict." In *Civil Wars, Insecurity, and Intervention*, edited by Barbara F. Walter and Jack L. Snyder. New York: Columbia University Press.

Fumagalli, Matteo. 2007. "Informal Ethnopolitics and Local Authority Figures in Osh, Kyrgyzstan." *Ethnopolitics* 6, no. 2: 211–33. https://doi.org/10.1080/17449050701345017.

Gaziyev, Jamshid. 2008. *Ethno-Nationalism and Ethnic Conflicts in Central Asia*. Doctoral thesis, Durham University, Durham.

Gersovitz, M., and N. Kriger. 2013. "What Is a Civil War? A Critical Review of Its Definition and (Econometric) Consequences." *The World Bank Research Observer* 28, no. 2: 159–90. https://doi.org/10.1093/wbro/lkt005.

Gieryn, Thomas F. 2000. "A Space for Place in Sociology." *Annual Review of Sociology* 26, no. 1: 463–96. https://doi.org/10.1146/annurev.soc.26.1.463.

Gleditsch, Nils Petter, Peter Wallensteen, Mikael Eriksson, Margareta Sollenberg, and HåVard Strand. 2002. "Armed Conflict 1946-2001: A New Dataset." *Journal of Peace Research* 39, no. 5: 615–37. https://doi.org/10.1177/0022343302039005007.

Greif, Avner. 1998. "Self-Enforcing Political Systems and Economic Growth: Late Medieval Genoa." In *Analytic Narratives*, edited by Robert H. Bates, 23–63. Princeton: Princeton University Press.

Halpern, David. 2005. *Social Capital*. Cambridge: Polity.

References

Hardin, Russell. 1997. *One for All: The Logic of Group Conflict*. Princeton: Princeton University Press.

Hartzell, Caroline, and Donald Rothchild. 1997. "Political Pacts as Negotiated Agreements: Comparing Ethnic and Non-Ethnic Cases." *International Negotiation* 2, no. 1: 147–71. https://doi.org/10.1163/15718069720847906.

Heathershaw, John. 2009. *Post-Conflict Tajikistan: The Politics of Peacebuilding and the Emergence of Legitimate Order*. Central Asian Studies Series 16. London: Routledge.

Higley, John, and Michael G. Burton. 1989. "The Elite Variable in Democratic Transitions and Breakdowns." *American Sociological Review* 54, no. 1: 17. https://doi.org/10.2307/2095659.

Hirsch, Francine. 2005. *Empire of Nations: Ethnographic Knowledge & the Making of the Soviet Union*. Ithaca: Cornell University Press.

Horowitz, Donald L. 1985. *Ethnic Groups in Conflict*. Berkeley: University of California Press.

– 2001. *The Deadly Ethnic Riot*. Berkeley: University of California Press.

HRW. 2010. "'Where Is the Justice?' Interethnic Violence in Southern Kyrgyzstan and Its Aftermath." Human Rights Watch.

– 2018. "Nigeria: Rising Toll of Middle-Belt Violence." Human Rights Watch. https://www.hrw.org/news/2018/06/28/nigeria-rising-toll-middle-belt-violence.

Huntington, Samuel P. 1993. *The Third Wave: Democratization in the Late Twentieth Century*. The Julian J. Rothbaum Distinguished Lecture Series 4. Norman: University of Oklahoma Press.

ICG. 2010. "The Pogroms in Kyrgyzstan." Asia Report N°193. International Crisis Group. Brussels/Bishkek.

Joint Working Group. 2012. "On Circumstances and Chronology of the Tragic Events in May–June 2010 in Osh and Jalalabat." 2012. http://www.fergananews.com/articles/7389.

Jones Luong, Pauline. 2002. *Institutional Change and Political Continuity in Post-Soviet Central Asia: Power, Perceptions, and Pacts*. Cambridge Studies in Comparative Politics. Cambridge: Cambridge University Press.

Kalyvas, Stathis N. 2006. *The Logic of Violence in Civil War*. Cambridge Studies in Comparative Politics. Cambridge: Cambridge University Press.

– 2008. "Promises and Pitfalls of an Emerging Research Program: The Microdynamics of Civil War." In *Order, Conflict, and Violence*, edited by Stathis N. Kalyvas, Ian Shapiro, and Tarek E. Masoud, 397–421. Cambridge: Cambridge University Press.

Kaplan, Cynthia S. 1998. "Ethnicity and Sovereignty: Insights from Russian Negotiations with Estonia and Tatarstan." In *The International Spread of Ethnic Conflict: Fear, Diffusion, and Escalation*, edited by David A. Lake and Donald S. Rothchild, 251–74. Princeton: Princeton University Press.

Kaplan, Oliver Ross. 2017. *Resisting War: How Communities Protect Themselves.* Cambridge: Cambridge University Press.

Karl, Terry Lynn. 1990. "Dilemmas of Democratization in Latin America." *Comparative Politics* 23, no. 1: 1. https://doi.org/10.2307/422302.

Khamidov, Alisher. 2006. "IPP: Как Восстановить Узы Доверия: Узбекская Община и Власть в Кыргызстане." (How to Restore the Bonds of Trust: The Uzbek Community and Power in Kyrgyzstan) 2006. http://www.tazar.kg/news.php?i=2096.

Khamidov, Alisher, Nick Megoran, and John Heathershaw. 2017. "Bottom-up Peacekeeping in Southern Kyrgyzstan: How Local Actors Managed to Prevent the Spread of Violence from Osh/Jalal-Abad to Aravan, June 2010." *Nationalities Papers*, August, 1–17. https://doi.org/10.1080/00905992.2017.1335695.

KIC. 2011. "Report of the Independent International Commission of Inquiry into the Events in Southern Kyrgyzstan in June 2010." Kyrgyzstan Inquiry Commission.

Kirschner, Shanna. 2014. *Trust and Fear in Civil Wars: Ending Intrastate Conflicts.* Lanham, Maryland: Lexington Books.

Kılavuz, İdil Tunçer. 2009. "The Role of Networks in Tajikistan's Civil War: Network Activation and Violence Specialists." *Nationalities Papers* 37, no. 5: 693–717. https://doi.org/10.1080/00905990903122909.

Klaus, Kathleen, and Matthew I. Mitchell. 2015. "Land Grievances and the Mobilization of Electoral Violence: Evidence from Côte d'Ivoire and Kenya." *Journal of Peace Research* 52, no.5: 622–35. https://doi.org/10.1177/00223 43315580145.

Klinken, Gerry van. 2009. *Communal Violence and Democratization in Indonesia: Small Town Wars.* London: Routledge.

Krause, Jane. 2018. Resilient Communities: Non-Violence and Civilian Agency in Communal War. https://doi.org/10.1017/9781108675079.

Kuran, Timur. 1998. "Ethnic Dissimilation and Its International Diffusion." In *The International Spread of Ethnic Conflict: Fear, Diffusion, and Escalation*, edited by David A. Lake and Donald S. Rothchild, 35–60. Princeton: Princeton University Press.

Kutmanaliev, Joldon. 2015. "Public and Communal Spaces and Their Relation to the Spatial Dynamics of Ethnic Riots: Violence and Non-Violence in the City of Osh." *International Journal of Sociology and Social Policy* 35, no. 7/8: 449–77. https://doi.org/10.1108/IJSSP-02-2015-0027.

– 2017. "Ethnic Violence and Peace in Southern Kyrgyzstan: Intragroup Policing and Intergroup Non-Aggression Pacts." Florence: European University Institute.

– 2018. "Spatial Security during Ethnic Riots in Osh: How Spatial Factors and the Built Environment Affect the Local Dynamics of Violence and Neighborhood Security." In *Interrogating Illiberal Peace in Eurasia: Critical Perspectives on Peace and Conflict*, edited by Catherine Owen, 195–222. Global Dialogues: Developing Non-Eurocentric IR and IPE. Lanham: Rowman & Littlefield.

– 2020. "Communal Violence in Kyrgyzstan." In *Post-Soviet Conflicts: The Thirty Years' Crisis*, edited by Ali Askerov, Stefan Brooks, and Lasha Tchantouridzé, 225–42. Lanham: Lexington Books.

Kylym Shamy. 2010. "Victims of the June 2010 Events in the South of the Republic of Kyrgyzstan." Bishkek.

– 2011. "Ensuring Safety of Firearms, Military Equipment and Ammunition during Mass Disorders. Research, Conclusions, and Recommendations." Bishkek.

Kyrgyzstan census. 2009. National Statistics Committee of the Kyrgyz Republic, 2009 data. Bishkek. http://www.stat.kg/rus/part/census.htm.

Lake, David A., and Donald S. Rothchild. 1996. "Containing Fear: The Origins and Management of Ethnic Conflict." *International Security* 21, no. 2: 41–75. https://doi.org/10.2307/2539070.

– 1998. "Spreading Fear: The Genesis of Transnational Ethnic Conflict." In *The International Spread of Ethnic Conflict: Fear, Diffusion, and Escalation*, edited by David A. Lake and Donald S. Rothchild, 3–32. Princeton: Princeton University Press.

Leitner, Helga, Eric Sheppard, and Kristin M. Sziarto. 2008. "The Spatialities of Contentious Politics." *Transactions of the Institute of British Geographers* 33, no. 2: 157–72. https://doi.org/10.1111/j.1475-5661.2008.00293.x.

Lemarchand, René. 1996. *Burundi: Ethnic Conflict and Genocide*. 1st paperback edition. Woodrow Wilson Center Series. Cambridge: Woodrow Wilson Center Press and Cambridge University Press.

– 2009. *The Dynamics of Violence in Central Africa*. National and Ethnic Conflict in the Twenty-First Century. Philadelphia: University of Pennsylvania Press.

Lewis, David G., and Saniya Sagnayeva. 2020. "Corruption, Patronage and Illiberal Peace: Forging Political Settlement in Post-Conflict Kyrgyzstan." *Third*

World Quarterly 41, no. 1: 77–95. https://doi.org/10.1080/01436597
.2019.1642102.

Lichterman, Paul. 2002. "Seeing Structure Happen: Theory-Driven Participant Observation." In *Methods of Social Movement Research*, edited by Bert Klandermans and Suzanne Staggenborg, 118–45. Social Movements, Protest, and Contention, vol. 16. Minneapolis: University of Minnesota Press.

Licklider, Roy. 1995. "The Consequences of Negotiated Settlements in Civil Wars, 1945–1993." *American Political Science Review* 89, no. 03: 681–90. https://doi.org/10.2307/2082982.

Little, Richard. 2007. *The Balance of Power in International Relations: Metaphors, Myths, and Models*. New York: Cambridge University Press.

Liu, Morgan Y. 2012. *Under Solomon's Throne: Uzbek Visions of Renewal in Osh*. Pittsburgh: University of Pittsburgh Press.

Lubin, Nancy, Council on Foreign Relations, Century Foundation, and Center for Preventive Action. 1999. *Calming the Ferghana Valley: Development and Dialogue in the Heart of Central Asia: Report of the Ferghana Valley Working Group of the Center for Preventive Action*. Preventive Action Reports, vol. 4. New York: Century Foundation Press.

Madueke, Kingsley L. 2018. "Routing Ethnic Violence in a Divided City: Walking in the Footsteps of Armed Mobs in Jos, Nigeria." *The Journal of Modern African Studies* 56, no. 3: 443–70. https://doi.org/10.1017/S0022278X18000320.

— 2019. "The Emergence and Development of Ethnic Strongholds and Frontiers of Collective Violence in Jos, Nigeria." *African Studies Review* (May): 1–25. https://doi.org/10.1017/asr.2018.115.

Madueke, Kingsley L., and Floris F. Vermeulen. 2018. "Frontiers of Ethnic Brutality in an African City: Explaining the Spread and Recurrence of Violent Conflict in Jos, Nigeria." *Africa Spectrum* 53, no. 2: 37–63. https://doi.org/10.1177/000203971805300203.

Martin, Deborah G., and Byron Miller. 2003. "Space and Contentious Politics." *Mobilization: An International Quarterly* 8, no. 2: 143–56.

Martin, Terry. 2001. *The Affirmative Action Empire: Nations and Nationalism in the Soviet Union, 1923–1939*. Ithaca; London: Cornell University Press.

Matveeva, Anna, Igor Savin, and Bahrom Faizullaev. 2012. "Kyrgyzstan: Tragedy in the South." Ethnopolitics Papers, 17, University of Exeter, Exeter.

McAdam, Doug, and William H. Jr Sewell. 2001. "It's About Time: Temporality in the Study of Social Movements and Revolutions." In *Silence and Voice in the Study of Contentious Politics*, edited by Ronald Aminzade, Jack A. Goldstone,

Elizabeth J. Perry, William H. Jr Sewell, Sidney Tarrow, Charles Tilly, and Doug McAdam, 89–125. Cambridge: Cambridge University Press.

McAdam, Doug, Sidney G. Tarrow, and Charles Tilly. 2001. *Dynamics of Contention*. Cambridge Studies in Contentious Politics. Cambridge: Cambridge University Press.

McFaul, Michael. 2002. "The Fourth Wave of Democracy and Dictatorship: Noncooperative Transitions in the Postcommunist World." *World Politics* 54, no. 2: 212–44. https://doi.org/10.1353/wp.2002.0004.

Megoran, Nick. 2013. "Shared Space, Divided Space: Narrating Ethnic Histories of Osh." *Environment and Planning A* 45, no. 4: 892–907. https://doi.org/10.1068/a44505.

— 2017. *Nationalism in Central Asia: A Biography of the Uzbekistan-Kyrgyzstan Border*. Central Eurasia in Context Series. Pittsburgh: University of Pittsburgh Press.

Melvin, Neil. 2011. "Promoting a Stable and Multiethnic Kyrgyzstan: Overcoming the Causes and Legacies of Violence." Central Eurasion project No. 3. Occasional Papers Series. Open Society Foundations. New York.

Memorial. 2012. "A Cronicle of Violence. The Events in the South of Kyrgyzstan in June 2010 (Osh Region)." Memorial Human Rights Center, Norwegian Helsinki Committee, Freedom House. Oslo.

Moravcsik, Andrew M. 1993. "Introduction: Integrating International and Domestic Theories of International Bargaining." In *Double-Edged Diplomacy: International Bargaining and Domestic Politics*, edited by Peter B. Evans, Harold Karan Jacobson, and Robert D. Putnam, 3–42. Studies in International Political Economy 25. Berkeley: University of California Press.

Morenoff, Jeffrey D., Robert J. Sampson, and Stephen W. Raudenbush. 2001. "Neighborhood Inequality, Collective Efficacy, and the Spatial Dynamics of Urban Violence." *Criminology* 39, no. 3: 517–58. https://doi.org/10.1111/j.1745-9125.2001.tb00932.x.

Murthi, Meera. 2009. "Who Is to Blame? Rape of Hindu-Muslim Women in Interethnic Violence in India." *Psychology of Women Quarterly* 33, no. 4: 453–62. https://doi.org/10.1111/j.1471-6402.2009.01523.x.

National Commission. 2011. "The Report by the National Commission for Investigation of Causes and Consequences of the June Events." Bishkek.

Niou, Emerson M.S., Peter C. Ordeshook, and Gregory F. Rose. 1989. *The Balance of Power: Stability in International Systems*. Cambridge: Cambridge University Press.

O'Connor, Francis. 2015. "Radical Political Participation and the Internal Kurdish Diaspora in Turkey." *Kurdish Studies* 3, no. 2: 151–71.
- 2021. *Understanding Insurgency: Popular Support for the PKK in Turkey.* 1st ed. Cambridge University Press. https://doi.org/10.1017/9781108975087.
O'Donnell, Guillermo A. 1986. "Introduction to the Latin American Cases." In *Transitions from Authoritarian Rule. Latin America,* edited by Guillermo A. O'Donnell, Philippe C. Schmitter, and Laurence Whitehead, 3–18. Baltimore: Johns Hopkins University Press.
O'Donnell, Guillermo A., and Philippe C. Schmitter. 1986. *Transitions from Authoritarian Rule. Tentative Conclusions about Uncertain Democracies.* Baltimore: Johns Hopkins University Press.
Olzak, Susan. 1992. *The Dynamics of Ethnic Competition and Conflict.* Stanford: Stanford University Press.
Ostrom, Elinor. 1990. *Governing the Commons: The Evolution of Institutions for Collective Action.* The Political Economy of Institutions and Decisions. Cambridge: Cambridge University Press.
Owen, Catherine, Juraev, Shairbek, Lewis, David, Megoran, Nick, and Heathershaw, John, eds. 2018. *Interrogating Illiberal Peace in Eurasia: Critical Perspectives on Peace and Conflict.* Global Dialogues: Developing Non-Eurocentric IR and IPE. Lanham: Rowman & Littlefield.
Petersen, Roger Dale. 2001. *Resistance and Rebellion: Lessons from Eastern Europe.* Studies in Rationality and Social Change. Cambridge: Cambridge University Press.
Porta, Donatella della, Abby Peterson, and Herbert Reiter, eds. 2006. *The Policing of Transnational Protest.* Advances in Criminology. Aldershot and Burlington: Ashgate.
Porta, Donatella della, and Herbert Reiter, eds. 1998. *Policing Protest: The Control of Mass Demonstrations in Western Democracies.* Social Movements, Protest, and Contention, vol. 6. Minneapolis: University of Minnesota Press.
- 2006. "The Policing of Transnational Protest: A Conclusion." In *The Policing of Transnational Protest,* edited by Donatella della Porta, Abby Peterson, and Herbert Reiter, 175–89. Advances in Criminology. Aldershot: Ashgate.
Posen, Barry R. 1993. "The Security Dilemma and Ethnic Conflict." *Survival* 35, no. 1: 27–47. https://doi.org/10.1080/00396339308442672.
Przeworski, Adam. 1991. "Some Problems in the Study of the Transition to Democracy." In *Transitions from Authoritarian Rule: Comparative Perspectives,* edited by Guillermo O'Donnell, Philippe C. Schmitter, and Laurence Whitehead, 3rd print, 47–63. Baltimore: Johns Hopkins University Press.

Putnam, Robert D. 1988. "Diplomacy and Domestic Politics: The Logic of Two-Level Games." *International Organization* 42, no. 03: 427. https://doi.org/10.1017/S0020818300027697.

Putnam, Robert D., Robert Leonardi, and Raffaella Y. Nanetti. 1994. *Making Democracy Work: Civic Traditions in Modern Italy.* 5th print. Princeton: Princeton University Press.

Radnitz, Scott. 2012. *Weapons of the Wealthy: Predatory Regimes and Elite-Led Protests in Central Asia.* 1st print, Cornell paperbacks. Ithaca: Cornell University Press.

Raleigh, Clionadh. 2015. "Urban Violence Patterns across African States." *International Studies Review* 17, no. 1: 90–106. https://doi.org/10.1111/misr.12206.

Reeves, Madeleine. 2014. *Border Work: Spatial Lives of the State in Rural Central Asia.* Culture and Society after Socialism. Ithaca: Cornell University Press.

Roessler, Philip G. 2016. *Ethnic Politics and State Power in Africa: The Logic of the Coup-Civil War Trap.* Cambridge: Cambridge University Press.

Rothchild, Donald S., and David A. Lake. 1998. "Containing Fear: The Management of Transnational Ethnic Conflict." In *The International Spread of Ethnic Conflict: Fear, Diffusion, and Escalation*, edited by David A. Lake and Donald S. Rothchild, 203–26. Princeton: Princeton University Press.

Roy, Ananya. 2012. "Urban Informality: The Production of Space and Practice of Planning." In *The Oxford Handbook of Urban Planning*, edited by Randall Crane and Rachel Weber, 691–705. New York: Oxford University Press.

Sambanis, Nicholas. 2004. "What Is Civil War? Conceptual and Empirical Complexities of an Operational Definition." *Journal of Conflict Resolution* 48, no. 6: 814–58. https://doi.org/10.1177/0022002704269355.

Sampson, Robert J., Jeffrey D. Morenoff, and Thomas Gannon-Rowley. 2002. "Assessing 'Neighborhood Effects': Social Processes and New Directions in Research." *Annual Review of Sociology* 28, no. 1: 443–78. https://doi.org/10.1146/annurev.soc.28.110601.141114.

Sampson, Robert J., and Stephen W. Raudenbush. 1999. "Systematic Social Observation of Public Spaces: A New Look at Disorder in Urban Neighborhoods." *American Journal of Sociology* 105, no. 3: 603–51. https://doi.org/10.1086/210356.

Sampson, Robert J., and Per-Olof H. Wikstrom. 2008. "The Social Order of Violence in Chicago and Stockholm Neighborhoods: A Comparative Inquiry." In *Order, Conflict, and Violence*, edited by Stathis N. Kalyvas, Ian Shapiro, and Tarek E. Masoud, 97–119. Cambridge: Cambridge University Press.

Sewell, William H. 1996. "Historical Events as Transformations of Structures:

Inventing Revolution at the Bastille." *Theory and Society* 25, no. 6: 841–81. https://doi.org/10.1007/BF00159818.

— 2001. "Space in Contentious Politics." In *Silence and Voice in the Study of Contentious Politics*, edited by Ronald Aminzade, Jack A. Goldstone, Doug McAdam, Elizabeth J. Perry, William H. Jr. Sewell, Sidney G. Tarrow, and Charles Tilly, 51–88. Cambridge: Cambridge University Press.

Straus, Scott. 2006. *The Order of Genocide: Race, Power, and War in Rwanda*. Ithaca: Cornell University Press.

— 2008. "Order in Disorder: A Micro-Comparative Study of Genocidal Dynamics in Rwanda." In *Order, Conflict, and Violence*, edited by Stathis N. Kalyvas, Ian Shapiro, and Tarek E. Masoud, 301–20. Cambridge: Cambridge University Press.

Tajima, Yuhki. 2014. The Institutional Origins of Communal Violence: Indonesia's Transition from Authoritarian Rule. New York: Cambridge University Press.

Tarrow, Sidney. 2007. "Inside Insurgencies: Politics and Violence in an Age of Civil War." *Perspectives on Politics* 5, no. 3: 587. https://doi.org/10.1017/S1537592707071575.

Thernborn, Göran. 2006. "Why and How Place Matters." In *The Oxford Handbook of Contextual Political Analysis*, edited by Robert E. Goodin and Charles Tilly, 509–33. Oxford Handbooks of Political Science. Oxford: Oxford University Press.

Tilly, Charles., and Sidney G. Tarrow. 2007. *Contentious Politics*. Oxford: Oxford University Press.

Tishkov, V. 1995. "'Don't Kill Me, I'm a Kyrgyz!': An Anthropological Analysis of Violence in the Osh Ethnic Conflict." *Journal of Peace Research* 32, no. 2: 133–49. https://doi.org/10.1177/0022343395032002002.

Toft, Monica Duffy. 2002. "Indivisible Territory, Geographic Concentration, and Ethnic War." *Security Studies* 12, no. 2: 82–119. https://doi.org/10.1080/09636410212120010.

— 2006. *The Geography of Ethnic Violence: Identity, Interests, and the Indivisibility of Territory*. Princeton Paperbacks. Princeton: Princeton University Press.

Trilling, David. 2010. "Inter-Ethnic Tension Rattles Bishkek." *EurasiaNet*, 20 April. http://www.eurasianet.org/node/60891.

UNITAR/UNOSAT. 2010. "Damage Assessment for Osh, Kyrgyzstan. 25 June 2010 - V1." UNITAR/UNOSAT.

Varshney, Ashutosh. 2001. "Ethnic Conflict and Civil Society: India and Beyond." *World Politics* 53, no. 3: 362–98. https://doi.org/10.1353/wp.2001.0012.

- 2002. *Ethnic Conflict and Civic Life: Hindus and Muslims in India.* New Haven: Yale University Press.
- 2007. "Ethnicity and Ethnic Conflict." In *The Oxford Handbook of Comparative Politics*, edited by Carles Boix and Susan Carol Stokes, 274–94. Oxford Handbooks of Political Science. Oxford: Oxford University Press.

Vinson, Laura Thaut. 2017. *Religion, Violence, and Local Power-Sharing in Nigeria.* Cambridge: Cambridge University Press.

Waddington, David P. 1989. *Flashpoints: Studies in Public Disorder.* London : Routledge.
- 2007. *Policing Public Disorder: Theory and Practice.* Cullompton: Willan.

Waddington, David P., Fabien Jobard, and Mike King, eds. 2009. *Rioting in the UK and France: A Comparative Analysis.* Cullompton: Willan.

Wahlström, Mattias, and Mikael Oskarsson. 2006. "Negotiating Political Protest in Gothenburg and Copenhagen." In *The Policing of Transnational Protest*, edited by Donatella della Porta, Abby Peterson, and Herbert Reiter, 117–43. Advances in Criminology. Aldershot: Ashgate.

Walter, Barbara F. 1999. "Introduction." In *Civil Wars, Insecurity, and Intervention*, edited by Barbara F. Walter and Jack L. Snyder, 1–12. New York: Columbia University Press.
- 2009. "Bargaining Failures and Civil War." *Annual Review of Political Science* 12, no. 1: 243–61. https://doi.org/10.1146/annurev.polisci.10.101405.135301.

Walter, Barbara F., and Jack L. Snyder, eds. 1999. *Civil Wars, Insecurity, and Intervention.* New York: Columbia University Press.

Weidmann, Nils B. 2009. "Geography as Motivation and Opportunity: Group Concentration and Ethnic Conflict." *Journal of Conflict Resolution* 53, no. 4: 526–43. https://doi.org/10.1177/0022002709336456.

Weidmann, Nils B., Jan Ketil Rød, and Lars-Erik Cederman. 2010. "Representing Ethnic Groups in Space: A New Dataset." *Journal of Peace Research* 47, no. 4: 491–99. https://doi.org/10.1177/0022343310368352.

Weidmann, Nils B., and Idean Salehyan. 2013. "Violence and Ethnic Segregation: A Computational Model Applied to Baghdad." *International Studies Quarterly* 57, no. 1: 52–64. https://doi.org/10.1111/isqu.12059.

Wilkinson, Steven. 2006. *Votes and Violence: Electoral Competition and Ethnic Riots in India.* Cambridge Studies in Comparative Politics. Cambridge: Cambridge University Press.
- 2009. "Riots." *Annual Review of Political Science* 12, no. 1: 329–43. https://doi.org/10.1146/annurev.polisci.12.041307.075517.

Wong, Bin R. 2006. "Detecting the Significance of Place." In *The Oxford Hand-*

book of Contextual Political Analysis, edited by Robert E. Goodin and Charles Tilly, 534–46. Oxford Handbooks of Political Science. Oxford: Oxford University Press.

Wood, Elisabeth Jean. 2003. *Insurgent Collective Action and Civil War in El Salvador*. Cambridge Studies in Comparative Politics. New York: Cambridge University Press.

Zhao, Dingxin. 1998. "Ecologies of Social Movements: Student Mobilization during the 1989 Prodemocracy Movement in Beijing." *American Journal of Sociology* 103, no. 6: 1493–1529. https://doi.org/10.1086/231399.

– 2013. "The Built Environment and Organization in Anti-US Protest Mobilization after the 1999 Belgrade Embassy Bombing." In *Spaces of Contention: Spatialities and Social Movements*, edited by Walter Nicholls, Justin Beaumont, and Byron Miller, 199–218. Farnham: Ashgate.

Index

Adolat, 64, 66, 67
aksakals, 83–4, 161–74, 181–5, 206–10
anti-social behaviour, 137, 170, 208, 225
armed conflict, 20–7, 92, 97, 126–9
armed groups, 24, 196, 202–4, 213
arrival of outsiders, 46, 169, 176–8, 181–8
asymmetric information, 227–8
asymmetry in power, 43–4
authority of leaders, 12, 39, 53, 131, 178–81, 208–17
avoided violence, 14, 139, 153, 231

Bakiev, Kurmanbek, 35, 59, 70–86, 192, 212, 232
Bargaining, 17, 39, 42, 239, 245–9; leverage, 188; power, 39, 44; problems, 50
barricades, 5–18, 92–104, 130–46, 154–61, 196–216
Batyrov, Kadyrjan, 71–86, 201–12, 233–5
bazaar, 93–5, 106, 126–49, 204–25

Bishkek-Osh highway, 103, 191, 192
breakdown of state, 8–9, 26, 34–7, 59, 85–7
brokerage, 14–40, 146–8, 216
built environment, 17–18, 28, 112, 125–49, 158, 214

Central Asia, 6, 60–4, 232
Cheremushki, 92–101, 131–43, 145–8, 156, 205, 234
civic engagement, 14, 31, 49, 148, 206, 229
civil society, 17, 54, 229, 230, 248
clans, 34, 39, 40, 85
clusters of destruction, 98–106
combatant groups, 145, 147, 196
commitment problem, 50, 54, 153
communal brokers, 150, 167, 223, 232
communal security, 10, 55; segregation, 49, 66; subgroups, 7, 19, 21
communications infrastructures, 130–1, 147
community response, 20, 28, 33–4, 45, 80, 103, 139, 201–25

contentious politics, 14, 126, 129, 147, 237, 243–5, 248
contingency, 28, 87, 131, 150, 215
contingent factors, 16–19, 148, 152, 156, 176–8, 220
counterproductive strategy, 101, 205, 214, 216
credible commitment, 12–54, 170, 173, 211, 228
criminal gangs, 75–6, 86, 100, 146
cross-neighbourhood analysis, 20–1, 30, 127–30
culprits, 11, 51, 170

damaged areas, 101, 181, 184
data reliability, 114–16
deadly ethnic riots, 23, 85, 90, 101
death toll, 69, 106–13, 232–3; threshold, 23–6
defensive strategy, 143, 158–9, 208, 215
diffusion of violence, 19, 28, 45–6, 87, 237–47
diplomacy, 21, 41, 162, 217, 229–31; preventive, 158, 187
disruptive negotiations, 156, 167
divergent outcomes, 7, 9, 33, 56, 150
divergent responses, 6–10, 190, 201, 219
domestic constituency, 158, 187
domestic constraints, 41, 156, 176–8
domestic forces, 41, 153, 187, 224

effective in-group policing, 11–16, 50–5, 150–2, 170–3, 186–8, 222–4

embittered refugees, 12, 131, 178, 181, 226
emerging anarchy, 8, 9, 36, 41, 59, 210–25
emerging violence, 6–10, 19, 27–8, 91, 172, 215, 219
emotions, 4, 18, 41, 104
enclaves, 4–9, 18, 47, 136
environmental conditions, 9, 16, 132, 148–51, 169, 178, 188
ethnic composition, 5, 10, 17, 190, 214–15, 219
ethnic cooperation, 31–3, 229
ethnic diplomacy, 229, 231
ethnic enclaves, 5, 18, 47, 136
ethnic entrepreneurs, 29, 41, 59, 72–3, 215
ethnic fears, 28, 74–6, 134, 189, 208, 219, 227
ethnic island, 159, 178, 210, 222
ethnic neighbourhoods, 4–13, 47, 48, 138, 186
ethnic segregation, 135–8, 216, 221, 229, 249
ethnic strongholds, 4, 47, 59, 201, 231
ethnic subgroups, 126–9, 219
external factor, 46, 49, 163, 228, 229
external threat, 9, 15, 28, 34–47, 222

failed pacts, 42, 150, 151, 178
failed self-policing, 46, 150–1, 176–85, 215, 226
firearms, 4, 27, 96–102, 192–8, 209
focal point, 18, 75, 78, 95, 138, 212, 235
frontier zones, 17, 48, 231

Furkat, 80–1, 89, 92, 97, 101–6, 154, 181–8, 205, 227

group behaviour, 20, 55, 117; fractionalization, 7, 21
guarantee of security, 11, 31–3, 54, 95, 167, 172, 202–3, 228–9

Hardliners, 43–4, 46
HBK. *See* Manas-Ata
hinterland zones, 47–8
hostages, 88–94, 100–2, 111, 132–5, 160, 200

impact of spatial factors, 6, 28, 125, 127, 150, 190
incursion of militants, 46, 147
individual unit houses, 55, 126, 135, 141, 189, 205, 212
infiltration of instigators, 158, 226
influx of outsiders, 12, 151–8, 187–8, 226
informal leaders, 18, 143–5, 196, 224–35
information failures, 39–41
information problems, 40, 50
in-group balance of power, 12–16, 39, 43–6, 150–88, 208, 226; control, 14, 52–6, 147, 158, 232; interactions, 40, 150, 219, 226–7; sanctions, 12–13, 50–1, 223, 228
insecurity, 10, 38, 41, 87
instigators, 143–4, 171–7, 182, 226
intercommunal negotiation environments, 152, 158, 163, 187
intercommunal negotiations, 150, 153, 160, 161, 187, 232

intercommunal tensions, 20, 35, 106, 170–3, 188, 197
interethnic alliances, 10, 14, 21, 177, 189, 217; cooperation, 10, 15, 49, 126, 170, 201–9; relations, 13, 49, 70–82; suspicions, 40–1, 53, 64, 74, 116
intergroup balance of power, 15–16, 41–9, 96–7, 174, 196, 209, 224
intermediaries, 34, 39, 101, 127
internal migrants, 12, 17, 67, 20 52, 6, 211
isolated ethnic enclaves, 5, 9, 10, 18, 143

Jiydalik, 93, 132–8, 178

Kalinin neighbourhood, 132, 139–48, 168, 234
Kojo Mahalla, 192–6, 204–16, 227
Krasin Street, 195, 200–6, 213–16
Kvartkom, 81, 115, 174, 212, 233, 236
kyrgyz leaders, 159, 169, 171–4, 187, 201–5, 211; minority, 68, 154, 183, 222; mobilization, 4, 95, 208–12; neighbourhoods, 151–9, 172–8, 187, 201, 211, 217
Kyrgyzstan-Uzbekistan border, 178, 188
Kyzyl-Kyshtak, 89–101, 156

large-scale destruction, 4, 24, 100, 153
law enforcement troops and authorities, 9, 80, 93, 100, 112
legitimate leaders and brokers, 12, 15, 34–9, 49, 174, 186, 228

Index

Manas-Ata, 93, 132–6, 168, 185–6
mass arson, 5, 94, 200
meso-level analysis and behaviour, 9, 14, 15, 55, 126, 209
micro-comparative research, 20–44, 221
microdynamics of violence, 6, 7, 20, 26, 29
micro-scale outcomes, 8, 10, 81, 220, 223
micro-spatial level analysis, 29–55
military depots, 4, 24, 93, 97, 195, 209
military intervention, 145, 163
military officers, 97, 112, 160, 183
mixed neighbourhoods, 10, 14, 32, 189, 205–7, 217–28
mixed patrols, 160, 203, 205, 221
moderate leaders, 16, 33, 49, 156, 165–77, 187, 224–8
moderates and radicals, 10, 42–5, 150, 156, 158
mountainous districts and areas, 65–8, 88, 103, 134–9, 212, 216

Nariman, 131, 136, 151–2, 176–88, 226
negotiation environment, 152, 158, 163–5, 176–8, 187
negotiation process, 29–33, 52, 56, 152–3, 163, 171, 176
neighbourhood committees, 79, 115, 135, 236
neighbourhood effects, 18, 19, 129, 221
neorealist studies, 9, 10, 27, 219
neutral brokers and mediators, 39, 40

neutrality, 24–5, 33, 38, 211, 231
nomads, 60–3, 232–3
non-occurrence of violence, 6, 125–6
nonviolent neighbourhoods, 7, 22, 112
nonviolent outcomes, 11, 16, 17, 52, 221
Nookat, 65–9, 75, 95, 156–69, 187
Nurdar, 80, 101, 178–86

opportunism, 12, 50, 94, 223, 228, 240
opportunist behaviour, 5, 18, 50, 93, 137, 138, 202, 222–5
Osh Aymagy, 64–7
Oshskii Raion, 132–49, 214, 225
Osh UNCC, 83–4, 164, 233
outsider groups, 4, 40, 46, 52–3, 65, 164–6

paired comparisons, 28, 130, 150–1, 186
patronage, 29, 35, 70, 86, 237, 243
peaceful intentions, 11, 13, 38, 43, 223, 229
peaceful outcomes, 11–12, 16, 32–3, 186, 201, 217, 228–9
peacemaking, 5, 55–6, 117, 239
physical security, 15, 31, 51, 227; self-isolation, 12, 18, 126, 143–7, 217; survival, 10, 32, 55
pogroms, 23–5, 68, 88–96, 100, 237, 241
police, 159, 192, 195, 196, 213; stations, 181, 183, 197
political violence, 26, 125, 146, 149
power shifts, 10, 16, 34, 42–53, 163, 177–8, 186–8, 208, 224

power vacuum, 27, 35, 59, 220
preemptive aggression, 8, 10, 14, 36–48, 189, 207–10, 215–27
pressure from radicals, 163, 177–8, 187
preventive diplomacy, 158, 177, 187
probability of occurrence, 16–17, 29, 42–3, 53, 224
property damage, 3, 99, 105–6, 119, 142, 194–9, 204–7
property destruction, 5, 26, 88–118, 139–41, 196
provocateurs, 72, 167
public space, 137–49, 247
punishment, 11, 44, 144, 166, 170

quantifiable indicators of violence, 113, 119
quarters, 6, 10, 11, 77–9, 201–25
quotidian links, 15, 206, 214, 222

radical groups, 43–51, 152, 187–8, 208, 228; leaders, 208, 226, 235; outsiders, 12, 46, 156–81
radicalization, 101, 224
radicals, 8–19, 32–56, 150–88, 208, 222–7
rape, 3–5, 88, 93, 101, 110, 119, 245
reconciliation, 82, 134, 162, 185
regime change, 9, 35, 59, 72, 85
regime transition, 27, 38, 48, 54, 72
regional road, 156, 158, 187, 235
republican-level UNCC, 79, 83, 86
residential mobility, 12, 17, 126, 214, 225
residential segregation, 138, 214
resistance, 24–5, 96

response strategy, 8, 38, 45, 47, 186
retaliation, 48, 50, 94, 116, 170, 175, 184
retaliatory attacks, 47, 95, 175, 222–7
revenge, 18, 74, 90, 202
rival groups, 11, 18, 36, 37, 40, 47, 150
roadblocks, 9, 14, 18, 92, 131, 155–67, 196–205
road communication, 138, 213
road infrastructure, 95, 106, 187
rural mobilization, 95, 210, 212
Russian colonization, 62

sanctions, 12–16, 50–6, 145, 159, 170, 175, 187, 223–8
sedentary population, 62–4
segregated neighbourhoods, 4, 12–21, 126–38, 186, 215–28; towns, 5, 18, 221–2
self-isolation strategy, 12, 143, 145, 205
separatist aspiration, 64, 85
sexual violence, 5, 18, 68, 110, 119, 237
shifts in power. *See* power shifts
snowball sampling, 114–16, 233
social capital, 15–17, 29, 148, 208, 229, 236, 240
social cohesion, 84, 152
social control, 17–18, 49–55, 129–45, 206–28
social norms, 12, 17, 49, 50, 81, 177–8, 211, 224–8
socio-spatial positionality, 146, 148
soldiers, 46, 97, 103, 112

spatial factors, 17, 30, 56, 125–48, 187–90, 212–21; agency, 126, 146; categories, 125–7, 146; characteristics, 28, 30, 145, 158, 159; conditions, 125, 150, 176; configuration, 132, 138; co-presence, 145, 147; differentiation, 6, 18, 112, 147, 177; mobility, 112, 145, 148; proximity, 17, 95, 128–38, 176–8, 187, 193; security, 125–49; structures, 28, 112, 125–39, 146–8
spatiality, 16, 125, 146–9, 214, 239
spillover effects, 6, 45–6, 131–54, 214, 226–8
sportspersons, 79, 84, 174
spread of violence, rumours, and fears, 18, 19, 76, 88, 136
Sputnik neighbourhood, 190–7, 211–17
state authorities, 9, 152, 182–8
strategic interactions, 12–43, 150, 220–7
strategic location, 95, 180, 221–2
strategic responses, 14, 218–25
street fights, 73, 85, 103
street mobilization, 77, 87
structural conditions, 19, 152, 176–7, 186, 214–29
structural constraints, 17, 225
subgroups, 7–22, 128–9, 219
Suzak, 75, 190–213

territorial council, 78–9, 115, 135–6, 174
traditional authority, 12, 131, 172–81, 208, 215
transformative events, 87, 89
trigger event, 80, 88–91, 226
two-level game, 11, 29, 40–3, 150–3, 227, 247

University of Peoples' Friendship (UDN), 191–216, 235
Uzbekistan's border, 131, 174, 191, 213
Uzbekistan's military, 88, 106, 163
Uzbek National Cultural Centers (UNCC), 79–86, 164–7, 233–5
Uzbeks: aksakals, 70–86, 151–74; armed groups, 196, 204, 213; mahallas, 78–95, 132–8, 180–98, 210–17; mediators, 117, 118; militants, 4, 104, 137; mobilization, 65–88, 106–38; refugees, 178–85; self-defense groups, 24, 85–100, 203–15
Uzgen, 14, 65–82, 102–17, 210–36

violent conflict, 15, 21–40, 128–9, 223–44
violent mobilization, 23, 81, 85, 126, 137, 138, 145, 149
violent riots, 26, 52, 87, 88
violent standoff, 89, 103, 196, 213, 214